Statistics in Psychology
An Historical Perspective

Statistics in Psychology
An Historical Perspective

Michael Cowles
York University

LAWRENCE ERLBAUM ASSOCIATES, PUBLISHERS
1989   Hillsdale, New Jersey   Hove and London

Lawrence Erlbaum Associates, Inc., Publishers
365 Broadway
Hillsdale, New Jersey 07642

BF
39
.C67
1989

Library of Congress Cataloging-in-Publication Data

Cowles, Michael, 1936–
    Statistics in psychology : an historical perspective / by Michael
Cowles.
        p.   cm.
    Bibliography: p.
    Includes indexes.
    ISBN 0-8058-0031-X
    1. Psychology—Statistical methods—History.   2. Social sciences—
Statistical methods—History.   I. Title.
BF39.C67   1989
150'.72—dc20   89-11628
                                                                          CIP

Printed in the United States of America

10   9   8   7   6   5   4   3   2   1

Contents

Preface

This book was written primarily for university students in psychology and the social sciences. Its origins lie in my efforts to inject into my courses in statistics and experimental design some feeling for the *life* that there is in the material. For mathematicians and mathematical statisticians the satisfaction of arriving successfully at the end of a proof, of seeing the structure of a particular logical development, is reward enough. But for many of the students that I encounter, statistics consists of the struggle to understand and apply a series of rules for data manipulation, and the reward that has been established by the social sciences comes when those manipulations provide *significant* outcomes. It became clear to me that this is not always reward enough and I therefore decided to try to examine the subject matter of the statistical recipe books from the standpoint of its origins and development. For students of the behavioral sciences the realization that the discipline of statistics was shaped by the *character* of its founders and their subscription to views that were sometimes personal and ideological, rather than *objective* and *scientific*, might provide ideas for future theses.

Some areas of statistics are hardly mentioned at all, particularly those that have been developed in relatively recent times. The book does not deal with multivariate techniques, the application of which has been spurred by the availability of computer packages such as SAS, SSPS^X, MINITAB, and BMDP. Factor analysis deserves its own historical account—an account that is not without drama. I have restricted this perspective to the statistical techniques that are to be found in the basic texts on statistics for psychology in the hope that it may encourage students to explore the tools they so readily apply and appreciate the tribulations of their beginnings. To all intents and purposes my account ends at about 1940, although on some occasions I have strayed into the 1950s.

There may be some who would quarrel with my inclusion of certain topics and criticize my omission of others. I can defend my synopsis but I realize that others are equally viable. I have made liberal use of quotations from both primary and secondary sources in the hope that they will encourage further exploration and alternative perspectives.

I have tried to make this account as nonmathematical as possible because I know that many of those who read it will have little experience of that discipline beyond high school. But mathematics cannot be totally avoided and I look forward to a day when social scientists recognize this in their training of students. The book will, I hope, be of use to students who have taken, or are taking, courses in statistics at both the undergraduate and graduate level, and, I trust, of interest to teachers and users of statistical methods. I have tried to make it uncomplicated and I fear that, at times, I may have been simplistic. The logic of statistical inference and its complex and fascinating history will continue to provide many scholars with academic papers for years to come. The development of applied statistics has provoked, and will continue to provoke, arguments that this account has missed, both by accident and design. It is also my hope that the book will offer, for those who have a feel for the endeavor, a starting point for a constructive reappraisal of the utility and rationale for the methods of data assessment that are of central importance to current psychological research. I have my own suggestions, but this particular work is not the one where they will be expressed.

I do not profess to be an historian. I am a psychologist, an average mathematician (who struggles!), and a teacher of statistics. Innumerable discussions with students and colleagues have shaped the book's perspective. In no sense is this a comprehensive and analytical history, it is a walk (I am tempted to say a ramble) through some of the historical trails of statistics and the views it proffers depend on the work of a great many scholars to whom I hope I have given due acknowledgment. The many of my friends and constructive critics who have helped me take the paths I traveled I cannot thank enough. The stumbles are my responsibility alone.

Among those who have offered comments and cogent criticisms and have helped to shape my views is Nick Wade whose late-night insights over chess and a bottle of malt scotch are among my academic highs. My good friend, coresearcher, and fiercest critic, Caroline Davis, has pushed me along when our work in general, and this work in particular, was going slowly. Graham Reed, a scholar who refuses to take himself or the world too seriously, is a pillar of intellect and good sense in the midst of cant. Jim Closs, Hy Day, Ray Fancher, Dave Ingram, Tim Johnson, Sandy and Pat Lovie, the late Bernard Singer, all, in one way or another, have contributed to this work. I must also thank two anonymous reviewers for their encouragement. They will, I hope, find that their comments have made this a better book. Finally I have to acknowledge my students who, in showing that they appreciated some account of the development of the statistical procedures that they grapple with, encouraged me to write this book.

My wife and family put up with my shutting myself away for hours on end and generously forgave my irritation when my work was interrupted or not going well. They know that the future will not be different and for that, and for the present and the past, I give my heartfelt thanks.

Michael Cowles

Acknowledgments

I wish to express my appreciation to a number of individuals, institutions, and publishers for granting permission to reproduce material that appears in this book:

Excerpts from Fisher Box, J. © 1978, *R. A. Fisher The life of a scientist*. Reprinted by permission of John Wiley & Sons Inc., the copyright holders.

Excerpts from a number of papers by R. A. Fisher. Reprinted by permission of Professor J. H. Bennett on behalf of the copyright holders, the University of Adelaide.

Excerpts, figures and tables by permission of Hafner Press, a division of Macmillan Publishing Company from *Statistical methods for research workers* by R. A. Fisher. Copyright © 1970 by University of Adelaide.

Excerpts from volumes of *Biometrika*. Reprinted by permission of the Biometrika Trustees.

Excerpts from MacKenzie, D. A. (1981). *Statistics in Britain 1865–1930*. Reprinted by permission of the Edinburgh University Press.

Two plates from Galton, F. (1885a). Regression towards mediocrity in hereditary stature. *Journal of the Anthropological Institute of Great Britain and Ireland, 15,* 246–263. Reprinted by permission of the Royal Anthropological Institute of Great Britain and Ireland.

Professor W. H. Kruskal, Professor F. Mosteller, and the International Statistical Institute for permission to reprint a quotation from Kruskal, W., & Mosteller, F. (1979). Representative sampling, IV: The history of the concept in statistics, 1895–1939. *International Statistical Review, 47,* 169–195.

Excerpts from Hogben, L. (1957). *Statistical theory.* London: Allen and Unwin; Russell, B. (1931). *The scientific outlook.* London: Allen and Unwin; Russell B. (1946). *History of western philosophy and its connection with political and social circumstances from the earliest times to the present day.* London: Allen and Unwin; von Mises, R. (1957). *Probability, statistics and truth.* (Second revised English Edition prepared by Hilda Geiringer) London: Allen and Unwin. Reprinted by permission of Unwin Hyman, the copyright holders.

Excerpts from Clark, R. W. (1971). *Einstein the life and times.* New York: World. Reprinted by permission of Peters, Fraser and Dunlop, Literary Agents.

Dr D. C. Yalden-Thomson for permission to reprint a passage from Hume, D. (1748). *An enquiry concerning human understanding.* (In D. C. Yalden-Thomson (Ed.). (1951). *Hume, Theory of Knowledge.* Edinburgh: Thomas Nelson).

Excerpts from various volumes of the *Journal of the American Statistical Association.* Reprinted by permission of the Board of Directors of the American Statistical Association.

An excerpt reprinted from *Probability, statistics, and data analysis* by O. Kempthorne and L. Folks, L. © 1971) Iowa State University Press, Ames, Iowa 50010.

Excerpts from De Moivre, A. (1756). *The doctrine of chances: or, A method of calculating the probabilities of events in play.* (3rd ed.), London: A. Millar. Reprinted from the edition published by the Chelsea Publishing Co., New York, © 1967 with permission and Kolmogorov, A. N. (1956). *Foundations of the theory of probability.* (N. Morrison, Trans.). Reprinted by permission of the Chelsea Publishing Co.

An excerpt reprinted with permission of Macmillan Publishing Company from *An introduction to the study of experimental medicine* by C. Bernard (H. C. Greene, Trans.), © 1927 (Original work published in 1865) and from *Science and human behaviour* by B. F. Skinner © 1953 by Macmillan Publishing Company, renewed 1981 by B. F. Skinner.

Excerpts from Galton, F. (1908). *Memories of my life.* Reprinted by permission of Methuen and Co.

An excerpt from Chang, W-C. (1976). Sampling theories and sampling practice. In D. B. Owen (Ed.), *On the history of statistics and probability* (pp. 299–315). Reprinted by permission of Marcel Dekker, Inc. New York.

An excerpt from Jacobs, J. (1885). Review of Ebbinghaus's *Ueber das Gedächtnis. Mind, 10,* 454–459 and from Hacking, I. (1971). Jacques Bernoulli's *Art of Conjecturing. British Journal for the Philosophy of Science, 22,* 209–229. Reprinted by permission of Oxford University Press and Professor Ian Hacking.

Excerpts from Lovie, A. D. (1979). The analysis of variance in experimental psychology: 1934–1945. *British Journal of Mathematical and Statistical Psychology, 32,* 151–178 and Yule, G. U. (1921). Review of W. Brown and G. H. Thomson, *The essentials of mental measurement. British Journal of Psychology, 2,* 100–107. Reprinted by permission of the British Psychological Society.

Excerpts from Edgeworth, F. Y. (1887). Observations and statistics: An essay on the theory of errors of observation and the first principles of statistics. *Transactions of the Cambridge Philosophical Society, 14,* 138–169 and Neyman, J., & Pearson, E. S. (1933b). The testing of statistical hypotheses in relation to probabilities *a priori. Proceedings of the Cambridge Philosophical Society, 29,* 492–510. Reprinted by permission of the Cambridge University Press.

Excerpts from Cochrane, W. G. (1980). Fisher and the analysis of variance. In S. E. Fienberg, & D. V. Hinckley (Eds.), *R. A. Fisher: An Appreciation* (pp. 17–34) and from Reid, C. (1982). *Neyman—from life.* Reprinted by permission of Springer-Verlag, New York.

Excerpts and plates from *Philosophical Transactions of the Royal Society* and *Proceedings of the Royal Society of London.* Reprinted by permission of the Royal Society.

Excerpts from Laplace P. S. de (1820). *A philosophical essay on probabilities.* F. W. Truscott, & F. L. Emory, Trans.). Reprinted by permission of Dover Publications, New York.

Excerpts from Galton, F. (1889). *Natural inheritance,* Thomson, W. (Lord Kelvin). (1891). *Popular lectures and addresses,* and Todhunter, I. (1865). *A history of the mathematical theory of probability from the time of Pascal to that of Laplace.* Reprinted by permission of Macmillan and Co., London.

Excerpts from various volumes of the *Journal of the Royal Statistical Society,* reprinted by permission of the Royal Statistical Society.

An excerpt from Boring, E. G. (1957). When is human behavior predetermined? *The Scientific Monthly, 84,* 189–196. Reprinted by permission of the American Association for the Advancement of Science.

Data obtained from Rutherford, E., & Geiger, H. (1910). The probability variations in the distribution of α particles. *Philosophical Magazine, 20,* 698–707. Material used by permission of Taylor and Francis, Publishers, London.

Excerpts from various volumes of *Nature* reprinted by permission of Macmillan Magazines Ltd.

An excerpt from Forrest, D. W. (1974). *Francis Galton: The life and work of a Victorian genius.* London: Elek. Reprinted by permission of Grafton Books, a division of the Collins Publishing Group.

Excerpts from Fisher, R. A. (1935, 1966, 8th ed.). *The design of experiments.* Edinburgh: Oliver and Boyd. Reprinted by permission of the Longman Group, UK, Limited.

Excerpts from Pearson, E. S. (1966). The Neyman-Pearson story: 1926–34. Historical sidelights on an episode in Anglo-Polish collaboration. In F. N. David (Ed.). *Festschrift for J. Neyman.* London: Wiley. Reprinted by permission of John Wiley and Sons Ltd., Chichester.

1

The Development

of Statistics

EVOLUTION, BIOMETRICS, AND EUGENICS

The central concern of the life sciences is the study of variation. To what extent does this individual or group of individuals differ from another? What are the reasons for the variability? Can the variability be controlled or manipulated? Do the similarities that exist spring from a common root? What are the effects of the variation on the life of the organisms? These are questions asked by biologists and psychologists alike.

The life-science disciplines are defined by the different emphases placed on observed variation, by the nature of the particular variables of interest, and by the ways in which the different variables contribute to the life and behavior of the subject matter.

Change and diversity in nature rest upon an organizing principle, the formulation of which has been said to be the single most influential scientific achievement of the 19th century: the theory of evolution by means of natural selection. The explication of the theory is attributed, rightly, to Charles Darwin (1809–1882). His book, *The Origin of Species*, was published in 1859, but a number of other scientists had written on the principle, in whole or in part, and these men were acknowledged by Darwin in later editions of his work.

Natural selection is possible because there is variation in living matter. The struggle for survival within and across species then ruthlessly favors the individuals that possess a combination of traits and characters, behavioral and physical, that allows them to cope with the total environment, exist, survive, and reproduce.

Not all sources of variability are biological. Many organisms, to a greater or

1

lesser extent reshape their environment, their experience, and, therefore, their behavior through learning. In human beings this reshaping of the environment has reached its most sophisticated form in what has come to be called *cultural evolution*. A fundamental feature of the human condition, of human nature, is our ability to process a very great deal of information. Human beings have originality and creative powers that continually expand the boundaries of knowledge. And, perhaps most important of all, our language skills, verbal and written, allow for the accumulation of knowledge and its transmission from generation to generation. The rich diversity of human civilization stems from cultural, as well as genetic, diversity.

Curiosity about diversity and variability leads to attempts to classify and to measure. The ordering of diversity and the assessment of variation have spurred the development of measurement in the biological and social sciences, and the application of statistics is one strategy for handling the numerical data obtained.

As science has progressed, it has become increasingly concerned with quantification as a means of describing events. It is felt that precise and economical descriptions of events and the relationships among them are best achieved by *measurement*. Measurement is the link between mathematics and science and the apparent (at any rate to mathematicians!) clarity and order of mathematics fosters the scientist's urge to measure. The central importance of measurement was vigorously expounded by Francis Galton (1822–1911); "Until the phenomena of any branch of knowledge have been submitted to measurement and number it cannot assume the status and dignity of a Science."

These words formed part of the letterhead of the Department of Applied Statistics of University College, London, an institution that received much intellectual and financial support from Galton. And it is with Galton, who first formulated the method of *correlation*, that the common statistical procedures of modern social science began.

The nature of variation and the nature of inheritance in organisms were much-discussed and much-confused topics in the second half of the 19th century. Galton was concerned to make the study of heredity *mathematical* and to bring order into the chaos.

Francis Galton was Charles Darwin's cousin. Galton's mother was the daughter of Erasmus Darwin (1731–1802) by his second wife and Darwin's father was Erasmus's son by his first. Darwin, who was 13 years Galton's senior, had returned home from a 5-year voyage as the naturalist on board *H.M.S. Beagle* (an Admiralty expeditionary ship) in 1836 and by 1838 had conceived of the principle of natural selection to account for some of the observations he had made on the expedition. The careers and personalities of Galton and Darwin were quite different. Darwin painstakingly marshalled evidence and single-mindedly buttressed his theory, but remained diffident about it, apparently uncertain of its acceptance. In fact it was only the inevitability of the announcement of the independent discovery of the principle by Alfred Russell Wallace (1823–1913) that forced Darwin to publish, some 20 years after he had formed the idea. Galton, on the other hand, though a staid and formal Victorian, was not without vanity, enjoying the fame and recognition brought to him by his many publications on a bewildering variety of topics. The stream of publication continued unabated from 1850 until shortly before his death.

The notion of correlated variation was discussed by the new biologists. Darwin observes in *The Origin of Species*:

> Many laws regulate variation, some few of which can be dimly seen, . . . I will here only allude to what may be called correlated variation. Important changes in the embryo or larva will probably entail changes in the mature animal . . . Breeders believe that long limbs are almost always accompanied by an elongated head . . . cats which are entirely white and have blue eyes are generally deaf . . . it appears that white sheep and pigs are injured by certain plants whilst dark-coloured individuals escape . . . (Darwin, 1859. Mentor Edition, 1958, p. 34)

Of course, at this time, the hereditary mechanism was unknown, and, partly in an attempt to elucidate it, Galton began, in the mid-1870s, to breed sweet peas.[1] The results of his study of the size of sweet pea seeds over two generations were published in 1877. When a fixed size of parent seed was compared with the mean size of the offspring seeds, Galton observed the tendency that he called then *reversion* and later *regression* to the mean. The mean offspring size is not as extreme as the parental size. Large parent seeds of a particular size produce seeds that have a mean size that is larger than average, but not as large as the parent size. The offspring of small parent seeds of a fixed size have a mean size that is smaller than average but now this mean size is not as small as that of the fixed parent size. This phenomenon will be discussed later in more detail. For the moment, suffice it to say that it is an arithmetical artifact arising from the fact that offspring sizes do not match parental sizes absolutely uniformly. In other words, the *correlation* is imperfect.

Galton misinterpreted this statistical phenomenon as a real trend toward a reduction in population variability. Paradoxically, however, it lead to the formation of the *Biometric School* of heredity and thus encouraged the development of a great many statistical methods.

Over the next several years Galton collected data on inherited human characteristics by the simple expedient of offering cash prizes for family records. From these data he arrived at the *regression* lines for hereditary stature.

A common underlying theme in Galton's work, and later that of Karl Pearson (1857–1936), was a particular social philosophy. Ronald Fisher (1890–1962) also subscribed to it, although, it must be admitted, it was not, as such, a direct

---

[1]Mendel had already carried out his work with edible peas and thus begun the science of genetics. The results of his work were published in a rather obscure journal in 1866 and the wider scientific world remained oblivious of them until 1900.

influence upon his work. These three men are the founders of what are now called *classical* statistics and all were *eugenists*. They believed that the most relevant and important variables in human affairs are inherited. One's ancestors rather than one's environmental experiences are the overriding determinants of intellectual capacity and personality as well as physical attributes. Human well-being, human personality, indeed human society, could therefore, they argued, be improved by encouraging the most able to have more children than the least able. MacKenzie (1981) and Cowan (1972, 1977) have argued that much of the early work in statistics and the controversies that arose among biologists and statisticians reflects the commitment of the founders of *biometry*, Pearson being the leader, to the eugenics movement.

In 1884, Galton financed and operated an anthropometric laboratory at the *International Health Exhibition*. For a charge of threepence, members of the public were measured. Visual and auditory acuity, weight, height, limb span, strength, and a number of other variables were recorded. Over 9,000 data sets were obtained, and, at the close of the exhibition, the equipment was transferred to the South Kensington Museum where data collection continued. Francis Galton was an avid measurer.

Karl Pearson (1930) relates that Galton's first forays into the problem of correlation involved ranking techniques, although he was aware that ranking methods could be cumbersome. How could one compare different measures of anthropometric variables? In a flash of illumination, Galton realized that characteristics measured on scales based on their own variability (we would now say standard score units) could be directly compared. He recalls the occasion in *Memories of my Life*, published in 1908.

> As these lines are being written, the circumstances under which I first clearly grasped the important generalisation that the laws of heredity were solely con-cerned with deviations expressed in statistical units are vividly recalled to my memory. It was in the grounds of Naworth Castle, where an invitation had been given to ramble freely. A temporary shower drove me to seek refuge in a reddish recess in the rock by the side of the pathway. There the idea flashed across me and I forgot everything else for a moment in my great delight. (Galton, 1908, p. 300)[2]

This incident apparently took place in 1888 and before the year was out, *Co-relations and Their Measurement Chiefly From Anthropometric Data*, had been presented to the Royal Society. In this paper Galton defines co-relation; "Two variable organs are said to be co-related when the variation of one is accom-

---

[2]Karl Pearson (1914–1930) in the volume published in 1924, suggested that this spot deserves a commemorative plaque. Unfortunately it looks as though the inspiration can never be so marked, for Kenna (1973), investigating the episode, reports that, "In the grounds of Naworth Castle there are not any rocks, reddish or otherwise, which could provide a recess, . . . " (p. 229), and he suggests that the location of the incident might have been Corby Castle.

panied on the average by more or less variation of the other, and in the same direction" (Galton, 1888, p. 135).

The last five words of the quotation indicate that the notion of negative correlation had not then been conceived, but this brief, but important, paper shows that Galton fully understood the importance of his statistical approach. Shortly thereafter mathematicians entered the picture with encouragement from some, but by no means all, biologists.

Much of the basic mathematics of correlation had, in fact, already been developed by the time of Galton's paper, but the utility of the procedure itself in this context had apparently eluded everyone. It was Karl Pearson, Galton's disciple and later his biographer, who, in 1896, set the whole concept on a sound mathematical foundation and presented statistics with the best solution to the problem of representing covariation by means of a single numerical index, the *coefficient of correlation*.

From these beginnings spring the whole corpus of present-day statistical techniques. George Udny Yule (1871–1951), an influential statistician who was not a eugenist, and Pearson himself, elaborated the concepts of *multiple* and *partial* correlation. The general psychology of individual differences and research into the structure of human abilities and intelligence relied heavily on correlational techniques. The first third of the 20th century saw the introduction of *factor analysis* through the work of Charles Spearman (1863–1945), Sir Godfrey Thomson (1881–1955), Sir Cyril Burt (1883–1971), and Louis L. Thurstone (1887–1955).

A further prolific and fundamentally important stream of development arises from the work of Sir Ronald Fisher. The technique of *analysis of variance* was developed directly from the method of *intra-class correlation*—an index of the extent to which measurements in the same category or family are related, relative to other categories or families.

Fisher studied mathematics at Cambridge but also pursued interests in biology and genetics. In 1913 he spent the summer working on a farm in Canada. He worked for a while with a City investment company and then found himself declared unfit for military service because of his extremely poor eyesight. He turned to school-teaching for which he had no talent and which he hated. In 1919 he had the opportunity of a post at University College with Karl Pearson, then head of the Department of Applied Statistics, but chose instead to develop a statistical laboratory at the Rothamsted Experimental Station near Harpenden in England, where he developed experimental methods for agricultural research.

Over the next several years relations between Pearson and Fisher became increasingly strained. They clashed on a variety of issues. Some of their disagreements helped, and some hindered, the development of statistics. Had they been collaborators and friends, rather than adversaries and enemies, statistics might have had a quite different history. In 1933 Fisher became Galton Professor of Eugenics at University College, and, in 1943, moved to Cambridge where he was Professor of Genetics. *Analysis of variance*, which has had such far-reaching effects on experimentation in the behavioral sciences, was developed through attempts to tackle problems posed at Rothamsted.

It may be fairly said that the majority of texts on methodology and statistics in the social sciences are the offspring (diversity and selection notwithstanding!) of Fisher's books, *Statistical Methods for Research Workers*, first published in 1925(a),[3] and *The Design of Experiments*, first published in 1935(a).

In succeeeding chapters these statistical concepts will be examined in more detail and their development elaborated. But first the use of the term *statistics* will be explored a little further.

THE DEFINITION OF STATISTICS

In an everyday sense when we think of statistics we think of facts and figures, of numerical descriptions of political and economic *states* (from which the word is derived), and of inventories of the various aspects of our social organization. The history of statistical procedures in this sense goes back to the beginnings of human civilization. When trade and commerce began, when governments imposed taxes, numerical records were kept. The counting of people, goods, and chattels was regularly carried out in the Roman Empire, the Domesday Book attempted to describe the state of England for the Norman conquerors, and government agencies the world over expend a great deal of money and energy in collecting and tabulating such information in the present day. Statistics are used to describe and summarize, in numerical terms, a wide variety of situations.

But there is another more recently-developed activity subsumed under the term *statistics*; the practice of not only collecting and collating numerical facts, but also the process of reasoning about them. Going beyond the data, making inferences and drawing conclusions with greater or lesser degrees of certainty in an orderly and consistent fashion is the aim of modern applied statistics. In this sense statistical reasoning did not begin until fairly late in the 17th century and then only in a quite limited way. The sophisticated models now employed, backed by theoretical formulations that are often complex, are all less than 100 years old. Westergaard (1932) points to the confusions that sometimes arise because the word *statistics* is used to signify both collections of measurements and reasoning about them, and that in former times it referred merely to descriptions of states in both numerical and non-numerical terms.

In adopting the statistical inferential strategy the experimentalist in the life sciences is accepting the intrinsic variability of the subject matter. In recognizing a range of possibilities, the scientist comes four-square against the problem of

---

[3]Maurice Kendall (1963) says of this work, "It is not an easy book. Somebody once said that no student should attempt to read it unless he had read it before" (p. 2).

deciding whether or not the particular set of observations he or she has collected can reasonably be expected to reflect the characteristics of the total range. This is the problem of parameter estimation, the task of estimating population values (parameters) from a consideration of the measurements made on a particular population subset—the sample statistics. A second task for inferential statistics is hypothesis testing, the process of judging whether or not a particular statistical outcome is likely or unlikely to be due to chance. The statistical inferential strategy depends on a knowledge of probabilities.

This aspect of statistics has grown out of three activities which, at first glance, appear to be quite different but in fact have some close links. They are actuarial prediction, gambling, and error assessment, and each addresses the problems of making decisions, evaluating outcomes, and testing predictions in the face of uncertainty, and each has contributed to the development of probability theory.

PROBABILITY

Statistical operations are often thought of as practical applications of previously developed probability theory. The fact is, however, that almost all our present-day statistical techniques have arisen from attempts to answer real-life problems of prediction and error assessment and theoretical developments have not always paralleled technical accomplishments. Box (1984) has reviewed the scientific context of a range of statistical advances and shown that the fundamental methods evolved from the work of practicing scientists.

John Graunt, a London haberdasher, born in 1620, is credited with the first attempt to predict and explain a number of social phenomena from a consideration of actuarial tables. He compiled his tables from *Bills of Mortality*, the parish accounts of deaths that were regularly, if somewhat crudely, recorded from the beginning of the 17th century.

Graunt recognizes that the question might be asked,

To what purpose tends all this laborious buzzling, and groping? To know, 1. the number of the People? 2. How many *Males*, and *Females*? 3. How many Married, and single? . . . (Graunt, 1662. Arno Press Edition, 1975, p. 77)

and says:

To this I might answer in general by saying, that those, who cannot apprehend the reason of these Enquiries, are unfit to trouble themselves to ask them. (p. 77)

Graunt reassured readers of this quite remarkable work,

The *Lunaticks* are also but few, *viz.* 158 in 229250 though I fear many more than are set down in our *Bills*, . . .

So that, this *Casualty* being so uncertain, I shall not force my self to make any inference from the numbers, and proportions we finde in our Bills concerning it: onely I dare ensure any man at this present, well in his Wits, for one in the thousand, that he shall not die a *Lunatick* in *Bedlam*, within these seven years, because I finde not above one in about one thousand five hundred have done so. (pp. 35–36)

Here is an inference based on numerical data and couched in terms not so very far removed from those in reports in the modern literature. Graunt's work was immediately recognized as being of great importance and the King himself (Charles II) supported his election to the recently-incorporated Royal Society.

A few years earlier the seeds of modern probability theory were being sown in France.[4] At this time gambling was a popular habit in fashionable society and a range of games of chance was being played. For experienced players the *odds* applicable to various situations must have been appreciated, but no formal methods for calculating the chances of various outcomes were available. Antoine Gombauld, the Chevalier de Méré, a "man-about-town" and gambler with a scientific and mathematical turn of mind, consulted his friend, Blaise Pascal (1623–1662), a philosopher, scientist, and mathematician, hoping that he would be able to resolve questions on calculation of expected (probable) frequency of gains and losses, as well as on the fair division of the stakes in games that were interrupted. Consideration of these questions led to correspondence between Pascal and his fellow mathematician, Pierre Fermat (1601–1665). No doubt their advice aided de Méré's game.[5] More significantly, it was from this exchange that some of the foundations of probability theory and combinatorial algebra were laid.

Christian Huygens (1629–1695) published, in 1657, a tract *On Reasoning With Games of Dice*, which was partly based on the Pascal-Fermat correspondence, and, in 1713, Jacques Bernoulli's (1654–1705) book, *The Art of Conjecture*, developed a theory of games of chance.

Pascal had connected the study of probability with the *arithmetic triangle*,

---

[4]But note that there are hints of probability concepts in mathematics going back at least as far as the 12th century and that Girolamo Cardano wrote *Liber de Ludo Aleae*, (*The Book on Games of Chance*) a century before it was published in 1663 (see Ore, 1953). There is also no doubt that quite early in human civilization, there was an appreciation of long run relative frequencies, randomness, and degrees of likelihood in gaming, and some quite formal concepts are to be found in Greek and Roman writings.

[5]Poisson (1781–1840), writing of this episode in 1837 says, "A problem concerning games of chance, proposed by a man of the world to an austere Jansenist, was the origin of the calculus of probabilities" (quoted by Struik, 1954, p. 145). De Méré was certainly "a man of the world" and Pascal did become austere and religious, but at the time of De Méré's questions Pascal was in his so-called "worldly period" (1652–1654). I am indebted to my father-in-law, the late Professor Tom Fletcher, for many insights into the life of Pascal.

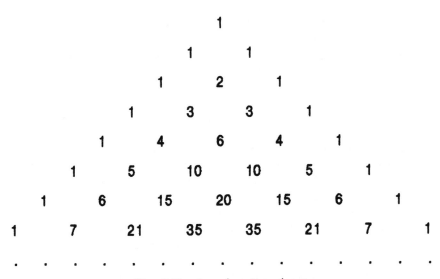

$$(\tfrac{1}{2} + \tfrac{1}{2})^4 = \tfrac{1}{16} + \tfrac{4}{16} + \tfrac{6}{16} + \tfrac{4}{16} + \tfrac{1}{16}$$

FIG. 1.1. Pascal's Triangle.

(Fig. 1.1) for which he discovered new properties, although the triangle was known in China at least 5 hundred years earlier. Proofs of the triangle's properties were obtained by *mathematical induction* or *reasoning by recurrence*.

Pascal's triangle, as it is known in the West, is a tabulation of the binomial coefficients that may be obtained from the expansion of $(P + Q)^n$ where $P = Q = \tfrac{1}{2}$. The expansion was developed by Sir Isaac Newton (1642–1727), and, independently, by the Scottish mathematician, James Gregory (1638–1675). Gregory discovered the rule about 1670. Newton communicated it to the Royal Society in 1676, although later that year he explained that he had first formulated it in 1664 while he was a Cambridge undergraduate. The example shown in Fig. 1.1 demonstrates that the expansion of $(\tfrac{1}{2} + \tfrac{1}{2})^4$ generates, in the numerators of the expression, the numbers in the fifth row of Pascal's triangle. The terms of this expression also give us the five expected frequencies of outcome (0, 1, 2, 3, or 4 heads) or the *probabilities* when a fair coin is tossed four times. Simple experiment will demonstrate that the actual outcomes in the "real world" of coin tossing closely approximate the distribution that has been calculated from a mathematical abstraction.

During the 18th century the theory of probability attracted the interest of many brilliant minds. Among them was a friend and admirer of Newton, Abraham De Moivre (1667–1754). De Moivre, a French Huguenot, was interned in 1685 after the revocation by Louis XIV of the Edict of Nantes, an edict which had guaranteed toleration to French Protestants. He was released in 1688, fled to England,

and spent the remainder of his life in London. De Moivre published what might be described as a gambler's manual entitled, *The Doctrine of Chances or a Method of Calculating the Probabilities of Events in Play*. In the second edition of this work, published in 1738, and in a revised third edition published posthumously in 1756, De Moivre demonstrated a method, which he had first devised in 1733, of approximating the sum of a very large number of binomial terms when n in $(P + Q)^n$ is very large (an immensely laborious computation from the basic expansion).

It may be appreciated that as n grows larger then the number of terms in the expansion also grows larger. The graph of the distribution begins to resemble a smooth curve (Fig. 1.2), a bell-shaped symmetrical distribution that held great interest in mathematical terms but little practical utility outside of gaming.

It is safe to say that no other theoretical mathematical abstraction has had such an important influence on psychology and the social sciences as that bell-shaped curve now commonly known by the name that Karl Pearson decided on—*The Normal Distribution*—although he was not the first to use the term.

Pierre Laplace (1749–1827) independently derived the function and brought together much of the earlier work on probability in *Theorie Analytique des Probabilites*, published in 1812. It was his work, as well as contributions by many others, that interpreted the curve as the *Law of Error* and showed that it could be applied to variable results obtained in multiple observations. One of the first applications of the distribution outside of gaming was in the assessment of errors in astronomical observations. Later the utility of the "law" in error assessment was extended to land surveying and even to range estimation problems in artillery fire. Indeed, between 1800 and 1820 the foundations of the theory of error distribution were laid.

Carl Friedrich Gauss (1777–1855), perhaps the greatest mathematician of all time, also made important contributions to work in this area. He was a consultant to the Governments of Hanover and of Denmark when they undertook geodetic surveys. The function that helped to rationalize the combination of observations is sometimes called the *Laplace-Gaussian Distribution*.

Following the work of Laplace and Gauss the development of mathematical probability theory slowed somewhat and not a great deal of progress was made until the present century. But it was during the 19th century, through the development of life insurance companies and through the growth of statistical approaches in the social and biological sciences, that the *applications* of probability theory burgeoned. Augustus De Morgan (1806–1871), for example, attempted to reduce the constructs of probability to straightforward rules of thumb. His work, *An Essay on Probabilities and on Their Application to Life Contingencies and Insurance Offices*, published in 1838, is full of practical advice and is commented on by Walker (1929).

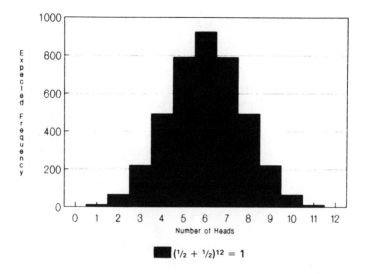

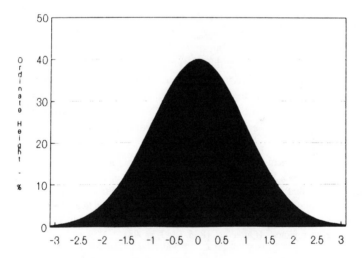

FIG. 1.2. The Binomial Distribution for N = 12 and the Normal Distribution.

THE NORMAL DISTRIBUTION

The normal distribution was so named because many biological variables when measured in large groups of individuals, and plotted as frequency distributions, do show close approximations to the curve. It is partly for this reason that the mathematics of the distribution are used in data assessment in the social sciences and in biology.

The responsibility, as well as the credit, for this extension of the use of calculations designed to estimate error or gambling expectancies into the examination of human characteristics rests with Lambert Adolphe Quetelet (1796–1874), a Belgian astronomer.

In 1835 Quetelet described his concept of the average man—*l'homme moyen*. *L'homme moyen* is Nature's ideal, an ideal that corresponds with a middle, measured value. But Nature makes errors, and in, as it were, missing the target, produces the variability observed in human traits and physical characters. More importantly, the extent and frequency of these errors often conforms to the law of frequency of error—the normal distribution.

John Venn (1834–1933), the English logician, objected to the use of the word *error* in this context; "When Nature presents us with a group of objects of every kind, it is using rather a bold metaphor to speak in this case also of a law of error" (Venn, 1888, p. 42), but the analogy was attractive to some.

Quetelet examined the distribution of the measurements of the chest girths of 5,738 Scottish soldiers, these data having been extracted from the thirteenth volume of the *Edinburgh Medical Journal*. There is no doubt that the measurements closely approximate to a normal curve. In another attempt to exemplify the law, Quetelet examined the heights of 100,000 French conscripts. Here he noticed a discrepancy between observed and predicted values.

> The official documents would make it appear that, of the 100,000 men, 28,620 are of less height than 5 feet 2 inches: calculation gives only 26,345. Is it not a fair presumption, that the 2,275 men who constitute the difference of these numbers have been fraudulently rejected? We can readily understand that it is an easy matter to reduce one's height a half-inch, or an inch, when so great an interest is at stake as that of being rejected. (Quetelet, 1835/1849, p. 98)

Whether or not the allegation stated here, that short (but not *too* short) Frenchmen have stooped so low as to avoid military service, is true is no longer an issue. A more important point is noted by Boring (1920),

> While admitting the dependence of the law on experience, Quetelet proceeds in numerous cases to analyze experience by means of it. Such a double-edged sword is a peculiarly effective weapon, and it is no wonder that subsequent investigators

were tempted to use it in spite of the necessary rules of scientific warfare. (Boring, 1920, p. 11)

The use of the normal curve in statistics is not, however, based solely on the fact that it can be used to describe the frequency distribution of many observed characteristics. It has a much more fundamental significance in inferential statistics as will be seen, and the distribution and its properties will appear in many parts of this book.

Galton first became aware of the distribution from his friend William Spottiswoode, who, in 1862, became Secretary of the Royal Geographical Society, but it was the work of Quetelet that greatly impressed him. Many of the data sets he collected approximated to the law and he seemed, on occasion, to be almost mystically impressed with it.

> I know of scarcely anything so apt to impress the imagination as the wonderful form of cosmic order expressed by the "Law of Frequency of Error." The law would have been personified by the Greeks and deified, if they had known of it. It reigns with serenity and in complete self-effacement amidst the wildest confusion. The huger the mob and the greater the apparent anarchy, the more perfect is its sway. It is the supreme law of Unreason. Whenever a large sample of chaotic elements are taken in hand and marshalled in the order of their magnitude, an unsuspected and most beautiful form of regularity proves to have been latent all along. (Galton, 1889, p. 66)

This rather theological attitude towards the distribution echoes De Moivre who, over a century before, proclaimed in *The Doctrine of Chances*,

> Altho' chance produces irregularities, still the Odds will be infinitely great, that in the process of Time, those irregularities will bear no proportion to the recurrency of that Order which naturally results from ORIGINAL DESIGN . . .
> Such Laws, as well as the original Design and Purpose of their Establishment, must all be from without . . . if we blind not ourselves with metaphysical dust, we shall be led, by a short and obvious way, to the acknowledgement of the great MAKER and GOVENOUR of all; Himself all-wise, all-powerful and good. (De Moivre, 1756, p. 251–252)

The ready acceptance of the normal distribution as a law of nature encouraged its wide application and also produced consternation when exceptions were observed.

Quetelet himself admitted the possibility of the existence of asymmetric distributions, and Galton was at times less lyrical, for critics had objected to the use of the distribution, not as a practical tool to be used with caution where it seemed appropriate, but as a sort of divine rule,

It has been objected to some of my former work, especially in *Hereditary Genius*, that I pushed the application of the Law of Frequency of Error somewhat too far. I may have done so, rather by incautious phrases than in reality; . . . I am satisfied to claim the Normal Law is a fair average representation of the observed Curves during nine-tenths of their course; . . . (Galton, 1889, p. 56)[6]

BIOMETRICS

In 1890, Walter F.R. Weldon (1860–1906) was appointed to the Chair of Zoology at University College, London. He was greatly impressed and much influenced by Galton's *Natural Inheritance*. Not only did the book show him how the frequency of the deviations from a "type" might be measured, it opened up for him, and for other zoologists, a host of biometric problems. In two papers published in 1890 and 1892, Weldon showed that various measurements on shrimps might be assessed using the normal distribution. He also demonstrated interrelationships (correlations) between two variables within the individuals.

But the critical factor in Weldon's contribution to the development of statistics was his professorial appointment, for this brought him into contact with Karl Pearson, then Professor of Applied Mathematics and Mechanics, a post Pearson had held since 1884. Weldon was attempting to remedy his weakness in mathematics so that he could extend his research and he approached Pearson for help. His enthusiasm for the biometric approach drew Pearson away from more orthodox work.

A second important link was with Galton, who had reviewed Weldon's first paper on variation in shrimps. Galton supported and encouraged the work of these two younger men until his death, and, under the terms of his will, left 45,000 pounds to endow a Chair of Eugenics at the University of London, together with the wish that the post might be offered first to Karl Pearson. The offer was made and accepted.

Pearson's contribution was monumental, for in less than 8 years, between 1893 and 1901, he published over 30 papers on statistical methods. The first was written as a result of Weldon's discovery that the distribution of one set of measurements of the characteristics of crabs, collected at the zoological station at Naples in 1892, was "double-humped." The distribution was reduced to the sum of two normal curves. Pearson (1894) proceeded to investigate the general problem of fitting observed distributions to theoretical curves. This work was to lead directly to the formulation of the χ^2 test of "goodness of fit" in 1900, one of the most important developments in the history of statistics.

Weldon approached the problem of discrepancies between theory and observation in a much more empirical way, tossing coins and dice and comparing the

---

[6]Note that this quotation and the previous one from Galton are 10 pages apart in the same work!

outcomes with the binomial model. These data helped to produce another line of development.

In a letter to Galton, written in 1894, Weldon asks for a comment on the results of 7,000 tossings of twelve dice collected for him by a clerk at University College.

> A day or two ago Pearson wanted some records of the kind in a hurry, in order to illustrate a lecture, and I gave him the record of the clerk's 7000 tosses . . . on examination he rejects them, because he thinks the deviation from the theoretically most probable result is so great as to make the record intrinsically incredible. (Quoted by E.S.Pearson, 1965, p. 11)

This incident set off a good deal of correspondence between Karl Pearson, F.Y. Edgeworth (1845–1926), an economist and statistician, and Weldon, the details of which are now only of minor importance. But, as Pearson remarked, "Probabilities are very slippery things" (quoted by E.S. Pearson, 1965, p. 14) and the search for criteria by which to assess the differences between observed and theoretical frequencies and whether or not they could be reasonably attributed to chance sampling fluctuations began. Statistical research rapidly expanded into careful examination of distributions other than the normal curve and eventually into the properties of sampling distributions, particularly through the work of Ronald Fisher.

In developing his research into the properties of the probability distributions of statistics, Fisher investigated the basis of hypothesis testing and the foundations of all the well-known tests of *statistical significance*. Fisher's assertion that $p = 0.05$ (1 in 20) is the probability that is convenient for judging whether or not a deviation is to be considered significant (i.e., unlikely to be due to chance), has profoundly affected research in the social sciences, although it should be noted that he was not the originator of the convention (Cowles & Davis, 1982a).

Of course the development of statistical methods does not end here, nor have all the threads been drawn together. Discussion of the important contribution of W.S. Gosset ("Student," 1876–1937) to small sample work and the refinements introduced into hypothesis testing by Karl Pearson's son, Egon S. Pearson (1895–1980) and Jerzy Neyman (1899–1981) will be found in later chapters when the earlier details have been elaborated.

Biometrics and Genetics

The early years of the biometric school were surrounded by controversy. Pearson and Weldon held fast to the view that evolution took place by the continuous selections of variations that were favorable to organisms in their environment. The rediscovery of Mendel's work in 1900 supported the concept that heredity depends on self-reproducing particles (what we now call *genes*), and that inherited variation is discontinuous and saltatory. The source of the development of higher types was occasional genetic jumps or mutations. Curiously enough, this was the view of evolution that Galton had supported. His misinterpretation of the purely statistical phenomenon of regression led him to the notion that a distinction had to be made between variations from the mean that regress and what he called "sports" (a breeder's term for an animal or plant variety that appears apparently spontaneously) that will not.

A champion of the position that mutations were of critical importance in the evolutionary process was William Bateson (1861–1926) and a prolonged and bitter argument with the biometricians ensued. The *Evolution Committee* of the Royal Society broke down over the dispute. *Biometrika* was founded by Pearson and Weldon, with Galton's financial support, in 1900, after the Royal Society had allowed Bateson to publish a detailed criticism of a paper submitted by Pearson before the paper itself had been issued. Britain's important scientific journal, *Nature*, took the biometricians' side and would not print letters from Bateson. Pearson replied to Bateson's criticisms in *Biometrika* but refused to accept Bateson's rejoinders, whereupon Bateson had them privately printed by the Cambridge University Press in the format of *Biometrika!*

At the British Association meeting in Cambridge in 1904, Bateson, then President of the Zoological Section, took the opportunity to deliver a bitter attack on the biometric school. Dramatically waving aloft the published volumes of *Biometrika* he pronounced them worthless and he described Pearson's correlation tables as, "a Procrustean bed into which the biometrician fits his unanalysed data." (Quoted by Julian Huxley, *Sunday Times*, 10th July, 1949).

It is even said that Pearson and Bateson refused to shake hands at Weldon's funeral. Nevertheless, after Weldon's death the controversy cooled. Pearson's work became more concerned with the theory of statistics, although the influence of his eugenic philosophy was still in evidence, and by 1910, when Bateson became Director of the John Innes Horticultural Institute, the argument had died.

However, some statistical aspects of this contentious debate predated the evolution dispute and echoes of them, indeed, marked reverberations from them, are still around today, although of course Mendelian and Darwinian thinking are completely reconciled.

STATISTICAL CRITICISM

Statistics has been called the "science of averages" and this definition is not meant in a kindly way. The great physiologist Claude Bernard (1813–1878) maintained that the use of averages in physiology could not be countenanced,

> . . . because the true relations of phenomena disappear in the average; when dealing with complex and variable experiments, we must study their various cir-

cumstances, and then present our most perfect experiment as a type, which, however, still stands for true facts.

. . . averages must therefore be rejected, because they confuse while aiming to unify, and distort while aiming to simplify. (Bernard, 1865/1927, p. 135)

Now it is, of course, true that lumping measurements together may not give us anything more than a picture of the lumping-together, and the average value may not be anything like any one individual measurement at all, but Bernard's ideal type fails to acknowledge the reality of individual differences. A rather memorable example of a very real confusion is given by Bernard:

A startling instance of this kind was invented by a physiologist who took urine from a railway station urinal where people of all nations passed, and who believed that he could thus present an analysis of *average* European urine! (Bernard, 1865/1927, pp. 134–135).

A less memorable, but just as telling, example is that of the social psychologist who solemnly reports "mean social class."

Pearson notes that,

One of the blows to Weldon, which resulted from his biometric view of life, was that his biological friends could not appreciate his new enthusiasms. They could not understand how the Museum "specimen" was in the future to be replaced by the "sample" of 500 to 1000 individuals. (Pearson, 1906, p. 37)

The view is still not wholly appreciated. Many psychologists subscribe to the position that the most pressing problems of the discipline, and certainly the ones of most practical interest, are problems of *individual* behavior. A major criticism of the effect of the use of the statistical approach in psychological research is the failure to differentiate adequately between general propositions that apply to most, if not all, members of a particular group and statistical propositions that apply to some aggregated measure of the members of the group. The latter approach discounts the exceptions to the statistical aggregate, which not only may be the most interesting but may, on occasion, constitute a large proportion of the group.

Controversy abounds in the field of measurement, probability, and statistics, and the methods employed are open to criticism, revision, and downright rejection. On the other hand, measurement and statistics play a leading role in psychological research and the greatest danger seems to lie in a nonawareness of the limitations of the statistical approach and the bases of their development, as well as the use of techniques, assisted by the high-speed computer, as recipes for data manipulation.

Miller (1963) observed of Fisher, "Few psychologists have educated us as rapidly, or have influenced our work as pervasively, as did this fervent, clear-headed statistician" (Miller, 1963, p. 157).

Hogben (1957) certainly agrees that Fisher has been enormously influential but he objects to Fisher's confidence in his own intuitions,

> This intrepid belief in what he disarmingly calls common sense . . . has led Fisher . . . to advance a battery of concepts for the semantic credentials of which neither he nor his disciples offer any justification *en rapport* with the generally accepted tenets of the classical theory of probability. (Hogben, 1957, p. 504)

Hogben also expresses a thought often shared by natural scientists when they review psychological research that,

> Acceptability of a statistically *significant* result of an experiment on animal be-haviour in contradistinction to a result which the investigator can repeat before a critical audience naturally promotes a high output of publication. Hence the argu-ment that the techniques *work* has a tempting appeal to young biologists. (Hogben, 1957, p. 27)

Experimental psychologists may well agree that the tightly controlled experiment is the apotheosis of classical scientific method; but they are not so arrogant as to suppose that their subject matter will *necessarily* submit to this form of analysis and they turn, almost inevitably, to statistical, as opposed to experimental, control. This is not a muddle-headed notion but it does present dangers if it is accepted without caution.

A balanced, but not uncritical, view of the utility of statistics can be arrived at from a consideration of the forces that shaped the discipline and an examination of its development. Whether or not this is an assertion that anyone, let alone the author of this book, can justify remains to be seen.

> Yet there are Writers, of a Class indeed very different from that of *James Bernoulli*, who insinuate as if the *Doctrine of Probabilities* could have no place in any serious Enquiry; and that Studies of this kind, trivial and easy as they be, rather disqualify a man for reasoning on any other subject. Let the Reader chuse. (De Moivre, 1756, p. 254)

2

Science, Psychology, and Statistics

DETERMINISM

It is a popular notion that if psychology is to be considered a science, then it most certainly is not an *exact* science. The propositions of psychology are considered to be inexact because no psychologist on earth would venture a statement such as this, "All stable extraverts will, when asked, volunteer to participate in psychological experiments."[1] The propositions of the natural sciences are considered to be exact because all physicists would be prepared to attest (with some few cautionary qualifications) that, "fire burns" or, more pretentiously, that "e = mc^2." In short, it is felt that the order in the universe, that nearly everyone (though for different reasons) is sure must be there, has been more obviously demonstrated by the natural rather than the social scientists.

Order in the universe implies *determinism,* a most useful and a most vexing term, for it brings those who wonder about such things into contact with the philosophical underpinnings of the rather everyday concept of *causality*. No one has stated the situation more clearly than Laplace in his *Essai*.

> Present events are connected with preceding ones by a tie based upon the evident principle that a thing cannot occur without a cause which produces it. This axiom known by the name of *the principle of sufficient reason*, extends even to actions

---

[1]Not wishing to make pronouncements upon the probabilistic nature of the work of others, the writer is making an oblique reference to work in which he and a colleague (Cowles & Davis, 1987) found that there is an 80% chance that stable extraverts will volunteer to participate in psychological research.

19

which are considered indifferent; the freest will is unable without a determinative motive to give them birth; . . .

We ought then to regard the present state of the universe as the effect of its anterior state and as the cause of the one that is to follow. Given for one instant an intelligence which could comprehend all the forces by which nature is animated and the respective situations of the beings who compose it—an intelligence sufficiently vast to submit these data to analysis—it would embrace in the same formula the movements of the greatest bodies of the universe and those of the lightest atom; for it nothing would be uncertain and the future, as the past, would be present to its eyes. (Laplace, 1820. Translation by Truscott and Emory, 1951, pp. 3–4)

The assumption of determinism is simply the apparently reasonable notion that events are *caused*. Science discovers regularities in nature, formulates descriptions of these regularities, and provides explanations, that is to say, discovers causes. Knowledge of the past enables the future to be predicted. This is the popular view of science and it is also a sort of working rule of thumb for those engaged in the scientific enterprise. Determinism is *the* central feature of the development of modern science up to the first quarter of the 20th century. The successes of the natural sciences, particularly the success of Newtonian mechanics, urged and influenced some of the giants of psychology, particularly in North America, to adopt a similar mechanistic approach to the study of behavior. The rise of *behaviorism* promoted the view that psychology could be a science, "like other sciences." Formulae could be devised that would allow behavior to be predicted, and a technology could be achieved that would enable environmental conditions to be so manipulated that behavior could be controlled. The variability in living things was to be brought under *experimental* control, a program that leads quite naturally to the notion of the *stimulus* control of *behavior*. It follows that concepts such as *will* or *choice* or *freedom of action* could be rejected by behavioral science.

In 1913 John B. Watson (1878–1958) published a paper that became the behaviorists' manifesto. It begins, "Psychology as the behaviorist views it is a purely objective experimental branch of natural science. Its theoretical goal is the prediction and control of behavior" (Watson, 1913, p. 158).

Oddly enough this pronouncement coincided with work that began to question the assumption of determinism in physics, the undoubted leader of the natural sciences. In 1913 a laboratory experiment in Cambridge, England, provided spectroscopic proof of what is known as the Rutherford-Bohr model of the atom. Ernest Rutherford (later Lord Rutherford, 1871–1937) had proposed that the atom was like a miniature solar system with electrons orbiting a central nucleus. Niels Bohr (1885–1962), a Danish physicist, explained that the electrons moved from one orbit to another emitting or absorbing energy as they moved toward or away from the nucleus. The jumping of an electron from orbit to orbit appeared to be unpredictable. The totality of exchanges could only be predicted in a statistical, probabilistic fashion. That giant of modern physicists, Albert Einstein (1879–1955), whose work had helped to start the revolution in physics, was loath to abandon the concept of a completely causal universe and indeed never did entirely abandon it. In the 1920s Einstein made the statement that has often been paraphrased as, "God does not play dice with the world." Nevertheless he recognized the problem. In a lecture, given in 1928, Einstein said,

> Today faith in unbroken causality is threatened precisely by those whose path it had illumined as their chief and unrestricted leader at the front, namely by the representatives of physics . . . All natural laws are therefore claimed to be, "in principle," of a statistical variety and our imperfect observation practices alone have cheated us into a belief in strict causality. (Quoted by Clark, 1971, pp. 347–348)

But Einstein never really accepted this proposition, believing to the end that indeterminacy was to be equated with ignorance. Einstein may be right in subscribing ultimately to the inflexibility of Laplace's all-seeing demon, but another approach to indeterminacy was advanced by Werner Heisenberg (1902–1981) a German physicist who, in 1927, formulated his famous *uncertainty principle*. He examined not merely the practical limits of measurement but the *theoretical* limits, and showed that the act of observation of the position and velocity of a sub-atomic particle interfered with it so as to inevitably produce errors in the measurement of one or the other. This assertion has been taken to mean that, ultimately, the forces in our universe are random and therefore indeterminate. Bertrand Russell disagrees:

> Space and time were invented by the Greeks, and served their purpose admirably until the present century. Einstein replaced them by a kind of centaur which he called "space-time," and this did well enough for a couple of decades, but modern quantum mechanics has made it evident that a more fundamental reconstruction is necessary. The Principle of Indeterminacy is merely an illustration of this necessity, not of the failure of physical laws to determine the course of nature. (Russell, 1931, pp. 108–109)

The important point to be aware of is that Heisenberg's principle refers to the observer and the act of observation and *not* directly to the phenomena that are being observed. This implies that the phenomena have an existence outside their observation and description, a contention that, by itself, occupies philosophers. Nowhere is the demonstration that technique and method shape the way in which we conceptualize phenomena more apparent than in the physics of light. The progress of events in physics that led to the view that light was both wave and particle, a view that Einstein's work had promoted, began to dismay him when it was used to suggest that physics would have to abandon strict continuity and causality. Bohr responded to Einstein's dismay,

You, the man who introduced the idea of light as particles! If you are so concerned with the situation in physics in which the nature of light allows for a dual interpretation, then ask the German government to ban the use of photoelectric cells if you think that light is waves, or the use of diffraction gratings if light is corpuscular. (Quoted by Clark, 1971, p. 253)

The parallels in experimental psychology are obvious.

That eminent historian of the discipline, Edwin Boring, describes a colloquium at Harvard when his colleague, William McDougall who:

. . . believed in freedom for the human mind—in at least a little residue of freedom—believed in it and hoped for as much as he could save from the inroads of scientific determinism . . .

and he, a determinist, achieved, for Boring, an understanding:

McDougall's freedom was my variance. McDougall hoped that variance would always be found in specifying the laws of behavior, for there freedom might still persist. I hoped then—less wise than I think I am now (it was 31 years ago)—that science would keep pressing variance towards zero as a limit. At any rate this general fact emerges from this example: freedom, when you believe it is operating, always resides in an area of ignorance. If there is a known law, you do not have freedom. (Boring, 1957, p. 190)

Boring was really unshakeable in his belief in determinism, and that most influential of psychologists, B.F. Skinner, agrees with the necessity of assuming order in nature,

It is a working assumption which must be adopted at the very start. We cannot apply the methods of science to a subject matter which is assumed to move about capriciously. Science not only describes, it predicts. It deals not only with the past but with the future. . . . If we are to use the methods of science in the field of human affairs, we must assume that behavior is lawful and determined. (Skinner, 1953, p. 6)

Carl Rogers is among those who have adopted as a fundamental position the view that individuals are responsible, free, and spontaneous. Rogers believes that, "the individual chooses to fulfill himself by playing a responsible and voluntary part in bringing about the destined events of the world" (Rogers, 1962, quoted by Walker, 1970, p. 13).

The use of the word *destined* in this assertion somewhat spoils the impact of what most take to be the individualistic and humanistic approach that is espoused by Rogers. Indeed he has maintained that the concepts of scientific determinism and personal choice can peacefully coexist in the way in which the particle and wave theories of light coexist. The theories are true but incompatible.

These few words do little more than suggest the problems that are faced by the philosopher of science when he or she tackles the concept of *method* in both the natural and the social sciences. What basic assumptions *can* we make? So often the arguments presented by humanistic psychologists have strong moral or even theological undertones whereas those offering the determinist's view point to the regularities that exist in nature—even human nature—and aver that without such regularities behaviour would be unpredictable. Clearly beings whose behavior was completely unpredictable would have been unable to achieve the degree of technological and social cooperation that marks the human species. Indeed individuals of all philosophical persuasions tend to agree that someone whose behavior is generally not predictable needs some sort of treatment. On the other hand the notion of moral responsibility implies freedom. If I am to be praised for my good works and blamed for my sins, a statement that "nature is merely unfolding as it should" is unlikely to be accepted as a defense for the latter, and unlikely to be advanced by me as a reason for the former. One way out of the *impasse*, it is suggested, is to reject strict "100 percent" determinism and to accept statistical determinism. "Freedom" then becomes part of the error term in statistical manipulations. Grünbaum (1952) considers the arguments against both strict determinism and statistical determinism, arguments based upon the complexity of human behavior, the concept of moral choice and the assignment of responsibility, assertions that individuals are unique and that therefore their actions are not generalizable in the scientific sense, and that human beings via their goal seeking behavior themselves determine the future. He concludes, "Since the important arguments against determinism which we have considered are without foundation, the psychologist need not be deterred in his quest and can confidently use the causal hypothesis as a principle, undaunted by the *caveat* of the philosophical indeterminist" (Grünbaum, 1952, p. 676).

Feigl (1959) insists that freedom must not be confused with the absence of causality, and causal determination must not be confused with coercion or compulsion or constraint. "To be free means that the chooser or agent is an essential link in the chain of causal events and that no extraneous compulsion—be it physical, biological, or psychological—forces him to act in a direction incompatible with his basic desires or intentions" (Feigl, 1959, p. 116).

To some extent, and many modern thinkers would say to a large extent (and Feigl agrees with this), philosophical perplexities can be clarified, if not entirely resolved, by examining the *meaning* of the terms employed in the debate rather than arguing about *reality*.

Two further points might be made. The first is that variability and uncertainty in observations in the natural as well as the social sciences require a statistical approach in order to reveal broad regularities, and this applies to experimentation and observation *now*, whatever philosophical stance is adopted. If the very idea of regularity is rejected then systematic approaches to the study of the human condition are irrelevant. The second is that, at the end of the discussion, most will smile with Dr Samuel Johnson when he said, "I *know* that I have free will and there's an end on it."

SCIENCE AND INDUCTION

It is common to trace the Western intellectual tradition to two fountainheads, Greek philosophy, particularly Aristotelian philosophy, and Judaic/Christian theology. Science began with the Greeks in the sense that they set out its commonly accepted ground rules. Science proceeds systematically. It gives us a knowledge of nature that is public and demonstrable and, most importantly, open to correction. Science provides explanations that are rational and, in principle, testable, rather than mystical or symbolic or theological. The cold rationality that this implies has been tempered by the Judaic/Christian notion of the compassionate human being as a creature constructed in the image of God, and, by the belief that the universe is the creation of God and as such deserves the attention of the beings that inhabit it. It is these streams of thought that give us the debate about intellectual values and scientific responsibility and sustain the view that science cannot be metaphysically neutral nor value free.

But it is not true to say that these traditions have continuously guided Western thought. Christianity took some time to become established. Greek philosophy and science disappeared under the pragmatic technologists of Rome. Judaism, weakened by the loss of its home and the persecution of its adherents, took refuge in the refinement and interpretation of its ancient doctrines. When Christianity did become the intellectual shelter for the thinkers of Europe it embraced the view that God revealed what He wished to reveal and that nature everywhere was symbolic of a general moral truth known only to Him. These ideas, formalized by the first great Christian philosopher, St. Augustine (354–430), persisted up to, and beyond, the Renaissance, and simplistic versions may be seen in the expostulations of fundamentalist preachers today. For the best part of 1,000 years scientific thinking was not an important part of intellectual advance.

Aristotle's rationalism was revived by "the schoolmen," of whom the greatest was Thomas Aquinas (1225?–1274), but the influence of science and the shaping of the modern intellectual world began in the 17th century.

> The modern world, so far as mental outlook is concerned, begins in the seventeenth century. No Italian of the Renaissance would have been unintelligible to Plato or Aristotle; Luther would have horrified Thomas Aquinas, but would not have been difficult for him to understand. With the seventeenth century it is different: Plato and Aristotle, Aquinas and Occam, could not have made head or tail of Newton. (Russell, 1946, p. 512)

This is not to deny the work of earlier scholars. Leonardo da Vinci (1452–1519) vigorously propounded the importance of experience and observation, and enthusiastically wrote of causality and the "certainty" of mathematics. Francis Bacon (1561–1626) is a particular example of one who expressed the importance of system and method in the gaining of new knowledge and his contribution, though often underestimated, is of great interest to psychologists. Hearnshaw (1987) gives an account of Bacon that shows how his ideas can be seen in the foundation and progress of experimental and inductive psychology. He notes that although, "Bacon himself made few detailed contributions to general psychology as such, he saw more clearly than anyone of his time the need for, and the potentialities of, a psychology founded on empirical data, and capable of being applied to 'the relief of man's estate'" (Hearnshaw, 1987, p. 55).

A turning point for modern science arrives with the work of Copernicus (1473–1543). His account of the heliocentric theory of our planetary system was published in the year of his death and had little impact until the 17th century. The Copernican theory involved no new facts, nor did it contribute to mathematical simplicity. As Ginzburg (1936) notes, Copernicus reviewed the existing facts and came up with a simpler physical hypothesis than that of Ptolemaic theory which stated that the earth was the center of the universe.

The fact that PTOLEMY and his successors were led to make an affirmation in violence to the facts as then known shows that their acceptance of the belief in the immobility of the earth at the centre of the universe was not the result of incomplete knowledge but rather the result of a positive prejudice emanating from non-scientific considerations. (Ginzburg, 1936, p. 308)

This statement is one that scientists, when they are wearing their scientists' hats, would support and elaborate upon, but an examination of the state of the psychological sciences could not fully sustain it. Nowhere is our knowledge more incomplete than in the study of the human condition and nowhere are our interpretations more open to prejudice and ideology. The study of differences between the sexes, the nature-nurture issue in the examination of human personality, intelligence, and aptitude, the sociobiological debate on the interpretation of the way in which societies are organized, all are marked by undertones of ethics and ideology that the scientific purist would see as outside the notion of an autonomous science. Nor is this a complete list.

Science is not so much about *facts* as about interpretations of observation, and interpretations as well as observations are guided and molded by preconceptions. Ask someone to "observe" and he or she will ask what it is that is to be observed. To suggest that the manipulation and analysis of numerical data, in the sense of the actual *methods* employed, can also be guided by preconceptions seems very odd. Nevertheless, the development of statistics was heavily influenced by the ideological stance of its developers. The strength of statistical analysis is that its latter-day users do not have to subscribe to the particular views of the pioneers in order to appreciate its utility and apply it successfully.

A common view is that science proceeds through the process of *induction*. Put simply, this is the view that the future will resemble the past. The occurrence of an event *A* will lead us to expect an event *B* if past experience has shown *B* always following *A*. The *general principle* that *B* follows *A* is quickly accepted. Reasoning from particular cases to general principles is seen as the very foundation of science.

The concepts of *causality* and *inference* come together in the process of induction. The great Scottish philosopher, David Hume (1711–1776), threw down a challenge that still occupies the attention of philosophers.

As to past *experience*, it can be allowed to give *direct* and *certain* information of those precise objects only, and that precise period of time, which fell under its cognizance: but why this experience should be extended to future times, and to other objects, which for aught we know, may be only in appearance similar; this is the main question on which I would insist.

These two propositions are far from being the same, *I have found that such an object has always been attended with such an effect* and *I foresee that other objects, which are, in appearance, similar, will be attended with similar effects.* I shall allow, if you please, that the one proposition may justly be inferred from the other: I know, in fact, that it always is inferred. But if you insist that the inference is made by a chain of reasoning, I desire you to produce that reasoning. (Hume, 1748. Edited version 1951, Yalden-Thomson, pp. 33–34)

The arguments against Hume's assertion that it is merely the frequent conjunction or sequencing of two events that leads us to a belief that one *causes* the other have been presented in many forms and this account cannot examine them all. The most obvious counter is that Hume's own assertion invokes causality. Contiguity in time and space *causes* us to assume causality. Popper (1962) notes that the idea of repetition based on similarity as the basis of a belief in causality presents difficulties. Situations are never *exactly* the same. Similar situations are interpreted as repetitions from a particular point of view—and that point of view is a system of "expectations, anticipations, assumptions, or interests" (Popper, 1962, p. 45).

In psychological matters there is the additional factor of *volition*. I wish to pick up my pen and write. A chain of nervous and muscular and cognitive processes ensues and I *do* write. The fact that human beings can and do control their future actions leads to a situation where a general denial of causality flies in the face of common sense. Such a denial invites mockery.

Hume's argument that experience does not justify prediction is more difficult to counter. The course of natural events is not wholly predictable and the history of the scientific enterprise is littered with the ruins of theories and explanations that subsequent experience showed to be wanting. Hume's scepticism, if it was accepted, would lead to a situation where nothing could be learned from experience and observation. The history of human affairs would refute this, but the argument undoubtedly leads to a cautious approach. Predicting the future becomes a probabilistic exercise and science is no longer able to claim to be the way to certainty and truth.

Using the probability calculus as an aid to prediction is one thing, using it to assess the value of a particular theory is another. Popper (1962) regards statements about theories having a *high degree of probability* as misconceptions. Theories can be invoked to explain various phenomena and good theories are those that stand up to severe test. But, Popper argues, corroboration cannot be equated with mathematical probability:

> . . . all theories, including the best, have the same probability, namely zero.
>
> That an appeal to probability is incapable of solving the riddle of experience is a conclusion first reached long ago by David Hume.
> . . . experience does not consist in the mechanical accumulation of observations. Experience is creative. It is the result of free, bold and creative interpretations, controlled by severe criticism and severe tests. (Popper, 1962, pp. 192–193)

INFERENCE

Induction is, and will continue to be, a large problem for philosophical discussion. *Inference* can be narrowed down. Although the terms are sometimes used in the same sense and with the same meaning, it is useful to reserve the term *inference* for the making of explicit statements about the properties of a wider universe that are based on a much narrower set of observations. Statistical inference is precisely that, and the discussion just presented leads to the argument that *all* inference is probabilistic and therefore all inferential statements are statistical.

Statistical inference is a way of reasoning that presents itself as a mathematical solution to the problem of induction. The search for rules of inference from the time of Bernoulli and Bayes to that of Neyman and Pearson has provided the spur for the development of mathematical probability theory. It has been argued that the establishing of a set of recipes for data manipulation has led to a situation where researchers in the social sciences "allow statistics to do the thinking for them." It has been further argued that psychological questions that do not lend themselves to the collection and manipulation of quantitative data are neglected or ignored. These criticisms are not to be taken lightly but they can be answered. In the first place, statistical inference is only a part of formal psychological investigation. An equally important component is *experimental design*. It is the lasting contribution of Ronald Fisher, a mathematical statistician and a champion of the practical researcher, that showed us how the formulation of intelligent questions in systematic frameworks would produce data that, with the help of statistics, could provide intelligent answers. In the second place, the social sciences have repeatedly come up with techniques that have enabled qualitative data to be quantified.

In experimental psychology two broad strategies have been adopted for coping with variability. The *experimental analytic* approach sets out boldly to contain or to standardize as many of the sources of variability as possible. In the micro-universe of the Skinner box, shaping and observing the rat's behavior depends on a knowledge of the antecedent and present conditions under which a particular piece of behavior may be observed. The second approach is that of statistical inference. Experimental psychologists control (in the sense of standardize or equalize) those variables that they can control, measure what they wish to measure with a degree of precision, assume that noncontrolled factors operate randomly, and hope that statistical methods will tease out the "effects" from the "error." Whatever the strategy, experimentalists will agree that the knowledge they obtain is approximate. It has also been generally assumed that this *approximate science* is an interim science. Probability is part of scientific method but not part of knowledge. Some writers have rejected this view. Reichenbach (1938), for example, sought to devise a formal probability logic in which judgments of the truth or falsity of propositions is replaced by the notion of *weight*. Probability belongs to a class of events. Weight refers to a single event, and a single event can belong to many classes.

> Suppose a man forty years old has tuberculosis; . . . Shall we consider . . . the frequency of death within the class of men forty years old, or within the class of tubercular people?. . .
> We take the narrowest class for which we have reliable statistics . . . we should take the class of tubercular men of forty . . . the narrower the class the better the determination of weight . . . a cautious physician will even place the man in question within a narrower class by making an X-ray; he will then use as the weight of the case, the probability of death belonging to a condition of the kind observed on the film. (Reichenbach, 1938, pp. 316–317)

This is a frequentist view of probability and it is the view that is implicit in statistical inference. Reichenbach's thesis should have an appeal for experimental psychologists, although it is not widely known. It reflects, in formal terms, the way in which psychological knowledge is reported in the journals and textbooks, although whether or not the writers and researchers recognize this may be debated. The weight of a given proposition is relative to the state of our knowledge and statements about particular individuals and particular behaviors are prone to error. It is not that we are totally ignorant, but that many of our classes are too broad to allow for substantial weight to be placed on the evidence. Popper (1959) takes issue with Reichenbach's attempts to extend the relative frequency view of probability to include *inductive probability*. Popper, with Hume, maintains that a theory of induction is impossible,

> We shall have to get accustomed to the idea that we must not look upon science as a 'body of knowledge', but rather as a system of hypotheses; that is to say, as a

system of guesses or anticipations . . . of which we are never justified in saying that we know that they are 'true' or 'more or less certain' or even 'probable'. (Popper, 1959, p. 317)

Now Popper admits only that a system is scientific when it can be *tested* by experience. Scientific statements are tested by attempts to refute or falsify them. Theories that withstand severe tests are *corroborated* by the tests, but they are not proven, nor are they even made more probable. It is difficult to gainsay Popper's logic and Hume's scepticism. They are food for philosophical thought, but scientists who perhaps occasionally worry about such things will put them aside, if only because working scientists are practical people. The principle of induction is *the* principle of science and the fact that Popper and Hume can shout from the philosophical sidelines that the "official" rules of the game are irrational and that the "real" rules of the game are not fully appreciated, will not stop the game from being played.

Statistical inference may be defined as the use of methods based on the rules of *chance* to draw conclusions from quantitative data. It may be directly compared with exercises where numbered tickets are drawn from a bag of tickets with a view to making statements about the composition of the bag, or where a die or a coin is tossed with a view to making statements about its fairness. Suppose a bag contains tickets numbered 1, 2, 3, 4, and 5. Each numeral appears on the same, very large, number of tickets. Now suppose that 25 tickets are drawn, *at random and with replacement* from the bag and the sum of the numbers calculated. The obtained sum could be as low as 25 and as high as 125, but the *expected* value of the sum will be 75, because each of the numerals should occur on one fifth of the draws or thereabouts. The sum should be $5(1 + 2 + 3 + 4 + 5) = 75$. In practice, a given draw will have a sum that departs from this value by an amount above or below it that can be described as *chance error*. The likely size of this error is given by a statistic called the *standard error*, which is readily computed from the formula $\sigma(\sqrt{n})$, where σ is the standard deviation of the numbers in the bag. Leaving aside, for the moment, the problem of estimating σ when, as is usual, the contents of the bag are unknown, all *classical* statistical inferential procedures stem from this sort of exercise. The real variability in the bag is given by the standard deviation, and the *chance* variability in the *sums* of the numbers drawn is given by the standard error.

STATISTICS IN PSYCHOLOGY

The use of quantitative methods in the study of mental processes begins with Gustav Fechner (1801–1887) who set himself the problem of examining the relationship between stimulus and sensation. In 1860 he published *Elemente der Psychophysik* in which he describes his invention of a psychophysical law that describes the relationship between mind and body. He developed methods of measuring sensation based upon mathematical and statistical considerations, methods that have their echoes in present-day experimental psychology. Fechner made use of the *normal law* in his development of the method of constant stimuli, applying it in the Gaussian sense as a way of dealing with error and uncontrolled variation.

Fechner's basic assumptions and the conclusions he drew from his experimental investigations have been shown to be faulty. Stevens work in the 1950s and the later developments of *signal detection theory* have overtaken the work of the 19th century psychophysicists, but the revolutionary nature of Fechner's methods profoundly influenced experimental psychology. Boring (1950) devotes a whole chapter of his book on the history of experimental psychology to the work of Fechner.

Investigations of mental inheritance and mental testing began at about the same time with Galton who took the *normal law of error* from Quetelet and made it the centerpiece of his research. The error distribution of physics became a description of the distribution of values about a value that was "most probable." Galton laid the foundations of the method of correlation that was refined by Karl Pearson, work that will be examined in more detail later. At the turn of the century Charles Spearman (1863–1945) used the method to define mental abilities as *factors*. When two apparently different abilities are shown to be correlated, Spearman took this as evidence for the existence of a general factor G, a factor of general intelligence, and factors that were specific to the different abilities. Correlational methods in psychology were dominant for almost the whole of the first half of this century and the techniques of *factor analysis* were honed during this period. Dodd (1928) reviewed the considerable literature that had accumulated over the 23 years since Spearman's original work and Wolfle (1940) pushed this labor further. Wolfle quotes Thurstone on what he takes to be the most important use of factor analysis.

Factor analysis is useful especially in those domains where basic and fruitful concepts are essentially lacking and where crucial experiments have been difficult to conceive . . .

They enable us to make only the crudest first map of a new domain. But if we have scientific intuition and sufficient ingenuity, the rough factorial map of a new domain will enable us to proceed beyond the factorial stage to the more direct forms of psychological experimentation in the laboratory. (Thurstone, 1940, pp. 189–190)

The interesting point about this statement is that it clearly sees factor analysis as a method of data exploration rather than an experimental method. As Lovie (1984) points out, Spearman's approach was that of an experimenter using correlational techniques to confirm his hypothesis, but, from 1940 on, that view of the methods of factor analysis has not prevailed.

Of course, the beginnings of general descriptive techniques crept into the psychological literature over the same period. Means and probable errors are commonly reported and correlation coefficients are also accompanied by estimates of their probable error. And it was around 1940 that psychologists started to become aware of the work of R.A. Fisher and to adopt *analysis of variance* as *the* tool of experimental work. It can be argued that the progression of events that led to Fisherian statistics also led to a division in empirical psychology, a split between *correlational* and *experimental* psychology.

Cronbach (1957) chose to discuss the "two disciplines" in his APA presidential address. He notes that in the beginning,

All experimental procedures were tests, all tests were experiments.

. . . the statistical comparison of treatments appeared only around 1900 . . . Inference replaced estimation: the mean and its probable error gave way to the critical ratio. The standardized conditions and the standardized instruments remained, but the focus shifted to the single manipulated variable, and later, following Fisher, to multivariate manipulation. (Cronbach, 1957, p. 674)

Although there have been signs that the two disciplines can work together the basic situation has not changed much over 30 years. Individual differences are *error variance* to the experimenter, it is the between-groups or *treatment variance* that is of interest. Differential psychologists look for variations and relationships among variables *within* treatment conditions. Indeed, variation in the situation here leads to error.

It may be fairly claimed that these fundamental differences in approach have had the most profound effect on psychology. And it may be further claimed that the sophistication and success of the methods of analysis that are used by the two camps have helped to formalize the divisions. Correlation and ANOVA have led to mutiple regression analysis and MANOVA and yet the methods are based on the same model—the general linear model. Unfortunately, statistical consumers are frequently unaware of the fundamentals, frightened away by the mathematics, or bored and frustrated by the arguments on the rationale of the probability calculus, they avoid investigation of the general structure of the methods. When these problems have been overcome the face of psychology may change.

3

Measurement

IN RESPECT OF MEASUREMENT

In the late 19th century the eminent scientist, William Thomson, Lord Kelvin, (1824–1907) remarked,

> I often say that when you can measure what you are speaking about, and express it in numbers, you know something about it; but when you cannot measure it, when you cannot express it in numbers, your knowledge is of a meagre and unsatisfactory kind: it may be the beginning of knowledge, but you have scarcely, in your thoughts, advanced to the stage of *science* whatever the matter might be. (William Thomson, Lord Kelvin, 1891, p. 80)

This expression of the paramount importance of measurement is part of our scientific tradition. Many versions of the same sentiment, for example, that of Galton, noted in chapter 1, and that of S.S. Stevens, (1906–1973), whose work will be discussed later in this chapter, are frequently noted with approval. Clearly, measurement bestows scientific respectability, a state of affairs that does scant justice to the work of people like Harvey, Darwin, Pasteur, Freud, and James, who, it will be noted, if they are to be labeled "scientists," are biological or behavioral scientists. The nature of the data and the complexity of the systems studied by these men are quite different in quality from the relatively simple systems that were the domain of the physical scientist. This is not, of course, to deny the difficulty of the conceptual and experimental questions of modern physics, but the fact remains that, in this field, problems can often be dealt with in controlled isolation.

It is, perhaps, comforting to observe that, in the early years, there was a scepticism about the introduction of mathematics into the social sciences. Kendall (1968) quotes a writer in the *Saturday Review* of November 11th, 1871, who states,

> If we say that *G* represents the confidence of Liberals in Mr Gladstone and *D* the confidence of Conservatives in Mr Disraeli and x, y the number of those parties; and infer that Mr Gladstone's tenure of office depends upon some equation involving dG/dx, dD/dy, we have merely wrapped up a plain statement in a mysterious collection of letters. (Kendall, 1968, p. 271)

And for George Udny Yule, the most level-headed of the early statisticians,

> Measurement does not necessarily mean progress. Failing the possibility of measuring that which you desire, the lust for measurement may, for example, merely result in your measuring something else—and perhaps forgetting the difference—or in your ignoring some things because they cannot be measured. (Yule, 1921, pp. 106–107)

To equate science with measurement is a mistake. Science is about systematic and controlled observations and the attempt to verify or falsify those observations. And if the prescription of science demanded that observations *must* be quantifiable, then the natural as well as the social sciences would be severely retarded. The doubts about the absolute utility of quantitative description expressed so long ago could well be pondered on by today's practitioners of experimental psychology. Nevertheless, the fact of the matter is that the early years of the young discipline of psychology show, with some notable exceptions, a longing for quantification and, thereby, acceptance. In 1885 Joseph Jacobs reviewed Ebbinghaus's famous work on memory, *Ueber das Gedachtnis*. He notes "If science be measurement it must be confessed that psychology is in a bad way" (Jacobs, 1885, p. 454).

Jacobs praises Ebbinghaus's painstaking investigations and his careful reporting of his measurements,

> May we hope to see the day when school registers will record that such and such a lad possesses 36 British Association units of memory power or when we shall be able to calculate how long a mind of 17 'macaulays' will take to learn Book ii of *Paradise Lost*? If this be visionary, we may at least hope for much of interest and practical utility in the comparison of the varying powers of different minds which can now at last be laid down to scale. (Jacobs, 1885, p. 459)

The enthusiasm of the mental measurers of the first half of the 20th century reflects the same dream and, even today, the smile that Jacobs' words might bring to the faces of hardened test constructors and users contains a little of the old yearning. The urge to quantify our observations and to impose sophisticated statistical manipulations upon them is a very powerful one in the social sciences. It is of critical importance to remember that sloppy and shoddy measurement cannot be forgiven or forgotten by presenting dazzling tables of figures, clean and finely-drawn graphs, or by statistical *legerdemain*.

Yule (1921), reviewing Brown and Thomson's book on mental measurement, comments on the problem in remarks that are not untypical of the misgivings expressed, on occasion, by statisticians and mathematicians when they see their methods in action.

> . . . *measurement*! O dear! Isn't it almost an insult to the word to term some of these numerical data *measurements*? They are of the nature of estimates, most of them, and outrageously bad estimates often at that.
>
> And it should always be the aim of the experimenter not to revel in statistical methods (when he does revel and not swear) but steadily to diminish, by continual improvement of his experimental methods, the necessity for their use and the influence they have on his conclusions. (Yule, 1921, pp. 105–106)

The general tenor of this criticism is still valid but the combination of experimental design and statistical method introduced a little later by Sir Ronald Fisher provided the hope, if not the complete reality, of statistical as opposed to strict experimental control. The modern statistical approach more readily recognizes the intrinsic variability in living matter and its associated systems. Furthermore, Yule's remarks were made before it became clear that *all* acts of observation contain irreducible uncertainty (as was noted in chap. 2).

Nearly 40 years after Yule's review, Kendall (1959) gently reminded us of the importance of precision in observation and that statistical procedures cannot replace it. In an acute and amusing parody he tells the story of Hiawatha. It is a tragic tale. Hiawatha, a "mighty hunter," was an abysmal marksman although he did have the advantage of having majored in applied statistics. Partly relying on his comrades' ignorance of the subject, he attempted to show that his patently awful performance in a shooting contest was not significantly different from that of his fellows. Still, they took away his bow and arrows.

> In a corner of the forest
> Dwells alone my Hiawatha
> Permanently cogitating
> On the normal law of error.
> Wondering in idle moments
> Whether an increased precision
> Might perhaps be rather better
> Even at the risk of bias
> If thereby one, now and then, could
> Register upon the target.
> (Kendall, 1959, p. 24)

SOME FUNDAMENTALS

Measurement is the application of mathematics to events. We use numbers to designate objects and events and the relationships that obtain between them. On occasion the objects are quite real and the relationships immediately comprehensible; dining-room tables, for example, and their dimensions, weights, surface areas, and so on. At other times, we may be dealing with intangibles such as intelligence, or leadership, or self-esteem. In these cases our measurements are descriptions of behavior that, we assume, reflects the underlying construct. But the critical concern is the hope that measurement will provide us with precise and economical descriptions of events in a manner that is readily communicated to others. Whatever one's view of mathematics with regard to its complexities and difficulty, it is generally regarded as a discipline that is clear, orderly, and rational. The scientist attempts to add clarity, order, and rationality to the world about us by using measurement.

Measurement has been a fundamental feature of human civilization from its very beginnings. Division of labor, trade, and barter are aspects of our condition that separate us from the hunters and gatherers who were our forebears. Trade and commerce mean that accounting practices are instituted and the "worth" of a job or an artifact has to be labeled and described. When groups of individuals agreed that a sheep could fetch three decent-sized spears and a couple of cooking-pots we see that the species has made a quantum leap into a world of measurement. Counting, making a tally, represents the simplest form of measurement. Simple though it is, it requires that we have devised an orderly and determinate *number* system.

Development of early societies, like the development of children, must have included the mastery of signs and symbols for differences and sameness and, particularly, for oneness and twoness. Most primitive languages at least have words for "one," "two," and "many," and modern languages, including English, have extra words for one and two (single, sole, lone, couple, pair, and so on).

Trade, commerce, and taxation encouraged the development of more complex number systems that required more symbols. The simple tally recorded by a mark on a slate may be made more comprehensible by altering the mark at convenient groupings, for example at every five units. This system, still followed by some primitive tribes as well as by psychologists when constructing, by hand, frequency tables from large amounts of data, corresponds with a readily available and portable counting aid—the fingers of one hand.

It is likely that the familiar decimal system developed because the human hands together have 10 digits. However, vigessimal systems, based on 20, are known, and language once again recognizes the utility of 20 with the word *score* in English and *quatre-vingt* for 80 in French. Contrary to general belief, the decimal system is not the easiest to use arithmetically and it is unlikely that decimal schemes will replace *all* other counting systems. Eggs and cakes will continue to be sold in dozens rather than tens and the hours about the clock will still be 12. This is because 12 has more integral fractional parts than 10, that is, you can divide 12 by more numbers and get whole numbers and not fractions (which everyone finds hard) than you can 10. Viewed in this way the now-abandoned British monetary system of 12 pennies to the shilling and 20 shillings to the pound does not seem so odd or irrational.

Systems of number notation and counting have a *base* or *radix*. Base 5 (quinary), 10 (decimal), 12 (duodecimal), and 20 (vigessimal) have been mentioned but any base is theoretically possible. For many scientific purposes binary (base 2) is used because this system lies at the heart of the operations of the electronic computer. Its two symbols, 0 and 1, can readily be reproduced in the *off* and *on* modes of electrical circuitry. Octal (base 8) and hexadecimal (base 16) will also be familiar to computer users. The *base* of a number system corresponds to the number of symbols that it needs to express a number, provided that the system is a *place* system. A decimal number, say 304, means 3 × 100 plus 0 × 10 plus 4 × 1.

The symbol for zero signifies an empty place. The invention of zero, the earliest undoubted occurrence of which is in India over 1,000 years ago but which was independently used by the Mayas of Yucatan, marks an important step forward in mathematical notation and arithmetical operation. The ancient Babylonians, who developed a highly advanced mathematics some 4,000 years ago, had a system with a base of 60 (a base with many integral fractions) that did not have a zero. Their scripts did not distinguish between say, 125 and 7,205, and which one is meant often has to be inferred from the context. The absence of a zero in Roman numerals may explain why Rome is not remembered for its mathematicians, and the relative sophistication of Greek mathematics leads some historians to believe that zero may have been invented in the Greek world and thence transmitted to India.

Scales of Measurement

Using numbers to count events, to order events, and to express the relationship between events, is the essence of measurement. These activities have to be carried out according to some prescribed rule. S.S. Stevens (1951) in his classic piece on mathematics and measurement defines the latter as "the assignment of numerals to objects or events according to rules" (Stevens, 1951, p. 1).

This definition has been criticized on the reasonable grounds that it apparently does not exclude rules that do not help us to be informative, nor rules that ensure that the same numerals are always assigned to the same events under the same conditions. Ellis (1968) has pointed out that some such rule as, "Assign the first number that comes into your head to each of the objects on the table in turn," must be excluded from the definition of measurement if it is to be *determinative* and *informative*. Moreover, Ellis notes that a rule of measurement must allow for different numerals, or ranges of numerals, to be assigned to different things, or to the same things under different conditions. Rules such as "Assign the number 3 to everything" are degenerate rules. Measurement must be made on a scale, and we only have a scale when we have a nondegenerate, informative, determinative rule.

For the moment the historical narrative will be set aside in order to delineate and comment on the matter. Stevens distinguished four kinds of scales of measurement and he believes that all practical common scales fall into one or other of his categories. These categories are worth examining and their utility in the scientific enterprise considered.

The Nominal Scale

The nominal scale, as such, does not measure quantities. It measures identity and difference. It is often said that the first stage in a systematic empirical science is the stage of classification. Like is grouped with like. Events having characteristics in common are examined together. The ancient Greeks classified the constitution of nature into earth, air, fire, and water. Animal, vegetable, or mineral are convenient groupings. Mendeleev's (1834–1907) periodic table of the elements in chemistry, and plant and animal species classification in biology (the *Systema Naturae* of the great botanist Carl von Linne, known as Linnaeus {1707–1778}), and the many typologies that exist in psychology are further examples.

Numbers can, of course, be used to label events or categories of events. Street numbers, or house numbers, or numbers on football shirts "belong" to particular events, but there is, for example, no quantitative significance between player number 10 and player number 4, on a hockey team, in arithmetical terms. Player number 10 is not 2.5 times player number 4. Such arithmetical rules cannot be applied to the classificatory exercise. However, it is frequently the case that a tally, a count, will follow the construction of a taxonomy.

Clearly, classifications form a large part of the data of psychology. People may be labeled Conservative, Liberal, Democrat, Republican, Socialist, and so on, on the variable of "political affiliation," urban, suburban, rural, on the variable of "location of residence," and we could think of dozens, if not scores, of others.

The Ordinal Scale

The essential relationship that characterizes the ordinal scale is *greater than* (symbolized >) or *less than* (symbolized <). These scales of measurement have proved to be very useful in dealing with psychological variables. It might, for example, be comparatively easy to state that, according to some specified set of criteria, Bill is more neurotic than Zoe, who is more neurotic than John, or that

Mary is more musical than Sue who is more musical than Jane, and so on, even though we are not in possession of a precise measuring instrument that will determine by how much the individuals differ on our criteria. It follows that the numbers that we assign on the ordinal scale represent only an order.

In ordering a group of 10 individuals according to judgments in terms of a particular set of criteria for leadership, we may designate the one with the most leadership ability "1" and go through to the one with the least and rank this person "10," or we may start with the one with least ability and rank him or her "1," progressing to the one with most who we rank "10." Either method of ordering is permissible and both give precisely the same sort of information, provided that the one doing the ordering adheres to the system being used and communicates the rule to others.

The Interval and Ratio Scales

When the gaps between equal points, in the numerical sense, on the measurement scale are truly quantitatively equal, then the scale is called an *interval* scale. The difference between 130 cm and 137 cm is exactly the same as the difference between 137 cm and 144 cm. When this sort of scale starts at a true zero point, as in the distance or length scale just mentioned, Stevens designates them *ratio* scales. For example, an individual who is 180 cm tall is twice the height of the child of 90 cm who, in turn, is twice the length of the baby of 45 cm. But when the scale has an arbitrary zero point, for example the Fahrenheit and Celsius temperature scales, these ratio operations are not legitimate. It is neither meaningful nor correct to say that a temperature of 30 is three times as hot as a temperature of 10. This ratio does not represent three times any temperature-related characteristic. Perhaps a more readily-appreciated example is that of calendar time. Although it is true to say that 60 years is twice 30 years it is meaningless to say that 2000 A.D. will be twice 1000 A.D. in any description of "age." In 1000 A.D. the famous Parthenon in Athens was not twice as old as it was in 500 A.D.. Why not? Because it was built in about 440 B.C.. It follows from these examples that arithmetical operations on a ratio scale are conducted on the scale values themselves but on the interval scale with its arbitrary zero such operations are conducted on the interval values.

The higher-order interval and ratio scales have all the properties of the lower-order nominal and ordinal scales and may be so applied. Psychologists, however, strive where possible for interval measurement for it has the appearance at least of greater precision. This desire sometimes leads to conceptual difficulties and statistical misunderstandings. It is easy to see that the 3 cm by which a line *A* of 12 cm differs from a line *B* of 9 cm is the same as the 3 cm by which *B* exceeds the 6-cm-long line *C*. We are agreed on how we will define a centimeter and measurement of length in these units is comparatively straightforward.

But what of this statement? "Albert has an Intelligence Quotient (IQ) of 120,

Billy one of 110, and Colin of 100." The *meaning* of the 10 point differences between these individuals, even when the measuring instrument (the test) used is specified, is not so easy to see, nor is it possible to say with complete confidence that the gap in intelligence between Albert and Billy is precisely the same amount as the gap between Billy and Colin. Suppose that Question 1 on our test, say, of numerical ability, asks the respondent to add 123 to 456; Question 2, to divide 432 by 144; and Question 3 to add the square of 123 to the square root of 144. Few would argue that these demands exhibit the same degree of difficulty, and, by the same token, few would agree on the weighting that might be assigned to the marks for each question. These weightings would, to some extent, reflect the differing concepts of numerical ability. How much more numerically able is the individual who has grasped the concept of square root than the one who understands nothing beyond addition and subtraction? Although these examples could, quite justifiably, be described as exaggerated, they are given to show how difficult, indeed, impossible, it is to construct a true interval scale for a test of intelligence.

Leaving aside for the moment the fact that no perfectly reliable instrument exists for the measurement of IQ, we also know that there is no clear agreement on the definition of IQ. In other words, statements about the magnitude of the differences in length between lines *A*, *B*, and *C*, or in IQ between Albert, Billy, and Colin depend upon the existence of a standard unit of measurement and upon a constant unit of measurement, one that is the same over all points on the scale. In the case of the measurement of length, these conditions exist but in the measurement of IQ they do not.

Do our arithmetical manipulations of psychometric test scales, as though they were true interval scales, suggest that psychologists are prepared to ignore the imperfections in their scales for the sake of computational convenience? Certainly the situation just described emphasizes the responsibility of the measurer to report on how the scales he or she employs are used and to keep their limitations in mind.

Many, perhaps most, discussions of *scales of measurement* reveal a serious misconception that also arises from Stevens' examination. It is that the level of measurement, that is the specific measurement scale used in a particular investigation, governs the application of various statistical procedures when the data come to be analyzed. Briefly, the notion is abroad that an interval scale of measurement is required for the adhibition of parametric tests; the *t*-ratio, *F*-ratio, the Pearson correlation coefficient, and so on, all of which will be discussed later in this work. Gaito (1980) is one of a number of writers who have tried to expose the fallacy, noting that it is based on a confusion between measurement theory and statistical theory. Gaito reiterates some of the criticisms made by Lord (1953) who, in a witty and brilliant discussion, tells the story of a professor who computed the means and standard deviations of test scores behind locked doors because he had taught his students that such ordinal scores should not be added. Matters came to a head when the professor, in a story that should be read in the original, and not paraphrased, discovers that even the numbers on football jerseys behave as if they were "real," that is, interval scale, numbers. In fact, ". . . the numbers don't remember where they came from" (p. 751).

It is important to realize that the preceding remarks do not detract from Stevens' sterling contribution to the development of coherent concepts regarding scales in measurement theory. The difficulties arise when these are regarded as prescriptions for the choice and use of a wide variety of statistical techniques.

ERROR IN MEASUREMENT

All acts of measurement involve practical difficulties that are lumped together as the source of *measurement error*. From the statistical standpoint measurement error increases the variability in data sets, decreasing the precision of our summaries and inferences. It follows that scientists strive for accuracy by continually refining measuring techniques and instruments. The odd fact is that this strategy proceeds even though we know that absolutely precise measurement is impossible.

It is clear that a meter rule must be made from rigid material and that measuring tapes must not be elastic. Without this the instruments lack reliability and self-consistency and, put simply, separate and independent measurements of the same event are unlikely to agree with each other. Only very rarely do paper-and-pencil tests, or two forms of the same test (say a test of personality factors), give exactly the same results when given to an individual or group on two occasions. In a sense these tests are like elastic measuring tapes and the discrepancy between the outcomes is an index of their reliability. Perfect reliability is indexed 1. Poor reliability would be indexed 0.3 or less, and good reliability 0.8 or more. In accepting this latter figure as good reliability, the psychologist is accepting the inevitable error in measurement, being prepared to do so because he or she feels that a quantitative description better serves to grasp the concepts under investigation, to communicate ideas about the concepts more efficiently, and to describe the relationships between these concepts and others more clearly.

Reliability is not just a function of the quality of the instrument being used. In 1796, Maskelyne, Astronomer Royal and Director of the Royal Observatory at Greenwich, near London, England, dismissed Kinnebrook, one of the assistants, because Kinnebrook's timing of stellar transits differed from his, sometimes by as much as 1 sec.[1] The accuracy of such measurements is, of course, crucial to the calculation of the distance of the star from Earth. Some 20 years later this incident suggested to Bessel, the astronomer at Königsberg, that such errors were

---

[1]Kinnebrook was employed at the observatory from May 1794 to February 1796. For some more details of the incident and what happened to him see Rowe (1983).

the result of individual differences in observers and led to work on the *personal equation*. The astronomers believed that these discrepancies were due to physiological variability and early experiments on reaction time reflect this view. But, as scientific psychology has grown, the reaction time variable has been used to study choice and discrimination, predisposition, attitudes, and the dynamics of motivation. These events mark the beginnings of the psychology of individual differences. For the immediate argument, however, they illustrate the importance of both inter-observer and intra-observer reliability.

The circumstances of an exercise in measurement must remain constant for each separate observation. If we were, say, measuring the heights of individuals in a group, we would ensure that each of them stood up straight with heels together, chin in, chest out, head erect, no slouching, no tip-toeing, and so on. Quite simply, height has to be defined and our measurements are made in accord with that definition.

When a concept is defined in terms of the operations, manipulations, and measurements that are made in referring to it we have an *operational* definition. Intelligence might be defined as the score obtained on a particular test, a character trait like generosity might be defined as the proportion of one's income that one gives away. These sorts of definition serve to increase the precision of communication. They most certainly do not imply immediate agreement among scientists about the nature of the phenomena thus defined. Very few people would maintain that the above definitions of intelligence and generosity are entirely satisfactory.

Operationalism is closely allied to the philosophy of the *Vienna Circle*, a group, formed in the late 1920s, that aimed to clarify the logic of the scientific enterprise. The members of the Circle, mainly scientists and mathematicians, came to be known as *logical positivists*. They hoped to rid the language of science of all ambiguity and to confine the business of science to the testing of hypotheses about the observable world. In this philosophy, meaning is equated with verifiability and constructs that are not accessible to observation are meaningless. Psychologists will recognize this approach as closely akin to the doctrine of behaviorism. The view that theoretical constructs can be grasped via the measurement operations that describe them is an interesting one, for it challenges the contention that there can be no measurement without theory and that operations cannot be described in nontheoretical terms.

The logical positivist view is obviously attractive to the working scientist because it seems to be eminently "hard-nosed." The doctrine of operationalism demands an analysis of the nature of measurement and its contribution to the description of *facts*. To state that science is concerned with the verification of facts is to imply that there will be agreement among observers. It follows that new methods, new observational tools, as well as observer disagreement, will change the facts. The fact or reality of a tomato is quite different for the artist, the gourmet cook, and the botanist, and the botanical view changed dramatically when it became possible to view the cellular structure of the fruit through a high-power microscope.

In the broad view, this argument includes not only the idea of levels of agreement and verification, but also the validity of tools and measurements. Do they, in fact, measure what they were designed to measure? And what is meant by "designed to measure" must have some basis in a conceptual disposition if not a full-blown theory.

We must not only consider levels of measurement, but also the *limits* of measurement. In chapter 2 it was noted that observing a system disturbs the system, affects the act of measurement, and thus provokes an irreducible uncertainty in all scientific descriptions. This proposition is embodied in the *Uncertainty Principle* of Heisenberg. The nearer one tries to obtain an accurate measurement of either the momentum or the position of a sub-atomic particle, the less certain becomes the measurement of the other. Ultimately the principle applies to *all* acts of measurement.

The world of psychological measurement is beset with system-disturbing features. Experimenter-participant interactions and the arousing and motivating properties of the setting, be it the laboratory or the natural environment, contribute to variance in the data. These factors have been variously described as *experimenter effect*, *demand characteristics*, and, more generally, as *the social psychology of the psychological experiment*. They are examined at length by Rosenthal and Rosnow (1969) and Miller (1972).

Despite the difficulties, logical and practical, of the procedures, scientists will continue to measure. The behavioral scientist is trying to pin down, with as much rigor as possible, the variability of the properties of living matter that arise as a result of the interaction of environmental and genetic factors. As mentioned in chapter 1, Quetelet (1835) described these in terms of what we now call the *normal* distribution, using the analogy of Nature's "errors."

Now although Quetelet and Galton and others may be criticized for the promotion of the distribution as a "law of nature," their work recognized the irreducible variance in the properties of living matter. Once more this brings out the essential content of the statistical approach. It is that there can be no absolute accuracy in the measurement of a characteristic but only a judgment of accuracy in terms of the inherent variation within and between individuals. Statistics provide us with the tools for assessing the properties of these random fluctuations.

4

The Organization
of Data

THE EARLY INVENTORIES

The counting of people and livestock, hearths and homes, and goods and chattels is an exercise that has a long past. The ancient civilizations of Babylon and Egypt conducted censuses for the purposes of taxation and the raising of armies, perhaps 3,000 years before the birth of Christ, and indeed the birthplace of Christ himself was determined partly by the fact that Mary and Joseph traveled to Bethlehem in order to be registered for a Roman tax. Censuses were carried out fairly regularly by the Romans, but after the fall of Rome many centuries passed before they became part of the routine of government. It can be argued that these exercises are not really important in statistical history because they were not used for the purposes of making comparisons or for drawing inferences in the modern sense (that is, by using the probability calculus), but they are early examples of the descriptions of States.

When inferences were drawn they were informal. The utility of such descriptions was recognized by Aristotle who prepared accounts, that were largely non-numerical, of 158 states, listing details of their methods of administration, judicial systems, customs, and so on. Although almost all of these descriptions are lost, they clearly were intended to be used for comparative purposes and compiled as part of Aristotle's theory of the State. Such systematic descriptions became part of our intellectual tradition in Europe, particularly in the German States, during the 17th and 18th centuries. *Staatenkunde*, the comparative description of states, made for the purposes of throwing light on their organization, their power, and their weaknesses, became an important discipline promoted especially by Gottfried Achenwall (1719–1772) who was Professor at the Uni-

versity of Göttingen. Hans Anchersen (1700–1765) a Danish historian, introduced tables into his work, and although these early tables were largely non-
numerical, they form a bridge between the early comparative descriptions and
Political Arithmetic, where we see the first inferences based on vital statistics
(see Westergaard, 1932, for an account of these developments).

Some early statistical accounts were, until quite recently, thought to have
been made solely for the purposes of taxation. Notable among these is *Domesday
Book*, ordered in 1085 by William the Conqueror, ". . . to place the government
of the conquered on a written basis . . ." (Finn, 1973, p. 1). This massive
survey, which was completed in less than 2 years, is not just a tax roll, but an
administrative record made to assist in government. Morever, Galbraith (1961)
notes that the Domesday Inquest made no effort to preserve the ovewhelming
mass of original returns, "Instead, the practical genius of the Norman king
preserved in a 'fair copy' what was little more than an abstract of the total
returns," (Galbraith, 1961, p. 2), so that *Domesday Book* is perhaps one of the
earliest examples of a summary of a large amount of data.

POLITICAL ARITHMETIC

The student in statistics who develops an interest in their history will be aston-
ished if he or she visits a good library and searches out titles on the history of
statistics or old books with the word *statistics* or *statistical* in the title. Very
soon, for example, *The History of Statistics*, published in 1918 to commemorate
the 75th anniversary of *The American Statistical Association*, and edited by
Koren, will be discovered. But there are no means or variances or correlation
coefficients to be found here. This volume contains memoirs from contributors
from 15 countries detailing the development of the collection and collation of
economic and vital statistics, for all kinds of motives and using all kinds of
methods, within the various jurisdictions. Such works are not unusual and they
relate to a variety of endeavors concerned with the use of numerical data both for
comparative and inferential purposes. They reflect the layman's view of statistics
in the present day. *Political arithmetic* may be dated from the publication by
John Graunt (1620–1674) in 1662, of *Natural and Political Observations Mentioned in a Following Index and Made Upon the Bills of Mortality*, although the
name *political arithmetic* was apparently the invention of Graunt's friend,
William Petty (1623–1687). It has been reported that Petty was in fact the author
of the *Observations*, but this is not so. Petty's *Political Arithmetick* was written
in about 1672 but was not published until 1690. Petty's work was of interest to
government and surely had ruffled some feathers. Petty's son, dedicating his
father's book to the king, writes:

> He was allowed by all, to be the Inventor of this Method of Instruction; where the
> perplexed and intricate ways of the World are explain'd by a very mean peice of

Science; and had not the Doctrins of this Essay offended France, they had long
since seen the light, and had found Followers, as well as improvements before this
time, to the advantage perhaps of Mankind. (Lord Shelborne. Dedication in Petty,
1690).

That the work had the *imprimatur* of authority is given in its frontispiece.

Let this Book called *Political Arithmetick*, which was long since Writ by Sir
William Petty deceased, be Printed.
Given at the Court at Whitehall the *7th day of Novemb.* 1690.
                                    Nottingham.

It was Karl Pearson's (1978) view, however, that Petty owed more to Graunt
than Graunt to Petty. Graunt was a well-to-do haberdasher who was influential
enough to be able to secure a professorship at Gresham College, London, for
Petty, a man who had a variety of posts and careers. Graunt was a cultured, self-
educated man and was friends with scientists, artists, and businessmen. The
publication of the *Observations* led to Charles II himself supporting his election
to the Royal Society in 1662. Graunt's work was the first attempt to interpret
social behavior and biological trends from counts of the rather crude figures of
births and deaths reported in London from 1604 to 1661. A continuing theme in
Graunt's work is the regularity of statistical summaries. He apparently accepted
implicitly the notion that when a statistical ratio was not maintained then some
new influence must be present, that some additional factor is there to be discovered. For example, he tried to show that the number of deaths from the plague
had been under-reported[1] and by examining the number of christenings reasoned
that the decrease in population of London because of the plague would be
recovered in 2 years. He attempted to estimate the population distribution by sex
and age and constructed a mortality table. Essentially, Graunt's work, and that of
Petty, emphasizes the use of mathematics to impose order on data and, by
extension, on society itself.

Petty was a founding member of the Royal Society which was granted its
charter in 1662. Although he had been a supporter of Cromwell and the Commonwealth, he was knighted in 1661 by Charles II. He was not so much concerned with the *vital statistics* studied by Graunt. Rather in his early work he
suggested ways in which the expenses of the state could be curtailed and the
revenue from taxes increased, and a continuing theme in his work is the estimation of wealth.

His *Political Arithmetick* (1690) compares England, France, and Holland in
terms of territory, trade, shipping, housing, and so on. His interest was in

---

[1]The weekly accounting of burials was begun to allay public fears about the plague. However, in
epidemic years when anxiety was at its highest, it appears that cases of the plague were concealed
because members of families with the illness were kept together, both the sick and the well.

practical political matters and money, topics that reflected his professional career as well as his philosophy.

In the context of the times, Graunt and Petty's work may be seen as a demonstration of their belief that quantification provided knowledge that was free from controversy and conflict. Buck (1977) discusses these efforts in the political climate of the times. The 17th century was, to say the least, a difficult time for the people of England. The Civil War, the execution of the King, the turmoil of the Commonwealth, religious conflict, the restoration, the weakness of the monarchs of the Stuart line, the *Glorious Revolution* that swept James II from the throne; all contributed to civil strife and political unease. And yet the post-restoration years saw the founding of the Royal Society, the establishment of the Royal Observatory at Greenwich, and the setting of the stage for the triumphs of Newtonian science in the 18th century. It was also the era of Restoration literature. Both John Evelyn (the diarist who gave the Society its name and its motto) and the poet, Dryden, were members of the Royal Society. Buck (1977) and others have argued that the philosophy underlying the contributions of Petty and Graunt differs from that of the 18th century in that it does not accept the existence of *natural order* in society. Indeed it could not, because the political mechanisms necessary for the maintenance of a relatively stable social system had not been established.

The practical effects of the work that was begun by Petty has its counterpart in the present-day agencies of the state that collect data for all manner of purposes. In this account of the development of statistics, however, this path will be left for now, in order to return to the enterprise that sprang from Graunt's mortality tables. Actuarial science has more to do with our perspective because it involves the early study of probability and risk and the use of these mathematics for inference.

VITAL STATISTICS

Actuarial science has been defined as the application of probability to insurance, particularly to life insurance. But to apply the rules of probability theory there have to be data, and these data are provided by mortality tables. Life expectancy tables go back as far as the 4th century when they were used under Roman law to estimate the value of annuities, but the major impetus to the systematic examination of the mathematics of tontines[2] and annuities is generally placed in 17th century Holland. John De Witt (1625–1672), the Grand Pensionary of Holland and West Friesland, applied probability principles to the calculation of annuities.

---

[2]Tontines were once a popular form of annuity. Subscribers paid into a joint fund and the income they received increased for the survivors as the members died off.

Dawson (1901) states that De Witt must be considered to be the founder of actuarial science, although his work was not rediscovered until 1852. More prominent is the work of De Witt's contemporaries, Christiaan Huygens (1629–1695) and John Hudde (1628–1704). Graunt's work influenced that of Huygens and his younger brother who debated the relative merits of estimating the mean duration of life and the probability of survival or death at a given age.

These attempts to bring rationality and order into the general area of life insurance was aided considerably by the work of Edmund Halley (1656–1742), the English astronomer and mathematician and patron of Newton. He published *An Estimate of the Mortality of Mankind, Drawn From Curious Tables of the Births and Funerals at the City of Breslaw; With an Attempt to Ascertain the Price of Annuities on Lives*, in *Philosophical Transactions* in 1693. He was a brilliant man and his clear exposition of the problems is remarkable on two counts. The first is that it was produced in order to fulfill a promise to the Royal Society to contribute material for the *Transactions*, which had resumed publication after a break of several years, and was a topic that was out of the mainstream of his work. The second is that the early life offices in England did not use the material, the common opinion being that insurance was largely a game of chance. The general realization that an understanding of probabilities helped in the actual determination of gains and losses in both games of chance and life insurance was not to come until almost the middle of the 18th century. The necessity of reliable systems for the determination of premiums for all kinds of insurance became more and more important in the rise of 18th century trade and commerce.

This account of the beginnings of actuarial science is by no means complete but the brief description highlights the utility of data organization and probability for the making of inferences and the business of practical prediction. As Karl Pearson (1978) noted in his lectures, there were two main lines of descent from Graunt; the probability-mathematicians and actuaries, and the 18th century political arithmeticians. Of the probability-mathematicians perhaps the most entertaining and enterprising was a physician, John Arbuthnot (1667–1735). He was able, he was intellectual, he was a wit, and he can be credited with the first use of an abstract mathematical proposition, the binomial theorem, to test the probability of an observed distribution, namely the proportion of male and female births. In fact, he appears to have been the first person to assess observed data, chance, and alternative hypotheses using a statistical test. Arbuthnot had, in 1692, published a translation of Huygens work on probability with additions of his own. In this book he observes that probability may be applied to Graunt's suggestion in the *Observations* that the greater number of male than female births was a matter of divine providence and not chance. In *An Argument for Divine Providence, Taken From the Constant Regularity Observ'd in the Births of Both Sexes*, published in 1710, Arbuthnott (sometimes, as he did here, he spelled his name with two t's) uses the binomial expansion to argue that the observed distribution of male and female christenings (which he equates with births) departs so much from equality as to be impossible, "from whence it follows that it is Art, not Chance, that governs" (p. 189). An excess of males is prevented by,

the wise Oeconomy of Nature; and to judge of the wisdom of the Contrivance, we must observe that the external Accidents to which Males are subject (who must seek their Food with danger) do make a great havock of them, and that this loss exceeds far that of the other Sex, occasioned by the Diseases incident to it, as Experience convinces us. To repair that Loss, provident Nature, by the Disposal of its wise Creator, brings forth more Males than Females; and that in almost constant proportion. (Arbuthnott, 1710, p. 188)

The resulting near-equal proportions of the sexes ensures that every male may have a female of suitable age, and Arbuthnot concludes, as did Graunt, that:

Polygamy is contrary to the Law of Nature and Justice, and to the Propagation of the Human Race; for where Males and Females are in equal number, if one Man takes Twenty Wives, Nineteen Men must live in Celibacy, which is repugnant to the Design of Nature; nor is it probable that Twenty Women will be so well impregnated by one Man as by Twenty. (Arbuthnott, 1710, p. 189)

which are as ingenious statements of what we now call *alternative hypotheses* as one could find anywhere.

The most outstanding of the probability-mathematicians of the era was Abraham De Moivre (1667–1754). He was born at Vitry in Champagne, a Protestant and the son of a poor surgeon. From an early age, although an able scholar of the humanities, he was interested in mathematics. After the repeal of the Edict of Nantes in 1685, he was interned and was faced with the choice of renouncing his religion or going into exile. He chose the latter and in 1688 went to England. By chance he met Isaac Newton and read the famous *Principia*, which had been published in 1687. He mastered the new infinitesimal calculus and passed into the circles of the great mathematicians, Bernoulli, Halley, Leibnitz, and Newton. Despite the efforts of his friends he was unable to obtain a secure academic position and supported himself as a peripatetic teacher of mathematics, ". . . and later in life sitting daily in Slaughter's Coffee House in Long Acre, at the beck and call of gamblers, who paid him a small sum for calculating odds, and of underwriters and annuity brokers who wished their values reckoned" (K. Pearson, 1978, p. 143).

De Moivre first published his treatise on annuities in 1725. Essentially and without going into the details, and some of the defects, of his procedures, De Moivre used the summation of series to compute compound interests and annuity values. The crucial factor was in applying the relatively straightforward mathematics to a mortality table. He examined Halley's Breslau table and concluded that the number of individuals who survived to a given age from a total starting out at an earlier age could be expressed as decreasing terms in an arithmetic series. In short, De Moivre combined probabilities and the interest factor to compute annuity values in a manner that pointed the way to modern actuarial science. Thomas Simpson (1710–1761) has been described as De Moivre's younger rival. He is certainly remembered in the history of life insurance as an innovator. He appears initially to have argued with De Moivre that mortality tables should be used as they were found and not fitted to mathematical rules. Simpson is dismissed by Pearson (1978) as a plagiarist who "set out to boil down De Moivre's work and sell the result at a lower price" (p. 176), whereas Dawson (1901) describes his book as "an attempt to popularize the science, never a popular movement among those who hope to profit by keeping it exclusive" (p. 102).

De Moivre was undoubtedly upset by Simpson's reproduction of his ideas but Pearson's view of Simpson's character is not shared by many historians of mathematics who have described him as a self-taught genius.

The application of mathematical rules to tables of mortality are the earliest examples of the use of theoretical abstractions for practical purposes. They are attempts to organize and make sense of data. The development of, and rationales behind, modern statistical summaries are of immediate interest.

GRAPHICAL METHODS

As knowledge increases amongst mankind and transactions multiply, it becomes more and more desirable to abbreviate and facilitate the modes of conveying information from one person to another and from one individual to the many.

I confess I was long anxious to find out whether I was actually the first who applied the principles of geometry to matters of finance as it had long before been applied to chronology with great success. I am now satisfied upon due inquiry, that I was the first:

As the eye is the best judge of proportion being able to estimate it with more accuracy than any other of our organs, it follows, that wherever *relative quantities* are in question, a gradual increase or decrease of any . . . value is to be stated, this mode of representing it is peculiarly applicable.

That I have succeeded in proposing and putting in practice a new and useful mode of stating accounts . . . and as much information may be *obtained* in five minutes as would require whole days to imprint on the memory, in a lasting manner, by a table of figures. (Playfair, 1801a, pp. ix-x)

These quotations are taken from Playfair's *Commercial and Political Atlas*, the third edition of which was published in 1801. They provide an unequivocal statement of his view, and the view of many historians, that he was the inventor of statistical graphical methods, methods which he termed *lineal arithmetic*. Also in 1801, Playfair's *Statistical Breviary; Shewing, on a Principle Entirely New, the Resources of Every State and Kingdom in Europe*, appeared. In these books we see in handsome hand-colored, copper-plate engravings, line and bar graphs in the *Atlas* and these, together with circle graphs and pie charts in the *Breviary*. They illustrate revenues, imports and exports, population distributions, taxes, and other economic data and they are accompanied by constant reminders of the utility of the graphical method for the examination of fiscal and trade matters.

William Playfair (1759–1823) was the younger brother of John Playfair, the mathematician. He had a variety of occupations beginning as an apprentice mechanical engineer and draftsman and later as a writer and rather unsuccessful businessman. In his examination of the history of graphical methods Funkhouser (1937), notes that the French translation of the *Atlas* was very well received on the continent, in fact much more attention was paid to it there than in England. He also suggests that this might account for the greater interest shown in graphical work by the French over the next century.

As a method of summarizing data we must give full credit to Playfair for the development of the graphical method, but there are examples of the use of graphs that predate his work by many centuries. Funkhouser (1937) mentions the use of coordinates by Egyptian surveyors and that latitudes and longitudes were used by the geographers and cartographers of ancient Greece. Nicole Oresme (c.1323–1382) developed the essentials of analytic geometry, which is René Descartes' (1596–1650) greatest contribution to mathematics, although it is of course true that graphs could have been used, and in fact occasionally were used, without any formal knowledge of the fact that the curve of a graph can be represented by a mathematical function. Funkhouser (1936) reports on a 10th century graph of planetary orbits as a function of time and, over the years, there have been other examples of the method, perhaps the most obvious of which is musical notation.

Despite Playfair's ingenuity and his attempts at the promotion of the technique, the use of graphs was surprisingly slow to develop. We find Jevons in 1874 describing the production of "best fit" curves by eye and suggesting the procuring or preparation of "paper divided into equal rectangular spaces, a convenient size for the spaces being one-tenth of an inch square" (p. 493), and not until the 11th edition, published in 1910, did *Encyclopaedia Britannica* devote an entry to graphical methods. Funkhouser (1937) suggests, and the suggestion is eminently plausible, that the collection of public statistics was affected by an ongoing controversy as to whether verbal descriptions of political and economic states were superior to numerical tables. If statistical tables were regarded with suspicion, then graphs would have been greeted with even more opprobrium. In

France and Germany the use of graphs was openly criticized by some statisticians.

In the social sciences the person who most helped to promote the use of the graph as a tool in statistical analysis was Quetelet who has already been mentioned. It has been noted that the use of the *Normal Curve* for the description of human characteristics begins with his work. The *law of error* and Quetelet's adaptation of it is of great importance.

5
Probability

A proposition that would find favor with most of us is that the business of life is concerned with attempts to do more or less the right thing at more or less the right time. It follows that a great deal of our thinking, in the sense of deliberating, about our condition is bound up with the problem of making decisions in the face of uncertainty. A traditional view of science in general, on the other hand, is that it searches for conclusions that are to be taken to be true, that the conclusions should represent an absolute certainty. If one of its conclusions fails then the failure is put down to ignorance, or poor methodology, or primitive techniques— the truth is still thought to be out there somewhere. In chapter 2 some of the difficulties that can arise in trying to sustain this position were discussed. Probability theory provides us with a means of reaching answers and conclusions when, as is the case in anything but the most trivial of circumstances, the evidence is incomplete or, indeed, can *never* be complete. Put simply, what is the best bet, what are the odds on our winning, and how confident can we be that we are right? The derivation of theories and systems that may be applied to assist us in answering these questions continues to present intellectual challenges.

THE EARLY BEGINNINGS

The early beginnings are very early indeed. David (1962) tells us that many archeological digs have produced quantities of astragali, animal heel bones, with the four flatter sides marked in various ways. These bones may have been used as counting aids, as children's toys, or as the forerunners of dice in ancient games. The astragalus was certainly used in board games in Egypt about 3,500 years before the birth of Christ. David suggests that *gaming* may have been developed from *game-playing* and reports that it is said to have been introduced in Greece just 300 years before Christ. She also suggests that gaming may have emerged from the wager, and the wager from divination and the interrogation of oracles with origins in religious ritual. We know that gaming was a common pastime in both Greece and Rome from at least 100 years before Christ. David notes that Claudius (10 B.C.-A.D. 54) wrote a book on how to win at dice which, regrettably, has not survived. David also comments on a remark in Cicero's *De Divinatione*, Book I:

> When the four dice produce the venus-throw [the outcome when four dice, or astragali, are tossed and the faces shown are all different] you may talk of accident: but suppose you made a hundred casts and the venus-throw appeared a hundred times; could you call that accidental? (David, 1962, p. 24)

This may be one of the earliest statements of the circumstances in which we might accept or reject the *null* hypothesis. Cicero quite clearly had some grasp of the concepts of *randomness* and *chance* and that rare events do occur in the long run. A variety of explanations may be advanced for the fact that these early insights did not lead to a mathematical calculus of probabilities. Greek philosophy, in the works of Plato and Aristotle, searched for order and regularity in the phenomena of the universe and, later, as Christianity spread, the Church promoted the idea of an omnipotent God who was unceasingly aware of, and responsible for, the slightest perturbation in natural affairs. Human beings were doomed to be ignorant of the succession of natural events and could achieve salvation only by submission to the will of an Almighty. A more mundane explanation may be provided by the fact that early arithmetic, at any rate in what we would now call Western culture, was hampered by the absence of a logical and efficient system of number notation. Whatever the reasons, and many others have been suggested (see, e.g., Acree, 1978; Hacking, 1975), we know that about 1,600 years elapsed before a foundation for probability theory was laid.

THE BEGINNINGS

The reader is referred to David's interesting book for a review of the contributions that emerged in Europe during the first millenium and beyond. In the 17th century Gerolamo Cardano's book *Liber de Ludo Aleae* [*The Book on Games of Chance*] was published (in 1663, some 87 years after the death of its author). A translation of this work by S.H. Gould is to be found in Ore (1953). The treatise is full of practical advice on both odds and personality, noting that persons who are renowned for wisdom, or old and dignified by civil honor or priesthood, should not play, but that for boys, young men, and soldiers, it is less of a reproach.

He also cautions that doctors and lawyers play at a disadvantage, for "if they win, they seem to be gamblers, and if they lose, perhaps they may be taken to be as unskilful in their own art as in gaming. Men of these professions incur the same judgment if they wish to practice music" (Ore, 1953, pp. 187–188).

It cannot be claimed that Cardano produced a theory with this book. However, it can be stated that he understood the importance of the relationship between theoretical reasoning and events in the "real world" of gaming.

The birth of the *mathematical theory* of probability, that is, "when the infant really sees the light of day" (Weaver, 1963, p. 31), took place in 1654. In that year Antoine Gombauld, Chevalier de Méré, (1607–1684) posed the questions to Blaise Pascal (1623–1662) that initiated the endeavor. The two may have met in the summer of 1652 and soon become friends, although there is some doubt about both the time and the circumstances of their meeting. David, in her book, deals rather harshly with de Méré. She dimisses him as having "a second-rate intelligence" and indicates that his writings do not show evidence of mathematical ability, "being literary pieces of not very high calibre" (David, 1962, p. 85). De Méré was not a mathematician, although there is no doubt that he held a good opinion of his abilities in a number of fields. What he appears to have been was France's leading arbiter of good taste and manners, a man who studied the ways of polite society with care and dedication.[1] His writings were sought after, and his opinions respected, by those who wished to maintain good standing in the drawing rooms of Paris. (See St. Cyres, 1909, pp. 136–158, for an account of de Méré). Pascal appears to have been a willing pupil, although toward the end of 1654 he underwent his second conversion to the religious life. The notion that, astonishingly, the calculus of probabilities was the offspring of a dilettante and an ascetic, which Poisson's remark (footnoted in chapter 1) has been taken to imply, is a not quite accurate reflection.

Every account of the history of the concept of probability shows how important the search for ways of assessing the odds in various gaming situations has been in shaping its development. There seems to be little doubt but that Pascal had spent sessions at the gaming tables and it seems unlikely that various situations had not been discussed with de Méré. What moved the matter into the realm of mathematical discourse was the correspondence between Pascal and his fellow mathematician, Pierre Fermat, sparked by specific questions that had been raised by de Méré.

An old gambling game involves the "house" offering a gambler even money that he or she will throw at least 1 six in 4 throws of a die. In fact the odds are slightly favorable to the house. De Méré's problem concerned the question of the odds in a situation where the bet was that a player would throw at least 1 double

---

[1]That David's judgment on the matter may be in error is likely. Michea (1938) maintains that Descarte's *bon sens* and Pascal's *coeur* can be equated with de Méré's *bon gout* and no one could find that Descartes and Pascal had second-rate intelligences.

six in 24 throws of 2 dice. Here the odds are, in fact, slightly against the house, even though 24 is to 36 as 4 is to 6. De Méré had solved this problem but used the outcome to argue to Pascal that it showed that arithmetic was self-contradictory![2] A second problem that de Méré was unable to solve, was the "problem of points" which concerns, for example, how the stakes or the "pot" should be divided among the players, according to the current scores of the participants, if a game is interrupted. This is an altogether more difficult question and the exchanges between Pascal and Fermat that took place over the summer of 1654 devote much space to it. The letters[3] show the beginning of the applications of combinatorial algebra and of the *arithmetic triangle*.

In 1655, Christiaan Huygens (1629–1695), a Dutch mathematician, visited Paris and heard of the Pascal-Fermat correspondence. There was enormous interest in the mathematics of chance but a seeming reluctance to announce discoveries and reveal the answers to questions under discussion, perhaps because of the material value of the findings to gamblers. Huygens returned to Holland and worked out the answers for himself. His short account *De Ratiociniis in Ludo Aleae* [*Calculating in Games of Chance*] was published in 1657 by Frans van Schooten (1615–1660) who was Professor of mathematics at Leyden. This book, the first on the probability calculus, was an important influence on James Bernoulli and De Moivre.

James (also referred to as Jacques or Jakob) Bernoulli (1654–1705) was one of an extended family of mathematicians who made many valuable contributions. It is his *Ars Conjectandi* [*The Art of Conjecture*], published in 1713 after editing by his nephew, Nicholas, that is of most interest. The first part of the book is a reproduction of Huygens' work with a commentary. The second and third parts deal with mathematics of permutations and combinations and its application to games of chance. In the fourth part of the book we find the theorem that Bernoulli called his "golden theorem," the theorem named "The Law of Large Numbers" by Poisson in 1837. In an excellent and most readable commentary Newman (1956) declares the theorem to be, "of cardinal significance to the theory of probability," for it, ". . . was the first attempt to deduce statistical measures from individual probabilities" (Vol. 3, p. 1448). Hacking (1971) has examined the whole work in some considerable depth.

Bernoulli likely did not anticipate *all* of the debates and confusions and misconceptions, both popular and academic, that his theorem would generate,

---

[2]The probability of *not* getting a six in a single throw of a die is $5/6$ and the probability of no sixes in four throws is $(5/6)^4$. The probability of at least 1 six in four throws is $1 - (5/6)^4$, which is 0.51775, which is favorable to the house. The probability of *not* getting 2 sixes in a single throw of two dice is $35/36$ and the probability of the event of at least once getting 2 sixes in 24 throws of two dice is $1 - (35/36)^{24}$, which is 0.49140, which is slightly unfavorable to the house.

[3]Translations of the Pascal-Fermat correspondence are to be found in David's (1962) book and in Smith (1929).

but that it was a source of intellectual puzzlement may be taken from the fact that its author states that he meditated on it for 20 years. In its simplest form the theorem states that if an event has a probability, p, of occurring on a single trial, and n trials are to be made, then the *proportion* of occurrences of the event over the n trials is also p. As n increases the probability that the proportion will differ from p by less than a given amount, no matter how small, also increases. It also becomes increasingly unlikely that the number of occurrences of the event will differ from pn by less than a fixed amount, however large. In a series of n tosses of a "fair" coin the probability of heads occurring close to 50% of the time ($0.5n$ occurrences) increases as n increases and there is a much greater probability of a difference of, say, 10 heads from what would be expected, in 1,000 tosses of the coin than in 100 tosses of the coin. Kneale (1949) notes that it is often supposed that the theorem is,

A mysterious law of nature which guarantees that in a sufficiently large number of trials a probability will be "realized as a frequency."

A misunderstanding of Bernoulli's theorem is responsible for one of the commonest fallacies in the estimation of probabilities, the fallacy of the maturity of the chances. When a coin has come down heads twice in succession, gamblers sometimes say that it is more likely to come down tails next time because "by the law of averages" (whatever that may mean) the proportion of tails must be brought to right some time. (Kneale, 1949, pp. 139–140)

The fact is, of course, that the theorem is no more and no less than a formal mathematical proposition and not a statement about realities and, as Newman (1956) puts it, " neither capable of validating 'facts' nor of being invalidated by them" (Vol. 3, p. 1450). Now this statement accurately represents the situation, but it must not be passed by without comment. If reality departs severely from the law then clearly we do not doubt reality, and nor do we doubt the law. What we might do, however, is to doubt some of our initial assumptions about the observed situation. If red were to turn up 100 times in a row at the roulette table it might be prudent to bet on red on the 101st spin because this sequence departs so much from expectation that we might conclude that the wheel is "stuck" on red. In fact we might use this observation as support for an assertion that the wheel is not fair. This example moves us away from probability theory and into the realm of practical statistical inference, an inference about reality that is based on probabilities indicated by an abstract mathematical proposition.

THE MEANING OF PROBABILITY

A problem has been raised. The difficulty inherent in any attempt to apply Bernoulli's theorem is that we assume that we know the *prior probability* p of a given event on a single trial, that, for example, we know that the value of p for the appearance of heads when a coin is tossed is $1/2$. If we do know p, then predictions can be made, and, given a series of observations, inferences may be drawn from them. The problem is to state the grounds for setting p at a particular value and this raises the question of what it is that we mean by *probability*. The issue was always there but it was not really confronted until the 19th century.

The title of this section is taken from Ernest Nagel's paper presented at the annual meeting of the American Statistical Association in 1935, and printed in its journal in 1936. Nagel's clear and penetrating account does not, as he admits, resolve the difficult problems raised in attempts to examine the concept, problems that are still the source of sometimes quite heated debate among mathematicians and philosophers. What it does is to present the alternative views and comment upon the conclusions that adoption of one or other of the positions entails.[4] Nagel first examines the methodological principles that can be brought to bear on the question, then he delineates the contexts in which ideas of probability may be found, and, finally, he examines the three interpretations of probability that are extant. What follows draws heavily on Nagel's review.

Appeals to probabilities are found in everyday discussion, in applied statistics and measurement, in physical and biological theories, in the comparison of competing theories, and in the mathematical probability calculus. The three important interpretations of the concept are, the classical; the notion of probability as "rational belief"; and the long-run relative frequency definition.

Laplace (1749–1827) and De Morgan (1806–1871) were the chief exponents of the classical view that regards probability as, in De Morgan's words, "a state of mind with respect to an assertion" (De Morgan, 1838). The strength of our belief about any given proposition is its probability. This is what is meant in everyday discourse when we say (though perhaps not *every* day!) that, "It is probable that gaming emerged from game-playing." In evaluating competing theories, this view is also evident as when it is said by some, for example, that, "Biologically based trait theories of personality are more probably correct than social learning theories." This interpretation is not what is meant when statistical assertions about the weather, the probability of precipitation, for example, or the outcome of an atomic disintegration are made.

John Maynard Keynes (later Lord Keynes, 1883–1946) interpreted probability as *rational belief* and it has been asserted that this is the most appropriate view for most applications of the term. Evidence about the moral character of witnesses would lead to statements about the probability of the truth of one person's testimony rather than another's or, in examining the results of evidence that attempted to show, for example, that a social learning theory interpretation of achievement motivation is more probable than one based on trait theory.

---

[4]Acree (1978) gives an extensive review that, for the present writer, is sometimes difficult to follow.

These statements rest on rational insights into the relationship between evidence and conclusion, not on statistical frequencies because we do not have such information. It is Nagel's view, and the view of others, that both the classical and the Keynesian views violate an important methodological principle—that of verifiability.

> On Keynes' view a degree of probability is assignable to a *single* proposition with respect to given evidence. But what *verifiable* consequences can be drawn from the statement that with respect to the evidence the proposition that on the *next* throw with a given pair of dice a 7 will appear, has a probability of 1/6? For on the view that it is significant to predicate a probability to the single instance there is nothing to be verified or refuted. (Nagel, 1936, p. 18)

The conclusion is that the views we have described "cannot be regarded as a satisfactory analysis of probability propositions in the sciences which claim to abide by this canon" (Nagel, 1936, p. 18).

The third interpretation of probability is the statistical notion of long-run relative frequency. Bolzano (1781–1841), Venn (1834–1923), Cournot (1801–1877), Peirce (1839–1914), and, more recently, von Mises (1883–1953) and Fisher (1890–1962) are among the scientists and mathematicians who supported this view. In a simple example, if you are told that your probability of survival and recovery after a particular surgical procedure is 80%, then this means that of 100 patients who have undergone this operation 80 have recovered.

The majority of working scientists in psychology who rely on statistical manipulations in the examination of data implicitly or explicitly subscribe to this meaning. Whether or not it is appropriate to the endeavor and whether or not the consequences of its acceptance are fully appreciated is a question to be considered. It is important to note, and here this is not meant to be facetious, that following the operation you are either alive or you are dead. In other words the probability statement is about a relationship between events, or rather *propositions* concerning the occurrence of events, not about a single event. In this respect the frequentists have no quarrel with the Keynesians.

The most common logical objection (in fact it is a class of objections) to the frequency view concerns the vague term *long-run*. Clearly, in order to establish a frequency ratio the run has to stop somewhere and yet probability values are defined as the limit of an infinite sequence. Nagel's answer to the objection, which von Mises (1957) also deals with at some length, is that empirically obtained ratios can be used as hypotheses for the true values of the infinite series and these hypotheses can be tested. Further, probability values might be arrived at by using some other theory than that obtained from a statistical series, for example using theoretical mechanics to predict the probability of a fair coin turning up heads. And again the predicted probability can be tested empirically. Nagel also argues that Keynesian examples about the credibility of witnesses *could* be examined in frequency terms, for instance, "the relative frequency with which a regular church-goer tells lies on important occasions is a small number considerably less than 1/2" (Nagel, 1936, p. 23).

It is obviously the case that there is more than one conception of probability and that each one has value in its particular context, but Nagel concludes that the frequency view is the most satisfactory for, "every-day discourse, applied statistics and measurement, and within many branches of the theoretical sciences" (p. 26).

It has been noted that psychological scientists have accepted this view. Nevertheless, the fact that probability has to do both with frequencies and with degrees of belief is the aleatory and epistemological duality that is clearly and cogently discussed by Hacking (1975). We blur the issue as we compute our statistics and speak of the confidence we have in our results. The fact that the answer to the question, "Who, in practice, cares?" is, "Probably very few," is based on an admittedly informal frequency analysis but it is one in which we can believe!

Probability and the Foundations of Error Estimation

The practical spur to the development of probability theory was simply the attempt to formulate rules that, if followed assiduously, would lead to a gambler making a profit over the long run, although, of course, it was not possible to assert how long the run might have to be for profit to be assured. Probability was therefore bound up with the notion of *expectancies* and the 150 years that followed the end of the 17th century saw its constructs being applied to expectancies in life insurance and the sale of annuities. John de Witt (1625–1672) and John Hudde (1628–1704), who calculated annuities based on mortality statistics and whose work was mentioned earlier, corresponded and consulted with Huygens and drew heavily on his writings.

An important figure in the history of probability, though the extent of his contribution was not fully recognized until long, long after his death, was Abraham De Moivre (1667–1754). His book, *The Doctrine of Chances: or A Method of Calculating the Probabilities of Events in Play*, was first published in 1718, but it is the second (1738) and third (1756) editions of the work that are of most interest here. De Moivre's *A Treatise of Annuities on Lives*, editions of which were published in 1724, 1743, and 1750, applies *The Doctrine of Chances* to the "valuation of annuities." The *Treatise* is to be found bound together with the 1756 edition of the *Doctrine*.

Here the problems of the gaming rooms and the questions of actuarial prediction in the mathematics of expectancies are linked. A third strand was not to emerge for over 50 years with investigations on the estimation of error. This latter is associated most closely with the work of Laplace (1749–1827) and Gauss (1777–1855) and the derivation of "The Law of Frequency of Error," or the *normal* curve as it came to be known. And yet we now know that this fundamental function had, in fact, been demonstrated by De Moivre who first published it in 1733 (the *Approximatio ad Summam Terminorum Binomii* $(a+b)^n$ *in Seriem Expansi*) and English translations of the work are to be found in the last two editions of *The Doctrine of Chances*. The *Approximatio* is examined by Todhunter (1820–1884) whose monumental *History of the Mathematical Theory of Probability From the Time of Pascal to That of Laplace*, published in 1865, still stands as one of the most comprehensive and one of the dullest books on probability. Todhunter devotes considerable space in his book to De Moivre's work, but, according to Karl Pearson (1926), he "misses entirely the epoch-making character of the 'Approximatio' as well as its enlargement in the 'Doctrine.' He does not say: Here is the original of Stirling's Theorem, here is the first appearance of the normal curve, here De Moivre anticipated Laplace as the latter anticipated Gauss" (Pearson, 1926, p. 552).

It is true that Todhunter does not state any of the above *precisely* and it is therefore now often reported that Karl Pearson discovered the importance of the *Approximatio* in 1922 while he was preparing for his lecture course on the history of statistics that he gave at University College London between 1921 "and certainly continuing up till 1929" (Pearson & Kendall, 1970, p. 479). Karl Pearson published an article on the matter in 1924(a) and some details are provided by Daw and Pearson (1972). Quite how much credit we can give Pearson for the revelation and how justified he was in his judgment that, "Todhunter fails almost entirely to catch the drift of scientific evolution . . ." (Pearson, 1926, p. 552) can be debated. It is certainly the case that one is not carried along by the excitement of the progression of discovery as one ploughs one's way through Todhunter's book, but he does say in a section where he refers to the pages of the third edition of the *Doctrine*, which give the *Approximatio*, and show an important result:

> Thus we have seen that the principal contributions to our subject from De Moivre are his investigations respecting the Duration of Play, his Theory of Recurring Series, and his extension of the value of Bernoulli's Theorem by the aid of Stirling's Theorem. Our obligations to De Moivre would have been still greater if he had not concealed the demonstrations of the important results which we have noticed . . . ; but it will not be doubted that the Theory of Probability owes more to him than to any other mathematician, with the sole exception of Laplace. (Todhunter, 1865, pp. 192–193)

It is also worth noting that De Moivre's contribution was remarked on by the American historian of psychology, Edwin Boring, in 1920, before Pearson, and without so much fuss. In a footnote referring to the "normal law of error" he says, "The so-called "Gaussian" curve. The mathematical propadeutics for this function were prepared as long ago as the beginning of the 18th century (De Moivre, 1718 [*sic*]). See Todhunter . . ." (Boring, 1920, p. 8).

A more detailed discussion of the *Approximatio* and the properties of the normal distribution is given in the next chapter. The roles of Laplace and Gauss in the derivation and applications of probability theory are of very great importance. Laplace brought together a great deal of work that had been published separately as memoirs in his great work *Theorie Analytique des Probabilités*, first published in 1812, with further editions appearing in 1814 and 1820. Todhunter (1865) devotes almost one quarter of his book to Laplace's work. From the standpoint of statistics as they developed in the social sciences, it is perhaps only necessary to mention two of his contributions; the derivation of the "Law of Error" and the notion of *inverse* probability. Laplace's theorem, the proof of which, in modern terms, may be found in David (1949), and which had been anticipated by De Moivre, shows the relationship between the binomial series and the normal curve. Put very simply, and in modern parlance, as n in $(a+b)^n$ approaches infinity the shape of the discrete binomial distribution approaches the continuous bell-shaped normal curve. It is therefore possible to express the sum of a number of binomial probabilities by means of the area of the normal curve, and indeed the value of this sum derived from the familiar tables of proportions of area under the normal distribution is quite close to the exact value even for n of only 10. The details of this procedure are to be found in many of the elementary manuals of statistics.

Laplace's work gives a number of applications of probability theory to practical questions, but it is the bell-shaped curve as it is applied to the estimation of error that is of interest here. Both Gauss and Laplace investigated the question independently of each other. Errors are inescapable, even though they may not always be of critical importance, in all observations that involve measurement. Despite the most sophisticated of instruments and the most skilled users, measurements of, say, distances between stars in our galaxy at a particular time, or points on the surface of the earth, will, when repeated, not always produce *exactly* the same result. The assumption is made that the values that we require are definite and, to all intents and purposes, unchanging, that is to say that a true value exists. Variations from the true value are errors. Laplace assumed that every instance of an error arose because of the operation of a number of sources of error each one of which may affect the outcome one way or the other. The argument proceeds to maintain that the mathematical abstraction that we now call the *normal* law represents the distribution of the resultant errors.

Gauss's approach is essentially the same as Laplace's but has a more unashamedly practical flavor. He assumed that there was an equal probability of errors of over-estimation and under-estimation and showed, by the method of least squares, that it is the arithmetic mean of the distribution of measurements that best reflects the true value of the measurement we wish to make. The distribution of measurements, the variation in which represents error on these assumptions, is precisely that of Laplace's theorem, or the *normal* curve, or, as it is sometimes termed, the *Gaussian* distribution.

FORMAL PROBABILITY THEORY

From the 17th to the 20th century, mathematical approaches to probability have been algebraical and geometrical. The work of Pascal and Fermat led to combinatorial algebra. The invention of the calculus led to formal examinations of theoretical probability distributions. Gaussian methods are essentially geometrical. Always the probability calculus found itself in difficulties over the absence of a formal definition of probability that was universally accepted. Modern probability theory, but not, it must be noted, statistics, has escaped this difficulty by developing an arithmetical axiomatic model. The renowned German mathematician, David Hilbert (1862–1943), Professor of Mathematics at Göttingen, presented a remarkable paper to the International Congress of Mathematics meeting in Paris in 1900. In it he presented mathematics with a series of no less than 23 problems that, he believed, would be the ones that mathematics should address during the 20th century.[5] Among them was a call for a theory of probability based on axiomatic foundations. At that time, various attempts were being made to develop a theory of arithmetic based on a small number of fundamental postulates or *axioms*. These axioms have no basis in what is called the real world. Questions such as "What do they mean?" are excluded, ambiguity is avoided. The axioms themselves do not depend on any assumptions. For example, one of the best-known of the mathematical logicians, Guiseppe Peano (1858–1932), based his arithmetic on postulates such as "Zero is a number." This is not the place to attempt to discuss the difficulties that have been uncovered in the axiomatic approach or in *set theory* with which it is closely allied. Suffice it to say that modern mathematical probability theory is largely based on the work of Andrei Kolmogorov (1903–), a Russian mathematician whose book, *Foundations of the Theory of Probability* was first published in 1933. Set theory is most closely linked with the work of Georg Cantor (1845–1918) born in St Petersburg of Danish parents but who lived most of his life in Germany. Set theory grew out of a new mathematical conception of *infinity*. It is a theory that has profound philosophical as well as mathematical implications but its basis is easy to understand. It is a mathematical system that deals with defined collections, lists, or classes of objects or *elements*.

> The theory of probability, as a mathematical discipline, can and should be developed from axioms in exactly the same way as Geometry and Algebra. This means that after we have defined the elements to be studied and their basic relations, and have stated the axioms by which these relations are to be governed, all further propositions must be based exclusively on these axioms, independent of the usual concrete meaning of these elements and their relations.

---

[5]In the actual talk Hilbert only had time to deal with 10 of the problems, but the entire manuscript, in English, can be found in the *Bulletin of the American Mathematical Society* (1902).

. . . the concept of a *field of probabilities* is defined as a system of sets which satisfies certain conditions. What the elements of this set represent is of no importance in the purely mathematical development of the theory of probability. (Kolmogorov, 1933/1956, p. 1)

The system cannot be fully delineated here, but this chapter will end with an illustration of its mathematical elegance in arriving at the well-known rules of mathematical probability theory. This account follows Kolmogorov closely although it does not use his terminology and symbols precisely.

E is a collection of elements called elementary events. f is a set of subsets of E. The elements of f are *random events*.

The axioms:

1. f is a field of sets.
2. f contains the set E.
3. To each set A in f is assigned a non-negative real number p(A). This is called the probability of event A.
4. p(E) = 1.
5. If A and B have no element in common, then p(A + B) = p(A) + p(B)

In set theory A has a complementary set A'. In the language of random events, A' means the non-occurrence of A. To say that A is impossible is to write A = 0, and to say that A must occur is to write A = E.

Because A + A' = E and from the 4th and 5th axioms, p(A) + p(A') = 1 and p(A) = 1 − p(A') and because E = 0, p(0) = 0. Axiom 5 is the *addition* rule.

If p(A) > 0, then $p(B|A) = \dfrac{p(AB)}{p(A)}$, which is the *conditional* probability of the event B under condition A. From this follows the general formula known as the *multiplication rule*, p(AB) = p(A)p($B|A$), and, as we shall see in chapter 7, this leads to Bayes' theorem. Note that p($B|A$) ≥ 0, p($E|A$) = 1, and, p{(B + C)|A| = p($B|A$) + p($C|A$).

For readers of a mathematical inclination who wish to see more of the development of this approach (it does get a little more difficult), Kolmogorov's book is concise and elegant.

6

Distributions

When Graunt and Halley and Quetelet made their inferences, they made them on the basis of their examination of *frequency distributions*. Tables, charts and graphs—no matter how the information is displayed—all can be used to show a listing of data, or classifications of data, and their associated frequencies. These are frequency distributions. By extension, such depictions of the frequency of occurrence of observations can be used to assess the *expectation* of particular values, or classes of values, occurring in the future. Real frequency distributions can, then, be used as *probability distributions*. In general, however, the probability distributions that are familiar to the users of statistical techniques are *theoretical distributions*, abstractions based on a mathematical rule, that match, or approximate, distributions of events in the real world. When bodies of data are described, it is the graph and the chart that are used. But the theoretical distributions of statistics and probability theory are described by the mathematical rules or functions that define the relationships between data, both real and hypothetical, and their expected frequencies or probabilities.

Over the last 300 years or so, the characteristics of a great many theoretical distributions, all of which have been found to have some practical utility in one situation or another, have been examined. The following discussion is limited to three distributions that are familiar to users of basic statistics in psychology. An account of some fundamental *sampling distributions* will be given later.

THE BINOMIAL DISTRIBUTION

In the years 1665–1666, when Isaac Newton was 23 and had just earned his degree, his Cambridge College (Trinity) was closed because of the plague.

Newton went home to Woolsthorpe in Lincolnshire and began, in peace and leisure, a scientific revolution. These were the years in which Newton developed some of the most fundamental and important of his ideas; universal gravitation, the composition of light, the theory of fluxions (the calculus), and the *binomial theorem*.

The binomial coefficients for integral powers had been known for many centuries but fractional powers were not considered until the work of John Wallis (1616–1703), Savilian professor of geometry at Oxford, and the most influential of Newton's immediate English predecessors. However, expansions of expressions such as $(x - x^2)^{1/2}$ were achieved by Newton early in 1665. He announced his discovery of the binomial theorem in 1676 in letters written to the Secretary of the Royal Society, although he never formally published it nor did he provide a proof. Newton proceeded from earlier work of Wallis, who published the theorem, with credit to Newton, in 1685. The problem was to find the area under the curve with ordinates $(1 - x^2)^n$. When n is zero the first two terms are $x - 0/3(x^3)$, and when n is 1 they are $x - 1/3(x^3)$. Newton, using the method of interpolation employed so much by Wallis, reasoned that when n was $1/2$ the corresponding terms should be, $x - 1/2/3(x^3)$. He arrived at the series,

$$x - \frac{1/2(x^3)}{3} - \frac{1/8(x^5)}{5} - \frac{1/16(x^7)}{7} - \cdots$$

and then discovered that the same result could be obtained by deriving, and subsequently integrating,

$$(1 - x^2)^{1/2} = 1 - 1/2(x^2) - 1/8(x^4) - 1/16(x^8) - \cdots$$

which is the binomial expansion of $(1 - x^2)^{1/2}$. The interesting and important point to be noted is that Newton's discovery was not made by considering the binomial coefficients of Pascal's triangle but by examining the analysis of infinite series, a discovery of much greater generality and mathematical significance. Figure 6.1 shows the binomial distribution for $n = 7$.

Newton's discovery of the calculus in his "golden years" at Woolsthorpe establishes him as its originator, but it was Gottfried Wilhelm Leibniz (1646–1716), the German philosopher and mathematician, who has priority of publication and it is pretty well established that the discoveries were independent. However, a bitter quarrel developed over the claims to priority of discovery and allegations were made that, on a visit to London in 1673, Leibniz could have seen the manuscript of Newton's *De Analysi Aequationes Numero Terminorum Infinitas* which, though written in 1669, was not published until 1711. Abraham De Moivre was among those appointed by the Royal Society in 1712 to report on the dispute. De Moivre made extensive use of the method in his own work and it was his *Approximatio*, first printed and circulated to some friends in 1733, that links the binomial to what we now call the *normal* distribution. The

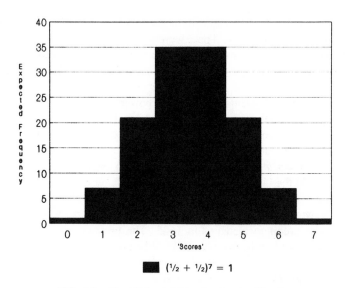

FIG. 6.1.   The Binomial Distribution for N = 7.

Approximatio is included in the second (1738) and third (1756) editions of the *Doctrine*.

It should be mentioned that a Scottish mathematician James Gregory (1638–1675), working at the time (1664–1668) in Italy, derived the binomial expansion and produced important work on the mathematics of infinite series, discovered quite independently of Newton.

THE POISSON DISTRIBUTION

Before the structure of the *normal* distribution is examined, the work of Siméon-Denis Poisson (1781–1840) on a useful special case of the binomial will be described. The Ecole Polytechnique was founded in Paris in 1794. It was the model for many later technical schools and its methods inspired the production of many student texts in mathematics and engineering which are the forerunners of present-day textbooks. Among the brilliant mathematicians of the Ecole during the earlier years of the 19th century was Poisson. His name is a familiar label in equations and constants in calculus, mechanics, and electricity. He was passionately devoted to mathematics and to teaching, and published over 400 works. Among these was *Recherche sur la Probabilité des Jugements* in 1837. This contains the *Poisson Distribution*, sometimes called Poisson's law of large numbers. It was noted earlier that as n in $(P + Q)^n$ increases, the binomial distribution tends to the normal distribution. Poisson considered the case where as n

increases toward infinity, P decreases toward zero, and nP remains constant. The resulting distribution has a remarkable application.

Data collected by insurance companies on relatively rare accidents, say, people trapping their fingers in bathroom doors, indicates that the probability of this event happening to any one individual is very low, in fact near zero. However, a certain number of such accidents (X) is reported every year and the number of these accidents varies from year to year. Over a number of years a statistical regularity is apparent, a regularity that can be described by Poisson's distribution.

If we set X at k, an integer, then,

$$p_x (k) = e^{-\lambda}\lambda^k/k!,$$

where λ is any positive number, e is the constant 2.7183 . . ., and $k!$ is factorial k.

Although the distribution is not commonly to be found in the basic statistics tests in psychology, it *is* used in the social sciences and it does have a surprising range of applications. It has been used to fit distributions in, for example, quality control (defects per number of units produced), numbers of patients suffering from certain specific diseases, earthquakes, wrong-number telephone connections, the daily number of hits by flying bombs in London during World War II, misprints in books, and many others.

Poisson attempted to extend the possible utility of probability theory, for he applied it to testimony and to legal decisions. These applications received much criticism but Poisson greatly valued them. Poisson formally discussed the concepts of a *random quantity* and *cumulative distribution functions* and these are significant theoretical contributions. But his name and work in probability does not occupy much space in the literature, perhaps because he was overshadowed by famous contemporaries such as Laplace and Gauss. Sheynin (1978) has given us a comprehensive review of his work in the area. An example of a Poisson distribution is given in Figure 6.2.

THE NORMAL DISTRIBUTION

The binomial and Poisson distributions stand apart from the normal distribution because they are applied to discrete frequency data. The invention of the calculus provided mathematics with a tool that allowed for the assessment of probabilities in *continuous distributions*. The first demonstration of integral approximation, to the limiting case of the binomial expansion, was given by De Moivre. In the *Approximatio* De Moivre begins by acknowledging the work of James Bernoulli.

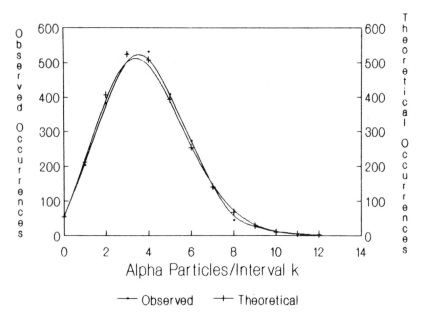

FIG. 6.2. The Poisson Distribution applied to Alpha emissions (Rutherford & Geiger, 1910).

Altho' the Solution of Problems of Chance often requires that several Terms of the Binomial $(a + b)^n$ [this is modern notation] be added together, nevertheless in very high Powers the thing appears so laborious, and of so great difficulty, that few people have undertaken that Task; for besides *James* and *Nicholas Bernoulli*, two great Mathematicians, I know of no body that has attempted it; in which, tho' they have shown very great skill, and have the praise which is due to their Industry, yet some things were farther required; for what they have done is not so much an Approximation as the determining very wide limits, within which they demonstrated that the Sum of the Terms was contained. (De Moivre, 1756, 3rd Ed., p. 243)

De Moivre proceeds to show how he arrived at the expression of the ratio of the middle term to the sum of all the terms in the expansion of $(1 + 1)^n$ when n is a very high power. His answer was $2/B\sqrt{n}$, where "B represents the Number of which the Hyperbolic Logarithm is $1 - 1/12 + 1/360 - 1/1260 + 1/1680$, &c." He acknowledges the help of James Stirling who had found that "B did denote the Square-root of the Circumference of a Circle whose Radius is Unity, so that if that Circumference be called c, the Ratio of the middle Term to the Sum of all the Terms will be expressed by $2/\sqrt{(nc)}$" (De Moivre, 1756, 3rd Ed., p. 244).

De Moivre had thus obtained (in modern notation) the expression,

$$\frac{Y_0}{2^n} = \frac{2}{\sqrt{2\pi n}}$$, for large n, where Y_0 is the middle term.

He also gives the logarithm of the ratio of the middle term to any term distant from it by an interval l as, $(m + l - 1/2)\log\{m + l - 1\} + (m - l + 1/2)\log\{m - l + 1\} - 2m\log m + \log\{(m + l)/m\}$, where $m = 1/2n$. and concludes, in the first of 9 corollaries numbered 1 through 6 and 8 through 10, 7 having been omitted from the numbering, that, "if m or $1/2n$ be a Quantity infinitely great, then the Logarithm of the Ratio, which a Term distant from the middle by the Interval l, has to the middle Term, is $-2ll/n$" (p. 245). This is merely the expression that,

$$Y_l = Y_0 e^{-2l^2/n}, \text{ for large } n.$$

The second corollary obtains the "Sum of the Terms intercepted between the Middle, and that whole distance from it . . . denoted by l", in modern terms, the sum of $Y_0 + Y_1 + Y_3 + \ldots + Y_l$, as

$$\frac{2}{\sqrt{(nc)}} \text{ into } l - \frac{2l^3}{1(3n)} + \frac{4l^5}{2(5nn)} - \frac{8l^7}{6(7n^3)} + \frac{16l^9}{24(9n^4)} - \frac{32l^{11}}{120(11n^9)} \text{ , \&c.}$$

which is the expansion of the integral,

$$\frac{2}{\sqrt{(2\pi n)}} \int_0^l e^{-2l^2/n} \, dl$$

When l is expressed as $S\sqrt{n}$, and S is interpreted as $1/2$, the sum becomes,

$$\frac{2}{\sqrt{c}} \text{ into } \frac{1}{2} - \frac{1}{3(4)} + \frac{1}{2(5)(8)} - \frac{1}{6(7)(10)} + \frac{1}{24(9)(32)} - \frac{1}{120(11)(64)} \text{ , \&c.}$$

. . . which converges so fast, that by help of no more than seven or eight Terms, the Sum required may be carried to six or seven places of Decimals: Now that Sum will be found to be 0.427812, independently from the common Multiplicator $2l / \sqrt{c}$, and therefore to the Tabular Logarithm of 0.427182, which is 9.6312529, adding the Logarithm of $2l/\sqrt{c}$, viz. 9.9019400, the sum will be 19.5331929, to which answers the number 0.341344. (De Moivre, 1756, 3rd Ed., p. 245)

This familiar final figure is the area under the curve of the normal distribution between the *mean* (which is, of course, also the middle value) and an ordinate one *standard deviation* from the mean. In the third corollary De Moivre says:

And therefore, if it was possible to take an infinite number of Experiments, the Probability that an Event which has an equal number of Chances to happen or fail, shall neither appear more frequently than $1/2n + 1/2\sqrt{n}$ times, nor more rarely than $1/2n - 1/2\sqrt{n}$ times, will be expressed by the double Sum of the number exhibited in the second Corollary, that is, by 0.682688, and consequently the Probability of the contrary . . . will be 0.317312, those two Probabilities together compleating Unity, which is the measure of Certainty. (De Moivre, 1756, 3rd Ed., p. 246)[1]

$^1/_2\sqrt{n}$ is what today we call the *standard deviation*. De Moivre did not name it but he did, in Corollary 6, say that $\sqrt{n}$ "will be as it were the *Modulus* by which we are to regulate our Estimation" (De Moivre, 1756, 3rd Ed., p. 248).

In fact what De Moivre does is to expand the exponential and to integrate from 0 to $S\sigma$.

In Corollary 6 De Moivre notes that if l is interpreted as $\sqrt{n}$ rather than $^1/_2\sqrt{n}$, then the series does not converge so fast and that more and more terms would be required for a reasonable approximation as l becomes a greater proportion to $\sqrt{n}$,

. . . for which reason I make use in this Case of the Artifice of Mechanic Quadratures, first invented by Sir *Isaac Newton*, . . . ; it consists in determining the Area of a Curve nearly, from knowing a certain number of its Ordinates A, B, C, D, E, F, &c. placed at equal Intervals, (De Moivre, 1756, 3rd Ed., p. 247).

He uses just 4 ordinates for his *quadrature* and finds, in effect, that the area between $\pm 2\sigma$ or $^1/_2 n \pm \sqrt{n}$ is 0.95428, and that the area in what we now call the *tails* is 0.04572. The true value is a little less than this but it is, nevertheless, familiar.

These results can be extended to the expansion of $(a + b)^n$ and where a and b are not equal.

If the Probabilities of happening and failing be in any given Ratio of inequality, the Problems relating to the Sum of the Terms of the Binomial $(a + b)^n$ will be solved with the same facility as those in which the Probabilities of happening and failing are in a Ratio of Equality. (De Moivre, 1756, 3rd Ed., p. 250)

In Corollary 9 De Moivre in effect, and in modern terms, introduces $\sqrt{(npq)}$, the expression we use today for the standard deviation of the normal approximation to the binomial distribution.

The sum and substance of the *Approximatio* is that it gives, for the first time, the function that was rediscovered much later, the function that dominates so-called classical statistical inference—the *normal distribution*—which in modern terminology is given by the density function,

$$f(X) = \frac{1}{\sqrt{(2\pi\sigma^2)}} \; e^{-(X - \mu)^2/2\sigma^2}$$

---

[1]The value for the proportion of area between $\pm 1\sigma$ is 0.6826894, so that De Moivre was out by one unit in the sixth decimal place.

Figure 6.3 shows the graph of the normal distribution. De Moivre's philosophical position is revealed in the sections headed "Remark I" in the 1738 edition of the *Doctrine* and an additional, and, much longer, "Remark II" in 1756. De Moivre sets his work in the philosophical context of an ordered determinate universe. His notion of *Original Design* (see the quotation in chap. 1) is a notion that persisted at least down to Quetelet. A powerful deity reveals the grand design through statistical averages and stable statistical ratios. Chance produces irregularities. As Pearson remarked:

> There is much value in the idea of the ultimate laws being statistical laws, though why the fluctuations should be attributed to a Lucretian 'Chance', I cannot say. It is not an exactly dignified conception of the Deity to suppose him occupied solely with first moments and neglecting second and higher moments! (Pearson, 1978, p. 160)

and elsewhere,

> The causes which led De Moivre to his "Approximatio" or Bayes to his theorem were more theological and sociological than mathematical, and until one recognizes that the post-Newtonian English mathematicians were more influenced by Newton's theology than by his mathematics, the history of science in the eighteenth century—in particular that of the scientists who were members of the Royal Society—must remain obscure. (Pearson, 1926, p. 552)

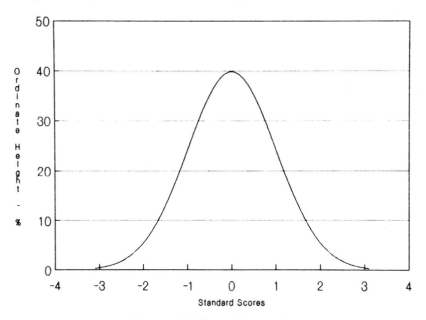

FIG. 6.3. The Normal Distribution.

It is interesting that this is precisely the sort of analysis that has been brought to bear on the work of Galton and Karl Pearson himself, save that it is the philosophy of *eugenics* that influenced their work rather than Christian theology. In Remark II, De Moivre takes up Arbuthnot's argument for the ratio of male to female births, which was discussed earlier, defending the argument against the criticisms that had been advanced by Nicholas Bernoulli who had noted that a chance distribution of the actual male/female birth ratio would be found if the hypothesized ratio (i.e., the ratio under what we would now call the *null* hypothesis) had been taken to be 18 : 17 rather than 1 : 1. But De Moivre insists,

> This Ratio once discovered, and *manifestly serving to a wise purpose*, we conclude the Ratio itself, or if you will the *Form of the Die*, to be an Effect of *Intelligence* and *Design*. As if we were shewn a number of Dice, each with 18 white and 17 black faces, which is Mr. *Bernoulli's* supposition, we should not doubt but that those Dice had been made by some Artist; and that their form was not owing to *Chance*, but was adapted to the particular purpose he had in View. (De Moivre, 1756, 3rd Ed., p. 253)

With the greatest respect to De Moivre this was clearly not Arbuthnot's argument and De Moivre's view that he *might* have said it is somewhat specious. Like Quetelet's use of the normal curve many years later De Moivre's view is a prejudgement and all findings must be made to fit it. Karl Pearson (1978) makes essentially the same point, but it is apparently a point that he did not recognize in his own work.

7

Practical Inference

Some of the philosophical questions surrounding *induction* and *inference* were dealt with in chapter 2. Here the foundations of practical inference will be considered.

INVERSE PROBABILITY AND THE FOUNDATIONS
OF INFERENCE

The first exercises in statistical inference arose from a consideration of statistical summaries such as those found in mortality tables. The development of theories of inference from the standpoint of the implications of mathematical theory can be dated from the work of Thomas Bayes (1702–1761), an English Nonconformist clergyman whose ministry was in Tunbridge Wells. Bayes was recognized as a very good mathematician, although he published very little, and he was elected to the Royal Society in 1742 (see Barnard, 1958, for a biographical note). Curiously enough the paper for which he is remembered was communicated to the Royal Society by his friend, Richard Price, over 2 years after his death and the celebrated forms of the theorem that bear his name, although they follow from the essay, do not actually appear in the work. *An Essay Towards Solving a Problem in the Doctrine of Chances* (Bayes, 1763) is still the subject of much discussion and controversy both as to its contents and implications and as to how much of its import was contributed by its editor, Richard Price. The problem that Bayes addressed is stated by Price in the letter accompanying his submission of the essay,

Mr De Moivre . . . has . . . after Bernoulli, and to a greater degree of exactness, given rules to find the probability there is, that if a very great number of trials be made concerning any event, the proportion of the number of times it will happen, to the number of times it will fail in those trials, should differ less than by small assigned limits from the proportion of the probability of its happening to the probability of its failing in one single trial. But I know of no person who has shewn how to deduce the solution of the converse problem to this; namely, "the number of times an unknown event has happened and failed being given, to find the chance that the probability of its happening should lie somewhere between any two named degrees of probability." (Bayes, 1763, pp. 372–373)

A demonstration of some simple rules of mathematical probability, using a frequency model, will help to derive and illustrate Bayes' Theorem. The probability of drawing a red card from a standard deck of playing cards is 26/52 or $p(R) = 1/2$. The probability of drawing a picture card from the deck is 12/52 or $p(P) = 3/13$. The probability of drawing a red picture card is 6/52 or $p(R \& P) = 3/26$. What is the probability of drawing *either* a red card *or* a picture card? The answer is, of course, 32/52 or $p(R \text{ or } P) = 8/13$. Note that:

$$p(R \text{ or } P) = p(R) + p(P) - p(R \& P), [8/13 = (1/2 + 3/13) - 3/26].$$

This is known as the *addition rule*.

Suppose that you draw a card from the deck, but you are not allowed to see it. What is the probability that it is a red picture card? We can calculate the answer to be 6/52. Now suppose that you are told that it is a red card. What now is the probability of it being a picture card? The probability of drawing a red card is 26/52. We also can figure out that if the card drawn *is* a red card then the probability of it also being a picture card is 6/26. In fact,

$$p(R \& P) = p(R)[p(P|R)], [6/52 = 26/52(6/26)]$$

$p(P|R)$ symbolizes the *conditional* probability of P, that is, the probability of P given that R has occurred and the expression denotes the *multiplication* rule. Note that $p(R \& P)$ is the same as $p(P \& R)$, and that this is equal to $p(P)[p(R|P)]$ or, $6/52 = 12/52(6/12)$. From this fact we see that:

$$p(P|R) = p(P) \frac{p(R|P)}{p(R)}$$

which is the simplest form of Bayes' Theorem. In current terminology the left hand side of this equation is termed the *posterior* probability, the first term on the right hand side, the *prior* probability, and the ratio, $p(R|P)/p(R)$, the *likelihood* ratio.

From the addition rule we can also show that the probability of a red card is the sum of the probabilities of a red picture card and a red number card minus the probability of a picture number card (which does not exist!), or,

$$p(R) = p(R \text{ \& } P) + p(R \text{ \& } N) - p(P \text{ \& } N).$$

But $p(P \text{ \& } N) = 0$ because the events *picture card* and *number card* are mutually exclusive. So that Bayes' Theorem may be written:

$$p(P|R) = p(P) \ \frac{p(R|P)}{p(P)[p(R|P)] + p(N)[p(R|N)]}$$

The fact that this formula is arithmetically correct may be checked by substituting the values we can obtain from the known distribution of cards in the standard deck. However, this does not demonstrate the alleged utility of the theorem for statistical inference. For that we must turn to another example after substituting D (for Data) in place of R, and H_1 (for Hypothesis 1) in place of P, and H_2 (for Hypothesis 2) in place of N, where H_1 and H_2 are two mutually exclusive and exhaustive hypotheses. We have:

$$p(H_1|D) = p(H_1) \ \frac{p(D|H_1)}{p(H_1)p(D|H_1) + p(H_2)p(D|H_2)}$$

Bayes' Theorem apparently provides a means of assessing the probability of a hypothesis given the data (or outcome) which is the inverse of assessing the probability of an outcome given a hypothesis (or rule), and of course we may envisage more than two hypotheses. In the original essay Bayes demonstrated his construct using as an example the probability of balls coming to rest on one or other of the parts of a plane table. Laplace who, in 1774, arrived at essentially the same result as Bayes, but provided a more generalized analysis, used the problem of the probability of drawing a white ball from an urn containing unknown proportions of black and white balls given that a sampling of a particular ratio has been drawn. Traditionally, writers on Bayes make heavy use of "urn problems," and tradition will be followed with a simple example. Phillips (1973) gives a comprehensive account of Bayesian procedures and shows how they can be applied to data appraisal in the social sciences. Suppose we are presented with two identical urns W and B. W contains 70 white and 30 black balls, B contains 40 white and 60 black balls. From one of the urns we are allowed to draw 10 balls, and we find that 6 of them are white and 4 of them are black. Is the urn that we have chosen more likely to be W or more likely to be B? Presumably most of us would opt for W. What is the probability that it *was* W?

$p(H_1|D)$ is the probability of W given the data, and $p(H_2|D)$ is the probability of B given the data. Now the probability of drawing a white ball from W is 7/10 and from B it is 4/10. The probability of the data given H_1 [$p(D|H_1)$] is $(0.7)^6(0.3)^4$, and $p(D|H_1)$ is $(0.4)^6(0.6)^4$.

Now we apply Bayes' Theorem:

$$p(H_1|D) = p(H_1) \ \frac{0.0009}{p(H_1)(0.0009) + p(H_2)(0.0005)}$$

In order to complete the calculation, we have to have values for $p(H_1)$ and $p(H_2)$—the prior probabilities. And here is the controversy. The objectivist view is that these probabilities are unknown and unknowable because the state of the urn that we have chosen is fixed. There are no grounds for saying that we have chosen W or B. The personalist would say that we can always state some degree of belief. If we are completely ignorant about which urn was chosen then both $p(H_1)$ and $p(H_2)$ can be expressed as 0.5. This is a formal statement of Laplace's *Principle of Insufficient Reason*, or *Bayes' Postulate*. If we put these values in our equation $p(H_1|D)$ works out to be 0.64, which matches common sense. This value could then be used to revise $p(H_1)$ and $p(H_2)$ and further data collected. For its proponents the strength of Bayesian methods lies in the claim that they provide formal procedures for revising many kinds of opinion in the light of new data in a direct and straightforward way, quite unlike the inferential procedures of Fisherian statistics. The most important point that has to be accepted however is the justification for the assignment of prior probabilities. Although, in this simple example there might seem to be little difficulty, in more complex situations, where probabilities, based on relative frequency,[1] hunches, or on opinion, cannot be assigned precisely or readily, the picture is far less clear. Furthermore, the principle of the *equal distribution of ignorance* has itself come under a great deal of philosophical attack. "It is rather generally believed that he [Bayes] did not publish because he distrusted his postulate, and thought his scholium defective. If so he was correct" (Hacking, 1965, p. 201).

Fisherian Inference

When the justification for the probabilistic basis of inference in the sense of revising opinion on the basis of data was thought of at all, it was the Bayesian approach that held sway until this century. Its foundations had come under attack primarily on the grounds that probability in any practical sense of the word must be based on relative frequency of observations and not on degrees of belief. Venn (1866) was perhaps the most insistent spokesman for this view. Sir Ronald Fisher (1890–1962), certainly the most influential statistician of all time, set out to replace it. In 1930 he published a paper that supposedly set out his notion of *fiducial* probability, claiming, "Inverse probability has, I believe, survived so long in spite of its unsatisfactory basis, because its critics have until recent times put forward nothing to replace it as a rational theory of learning by experience" (Fisher, 1930, p. 531).

There is no doubt that Fisher's methods, and the contributions of Neyman and Pearson that have been grafted on to them, have provided us with a set of inferential *procedures*. There seems to be considerable doubt as to whether he

---

[1]Presumably it could be argued that our urn with its unknown ratio of black and white balls is one of an infinite distribution of urns with differing make-ups.

provided us with a coherent non-Bayesian *theory*. Fisher himself asserted that the concept of the *likelihood* function was fundamental to his new approach and distinguished it from Bayesian probability. Kendall (1963) in his obituary of Fisher says this:

It appears to me that, at this point, [1922] his ideas were not very well thought out. Certainly his exposition of them was obscure. But, in retrospect, it becomes plain that he was thinking of a probability function $f(x,\theta)$ in two different ways: as the probability distribution of x for given θ, and as giving some sort of permissible range of θ for an observed x. To this latter he gave the the name of 'fiducial probability distribution' (later to be known as a fiducial distribution) and in doing so began a long train of confusion; for it is not a probability distribution to anyone who rejects Bayes's approach, and indeed, may not be a distribution of anything. Fisher nevertheless manipulated it as if it were, and thereafter maintained an attitude of rather contemptuous surprise towards anyone who was perverse enough to fail in understanding his argument.

The position on both sides has been restated *ad nauseam*, without much attempt at reconciliation or, as I think, without an explicit recognition of the real point, which is that a man's attitude towards inference, like his attitude towards religion, is determined by his emotional make-up, not by reason or mathematics. (Kendall, 1963, p. 4)

Richard von Mises (1957) is baffled also,

Fisher introduces the term [likelihood] in order to denote something different from probability. As he fails to give a definition for either word, i.e., he does not indicate how the value of either is to be determined in a given case, we can only try to derive the intended meaning by considering the context in which he uses these words.

I do not understand the many beautiful words used by Fisher and his followers in support of the likelihood theory. The main argument, namely, that p [the probability of the hypothesis] is not a variable but an "unknown constant," does not mean anything to me. (von Mises, pp. 157–158)

It is tempting to leave it at that but some attempt at capturing the flavor of Fisher's position must be made. Clearly if one has knowledge of a distribution of probabilities of events then that knowledge can be used to establish the probability of an event that has not yet been observed, for example the probability that the next roll of two dice will produce a seven ($p = 0.167$). What of the situation where an event has been observed—the roll did produce a seven—can we say anything about the plausibility of an event with $p = 0.167$ having occurred? This is a decidedly odd sort of question because the event has indeed occurred! Before the draw from a lottery with 1,000,000 tickets is made, the probability of my winning is 0.000001. It will be difficult to convince me *after* the draw, as I clutch the winning ticket, that what has happened is impossible, or even very, very unlikely to have occurred by chance, and, if you continue to insist I shall merely keep on showing you my ticket.

Fisher, in 1930, puts the situation in this way:

> There are two different measures of rational belief appropriate to different cases. Knowing the population we can express our incomplete knowledge of, or expectation of, the sample in terms of probability; knowing the sample we can express our incomplete knowledge of the population in terms of likelihood. (Fisher, 1930, p. 532)

Likelihood then is a numerical measure of rational belief different from probability. Whether or not the logic of the situation is understood, all users of statistical methods will recognize the reasoning as crucial to both estimation and hypothesis testing. The method of *maximum likelihood* that Fisher propounds (although it had been put forward by Daniel Bernoulli in 1777—see Kendall, 1961) justifies the choice of population parameter. The method simply says that the best estimate of the parameter is the value that maximizes the probability of the observations, or, that what has occurred is the most likely thing that could have occurred. A number of writers, for example Hogben (1957), have stated that this assumption cannot be justified without an appeal to inverse probability so that Fisher did not succeed in detaching inference from Bayes' Theorem. Nevertheless, the basic notion is that we can find the likelihood of a particular population parameter, say the correlation coefficient ρ, by defining it as a value that is proportional to the probability that from a population with that value we have obtained a sample with an observed value r.

There is no doubt that Fisher's argument will continue to be controversial and that many attempts to resolve the ambiguities will be made. Dempster (1964) is among those who have entered the fray and Hacking's (1965) rationale has resulted in one well-known statistician (Bartlett, 1966) to propose that the resulting theory be renamed "the Fisher-Hacking theory of fiducial inference."

8

Sampling
and Estimation

RANDOMNESS AND RANDOM NUMBERS

In common parlance to choose "at random" is to choose without bias, to make the *act of choosing* one without purpose even though the eventual outcome may be used for a decision. The emphasis here is on the act rather than the outcome. It is certainly not true to say that ordinary folk accept that random choice means absence of design in the outcome. Politicians, examining the polls, have been known to remark that the result was "in the cards." Primitive notions of fate, demons, guardian angels, and modern appeals to the "will of God," often lie behind the drawing of lots and the tossing of coins to "decide" if Mary loves John, or to take one course of action rather than another. It is absence of design in the *manner of choosing* that is important. The point must not be labored, but everyday notions of chance are still construed, even by the most sophisticated, in ways that are not too far removed from the random element in divination and sortilege practiced by the oracles and priests who were consulted by our remote, and not-so-remote, ancestors. And, as already noted, perhaps one of the reasons for the delay in the development of the probability calculus arose from a reluctance to attempt to "second-guess" the gods.

The concepts of *randomness* and *probability* are, therefore, inextricably intertwined in statistics. The difficulties inherent in defining probability, which were discussed earlier, are once more presented in an examination of randomness. It is commonly thought that everyone knows what randomness is. The great statistician Jerzy Neyman (1894–1981) states, "The method of random sampling consists, as it is known, in taking at random elements from the population which it is intended to study. The elements compose a sample which is then studied" (Neyman, 1934, p. 567).

It is unlikely that this definition would be given a high grade by most teachers of statistics. Later in this paper and, this inadequate definition notwithstanding, it is a paper of central and enormous importance, Neyman does note that random sampling means that each element in the population must have an equal chance of being chosen, but it is not uncommon for writers on the method to ignore both this simple directive and instructions as to the means of its implementation. Of course the use of the words "equal chance" in the definition brings us back to what we mean by *chance* and *probability*. For most purposes we fall back on the notion of long-run relative frequency rather than leaving these constructs as undefined ideas that make intuitive sense. Practical tests of *randomness* rest on the examination of the distribution of events in long series. It is also the case, as Kendall and Babington Smith (1938) point out, that random sampling procedures may follow a purposive process. For example, the number π is not a random number but its calculation generates a series of digits which *may* be random. These authors are among the earliest to set out the bases of random sampling from a straightforward practical viewpoint, and they were writing a mere 50 years ago. The concept of a formal random sample is a modern one; and concerns about its place and importance in scientific inference and significance testing paralleled the development of methods of experimental design and technical approaches to the appraisal of data. Nevertheless, informal notions of randomness that imply lack of partiality and "choice by chance" go back many centuries.

Stigler (1977) has researched the procedure known as "the trial of the Pyx," a sampling inspection procedure that has been in existence at the Royal Mint in London for almost 8 centuries. Over a period of time a coin would be taken daily from the batch that had been minted, and placed in a box called the Pyx. At intervals, sometimes separated by as much as 3 or 4 years, the Pyx was opened and the contents checked and assayed in order to ensure that the coinage met the specifications laid down by the Crown. Stigler quotes Oresme on the procedure followed in 1280:

> When the Master of the Mint has brought the pence, coined, blanched and made ready, to the place of trial, e.g. the Mint, he must put them all at once on the counter which is covered with canvas. Then, when the pence have been well turned over and thoroughly mixed by the hands of the Master of the Mint and the Changer, let the Changer take a handful in the middle of the heap, moving round nine or ten times in one direction or the other, until he has taken six pounds. He must then distribute these two or three times into four heaps, so that they are well mixed. (Stigler, 1977, p. 495)

The Master of the Mint was allowed a margin of error called *the remedy* and had to make good any deficit that was discovered. Although mathematical statistics played no part in these tests, and if they had they would have been more precise,[1] the procedure itself mirrors modern practice.

> The trial of the Pyx even in the Middle Ages consisted of a sample being drawn, a null hypothesis (the standard) to be tested, a two-sided alternative, and a test statistic and a critical region (the total weight of the coins and the remedy). The problem even carried with itself a loss function which was easily interpretable in economic terms. (Stigler, 1977, p. 499)

Random selections may be made from real, existent universes, for example, the population of Ontario, or from hypothetical universes, for example individuals who, over a period of time, have taken a particular drug as part of a clinical trial. In the latter case to talk of "selection" in any real sense of the word is stretching credulity but we do use the results based on the individuals actually examined to make inferences about the *potential* population that may be given the drug. In the same way the samples of convenience that are used in psychological research are hardly ever selected randomly in the formal sense. Undergraduate student volunteers are not labeled as automatically constituting random samples but they are often assumed to be *unbiased* with respect to the dependent variables of interest, an assumption that has produced much criticism. This latter statement emphasizes the fact that a sampling method, whatever it is, relates to the universe under study and the particular dependent variable or variables of interest. A questionnaire asking about attitudes to health and fitness given to members of the audience at, say, a symphony concert, may well be generalizable to the population of the city but the same instrument given to the annual convention of a weight watchers' club would not. These statements seem to be so obvious and yet, as we shall see, overlooking possible sources of bias either by accident or design has led to some expensive fiascos. Unfortunately the method of sampling can never be assuredly independent of the variable under study. Kendall and Babington-Smith (1938) note that; "The assumption of independence must therefore be made with more or less confidence on *a priori* grounds. It is part of the hypothesis on which our ultimate expression of opinion is based" (p. 152).

Kendall and Babington Smith comment on the use of "random" digits in random sampling and it is worth examining these applications because most of the present-day statistical cookbooks at least pay lip-service to the procedures by including tables of random numbers and some instruction as to their use. Individual units in the population are numbered in some convenient way and then numbers, taken from the tables, are matched with the individuals to select the

---

[1]Stigler notes that the *remedy* was specified on a per pound basis and that all the coin weights were combined. This, together with the central limit theorem, almost guarantees that the Master would not exceed the remedy.

sample. This procedure may result in a sample of individuals numbered 1, 2, 3, 4, 5, 6, 7, 8, 9, or 2, 4, 6, 8, 10, 12, 14, 16, 18, 20, groupings that may invite comment because they follow immediately recognizable orders but which nevertheless *could* be generated by a random selection. The fact that a random selection produces a grouping that *looks* to be biased or non-representative led to a great deal of debate in the 1920s and 1930s. The sequence 1, 4, 2, 7, 9, has the appearance of being random but the sequence 1, 4, 2, 7, 9, 1, 4, 2, 7, 9, has not. Finite sequences of *random numbers* are therefore only *locally random*. Even the famous tables of one million random digits produced by the RAND Corporation (1965) can only, strictly speaking, be regarded as anything other than locally random, for it may be that the sequence of one million was about to repeat itself. Random sequences may also be "patchy." Yule (1938b), for example, after examining Tippett's tables which had been constructed by taking numbers at random from census reports, gained the impression that they were rather patchy and proceeded to apply further tests that gave some support to his view. Tippett (1925) used his tables (not then published) to examine experimentally his work on the distribution of the range.

Simple tests for local randomness are outlined by Kendall and Babington Smith, tests that Tippett's tables had passed, and although much more extensive appraisals can be made today by using computers these prescriptions illustrate the sort of criteria that should be applied. Each digit should appear approximately the same number of times; no digit should tend to be followed by another digit; there are certain expectations in blocks of digits with regard to the occurrence of three, four, or five digits that are all the same; there are certain expectations regarding the *gaps* in the sequence between digits that are the same. Tests of this sort do not exhaust the many that can be applied. Whitney (1984) has recently noted that, "It has been said that more time has been spent generating and testing random numbers than using them" (p. 129).

COMBINING OBSERVATIONS

The notion of using a measure of the *average* as an adequate and convenient summary or description of a number of data is an accepted part of everyday discourse. We speak of average incomes and average prices, of average speeds and average gas consumption, of average men and average women. We are referring to some middling, nonextreme value that we take as a fair representation of our observations. The easy use of the term does not reflect the logical problems associated with the justification for the use of particular measures of the average. The term itself, we find from the Oxford Dictionary, refers, among other things, to notions of sharing labor or risk. So that old forms of the word refer to work done by tenants for a feudal superior or to shared risks among merchants for losses at sea. Modern conceptions of the word also include the notion of a sharing or evening out over a range of disparate values.

A large series of observations or measurements of the same phenomenon produces a distribution of values. Given the assumption that a single true value does, in fact, exist, the presence of different values in the series shows that there are errors. The assumption that over-estimations are as likely as under-estimations would provide support for the use of the middle value of the series, the *median*, as representing the true value. The assumption that the value we observe most frequently is likely the true value justifies the use of the *mode*, and the "evening out" of the different values is seen in the use of the *arithmetic mean*. It is this latter measure that is now the statistic of choice when observations are combined and there are a number of strands in our history that have contributed to the justification for its use. The employment of the arithmetic mean and the use of the *law of error* have sound mathematical underpinnings in the *Principle of Least Squares*, which will be considered shortly. First, however, a somewhat critical look at the use of the mean is in order.

The Arithmetic Mean

In the 1755 *Philosophical Transactions*, and in a revision in *Miscellaneous Tracts* of 1757, Thomas Simpson argues the case for the arithmetic mean in *An Attempt to Show the Advantage arising by Taking the Mean Of a Number of Observations in Practical Astronomy*. These are valuable contributions that discuss, for the first time, measurement errors in the context of probability and point the way toward the idea of a law of facility of error. Simpson (1755) complains that, "some persons, of considerable note, have been of opinion, and even publickly maintained, that one single observation, taken with due care, was as much to be relied upon as the Mean of a great number" (pp. 82–83).

In the revision, Simpson states as axioms that positive and negative errors are equally probable and that there are assignable limits within which errors can be taken to fall. He also diagrams the law of error as an isosceles triangle and shows that the mean is nearer to the true value than a single random observation.

The claim of the *arithmetic mean* to be the best representation of a large body of data is often justified by appeal to the principle of least squares and the law of error. This is high theory and in appealing to it there is a danger of overlooking the *logic* of the use of the mean. Simply, as John Venn (1891), who was mentioned in chapter 1, puts it;

Why do we resort to averages at all?

How can a single introduction of our own, and that a fictitious one, possibly take the place of the many values which were actually given to us? And the answer surely is, that it can *not* possibly do so; the one thing cannot take the place of the other for purposes in general, but only for this or that specific purpose. (pp. 429–430)

This seemingly obvious statement is one that has frequently been ignored in statistics in the social sciences. Venn points out the different kinds of averages that can be used for different purposes and notes cases where the use of any sort of average is misleading. Edgeworth (1887) had provided an attempt to examine the mathematical justifications for the different averages and Venn and many others refer to this treatment. Edgeworth's paper also examines the validity of the least squares principle in this context. Venn illustrates his argument with some straightforward examples. If two people reckoned the distance of Cambridge from London to be 50 and 60 miles, in the absence of any information that would lead us to suspect either of the measures, one would guess that 55 miles was the probable distance. However, if one person said that someone they knew lived in Oxford and another that the individual lived in Cambridge, the most probable location would not be at some place in between. In the latter case, in the absence of any other information, one would have a chance at arriving at the truth by choosing at random.

Edgeworth's papers on the *best mean* represent some of his most useful work. A particular service is rendered by his distinction between real or objective means and fictitious or subjective means. The former arise when we use the arithmetic mean as the true value underlying a group of measurements that are subject to error, the latter is a description of a set.

The mean of observations is a cause, as it were the source from which diverging errors emanate. The mean of statistics is a description, a representative of the group, that quantity which, if we must in practice put one quantity for many, minimises the error unavoidably attending such practice.

Observations are different copies of one original; statistics are different originals affording one 'generic portrait.' (Edgeworth, 1887, p. 139)

This formal distinction is clear. However, because the mathematics of the analysis of errors and the manipulations of modern statistics rest on the same principles, the logic of inference is sometimes clouded. It is Quetelet who brought the mathematics of error estimation in physical measurement into the assessment of the dispersion of human characteristics. Clearly something of the sort had been done before in the examination of mortality tables for insurance purposes, but we see Quetelet making a direct statement that only partially recognizes Edgeworth's later distinction.

Everything occurs then as though there existed a type of man, from which all other men differed more or less. Nature has placed before our eyes living examples of what theory shows us. Each people presents its mean, and the different variations from this mean which may be calculated *a priori*. (Quetelet, 1835/1849, p. 96)

The Principle of Least Squares

In its best-known form this famous principle states that the sum of squared differences of observations from the mean of those observations is a minimum, that is to say, it is smaller than the sum of squared differences from any other reference point.

Legendre (1752–1833) announced the *Principle of Least Squares* in 1805, but in *Theoria Motus Corporum Coelestium*, published in 1809, Gauss (1777–1855) discussing the method, refers to his work on it in 1795 (when he was a 17–year-old student preparing for his university studies). This claim to priority upset Legendre and led to some bitter dispute. Today the method is most frequently associated with Gauss who is often identified as the greatest mathematician of all time. That the method very quickly became a topic of much commentary and discussion may be demonstrated by the fact that in the 70 or so years following Legendre's publication no less than 193 authors produced 72 books, 23 parts of books, and 313 memoirs relating to it. Merriman (1877) provides a list of these titles together with some notes. Faced with such sources, to say nothing of the derivations, papers, commentaries, and monographs published in the last 110 years, the following represents perhaps one of a dozen ways of commenting on its origins.

Using the mean to combine a set of independent observations was a technique that had been used in the 17th century. Gauss, later, examined the problem of selecting from a number of possible ways of combining data the one that produced the least possible uncertainty about the "true value." Gauss noted that in the combination of astronomical observations the mathematical treatment depended on the method of combination. He approached the problem from the standpoint that the method should lead to the cancellation of random errors of measurement and that, as there was no reason to prefer one method over another, the arithmetic mean should be chosen. Having appreciated that the "best" in the sense of "most probable" value, could not be known unless the distribution of errors was known, he turned to an examination of the distribution which gave the mean as the most probable value. Gauss's approach was based on practical considerations, and because the procedures he examined did produce workable solutions in astronomical and geodetic observations the method was vindicated. In fact, the principle of least squares, as Gauss himself noted, can be considered independently of the calculus of probabilities.

If we have n observations $X1, X_2, X_3, \ldots X_n$, from a population with a mean μ, what is the *least squares estimate* of μ? It is the value of μ that minimizes,

$$(X_1 - \mu)^2 + (X_2 - \mu)^2 + (X_3 - \mu)^2 + \ldots + (X_n - \mu)^2$$
$$= \Sigma(X_i - \mu)^2.$$

Now $\Sigma(X_i - \mu)^2 = \Sigma(X_i - \bar{X} + \bar{X} - \mu)^2$, where $\bar{X}$ is the mean of the n observations.

$$\Sigma(X_i - \mu)^2 = \Sigma(X_i - \bar{X})^2 + 2(\bar{X} - \mu)\Sigma(X_i - \bar{X}) + n(\bar{X} - \mu)^2$$

But $\Sigma(X_i - \bar{X}) = 0$,

So that, $\Sigma(X_i - \mu)^2 = \Sigma(X_i - \bar{X})^2 + n(\bar{X} - \mu)^2$.

Clearly the right hand side of the latter expression is at a minimum when $\bar{X} = \mu$, which demonstrates the principle.

This easily obtained result provides a rationale for estimating the population mean from the sample mean that is intuitively sensible. The law of error enters the picture when we consider the arithmetic mean as the *most probable* result. In this case we find that the law is in fact given by the *normal distribution*, often referred to as the Laplace-Gaussian distribution. It has been stated on more than one occasion that Laplace assumed the normal law in arriving at the mean to provide what he described as the most advantageous combination of observations. Laplace certainly considered the case when positive and negative errors are equally likely and these cases rest on the error law being what we now call "normal" in form.

The threads of the argument are not always easy to disentangle but one of the better accounts, for those who are prepared to grapple with a little mathematics, was given by Glaisher as long ago as 1872. The crucial point is that of the rationale for the two fundamental constructs of statistics, the *mean*, $\bar{X}$, and the *variance*, $\Sigma(X_i - \bar{X})^2/n$. The essential fact is easily seen. Given that a distribution of observations is normal in form, and given that we know the mean and the variance of the distribution, then the distribution is completely and uniquely specified. All its properties can be ascertained given this information.

In the context of statistics in the social sciences both the *normal law* and the *least squares principle* are best understood in the context of the linear model. The model encompasses these constructs and brings together in a formal sense the mathematics of the combination of observations developed for use in error estimation and mathematical statistics as exemplified by *analysis of variance* and *regression analysis*. The linear model will be discussed later.

Representation and Bias

The earliest examples of the use of samples in social statistics we have seen in the work of Graunt, Petty, Halley, and the early actuaries. These samples were neither random nor representative and mistaken inferences were plentiful. In any event, it was not until much later, when attempts were made to collect information on populations, inferential exercises repeated, and the results compared, that critical examinations of the techniques employed could be made. Stephan (1948) reports that Sir Frederick Morton Eden estimated the population of Great Britain in 1800 to be about 9,000,000. This estimate, which was based on the number of births and the average number of inhabitants in each house (a number that was obtained by sampling), was confirmed by the first British census in 1801. Earlier attempts to estimate populations had been made in France and Laplace in 1802 made an attempt to do so that followed a scheme he had devised and published in 1786, a scheme that included a probability measure of the precision of the estimate. Specifically, Laplace averred that the odds were 1,161 to 1 that the error would not reach half a million. Westergaard (1932) provides some more details of these exercises. Elsewhere in Europe and in the United States the 19th century saw various censuses conducted, as well as attempts to estimate the size of the population from samples. In the United States the Constitution provided for a census every 10 years in order to determine Congressional representation, but a Bill introduced into the British Parliament in 1753 to establish an annual census was defeated in the House of Lords.

It appears that the probability mathematicians and the rising group of political arithmeticians never joined forces in the 19th century. The latter favored the institution of complete censuses and, generally speaking, were not mathematicians, and the former were scientists who had many other problems to test their mettle. Almost 100 years passed before scientific sampling procedures were properly investigated.

Stephan (1948) lists four areas where modern sampling methods could have been used to advantage; agricultural crop and livestock estimates, economic statistics, social surveys and health surveys, and public opinion polls. The latter will be considered in a little more detail because it is in this area that the accuracy of forecasts is so often and so quickly assessed and breakdowns in sampling procedures detected with the benefit of hindsight.

The *Raleigh Star* in Raleigh, North Carolina, conducted "straw votes" as early as 1824, covering political meetings and trying to discover the "sense of the people." By the turn of the century many newspapers in the United States were regularly conducting opinion polls, a common method being merely to invite members of the public to clip out a ballot in the paper and to mail it in. The same basic procedure was followed by all the publications. Then the large circulation magazines, notably *Literary Digest*, began to mail out ballots to very large numbers of people, sometimes as many as 11,000,000. In 1916 this publication correctly predicted the election of Wilson to the presidency and from then until 1936 enjoyed consistent and much admired success. Its predictions were very accurate. For example, in 1932 its estimate of the popular vote for each candidate in the presidential election came to within 1.4% of the actual outcome. In 1936 came disaster. For years *Literary Digest* had conducted polls on all kinds of issues, mailing out millions of ballots, at considerable expense, to telephone subscribers and automobile owners. In 1936 the magazine predicted that Alfred M. Landon would win the presidency on the basis of the return of over 2,300,000 replies from over 10,000,000 mailed ballots. The record shows that Franklin D. Roosevelt won the presidency with one of the largest majorities in American presidential history. The reasons for this disastrous mistake are now easy to see. Prior to 1936 preference for the two major political parties in the United States was not related to level of income. In that year it seems that it was. The telephone subscribers and car owners (and in 1936 these were the rather more affluent) who had received the *Literary Digest*'s ballots were, in the main, Republicans. In 1937 the magazine ceased publication. Crum (1931) and Robinson (1932, 1937) have commentaries on some of these early polls.

Fortune magazine fared no better in 1948, underestimating the vote for the Democrats and Harry Truman by close to 12% and, of course, failing to pick the winner. In 1936, with a much, much smaller sample than that of *Literary Digest* (less than 5,000) it had forecast Roosevelt's vote to within 1%. The explanation for its failure in 1948 rests with the swing of both decided and undecided voters between the September poll and the November election and failure to correct for a geographic sampling bias. Parten (1966) has some commentary on these and other polls. One of the most successful polling organizations, the *American Institute of Public Opinion*, headed by George Gallup, began its work in 1933. But the Gallup poll also predicted a win for Dewey over Truman in 1948, and many people have seen the *Life* photograph of a victorious president holding the *Chicago Daily Tribune* with its famous Type I error headline, "Dewey defeats Truman."

The result produced one of the first claims that the polls influenced the outcome, inducing complacency in the Republicans and a small turnout of their supporters, leading to the defeat of the Republican candidate. Today there is much controversy over the conducting and the use of polls. They will survive because in general they are correct much more often than not. Their success is due to the development of refined sampling techniques.

SAMPLING IN THEORY AND IN PRACTICE

Chang (1976) gives a quite thorough review of inferential processes and sampling theory and it is worth sketching in some of its development in the context of survey sampling. However, from the standpoint of statistics and sampling in psychology, there is no doubt but that the rationale of sampling procedures for hypothesis testing rather than parameter estimation is of greater import. But the two are related.

The early political arithmeticians held to the view that statistical ratios, for example, males to females, average number of children per family, and so on, were approximately constant, and, as a result, proceeded to draw inferences from figures collected in a single town or parish to whole regions and even countries. The early 19th century saw the introduction of the law of error by Gauss and Laplace and an awareness that *variability* was an important consideration in the assessment of data. Populations are now defined by two *parameters*, the mean and the variance. One of the earliest attempts to put a measure of precision onto a sampling exercise was that of Laplace in 1802. The sample he used was not random although he appears to have assumed that it was. *Communes* distributed across France were chosen to balance out climatic differences. Those having mayors known for their "zeal and intelligence" were also selected so that the data would be the most precise. Laplace also assumed that birth rate was homogeneous across the French population, exactly the sort of unwarranted assumption that was made by the early political arithmeticians. Nevertheless, Laplace estimated the population total from his figures and, appealing to the *central limit theorem* (which he had discussed in 1783), approximated the distribution of estimation errors to the normal curve.

Survey sampling for all kinds of social investigations owes a great deal to Sir Arthur Lyon Bowley (1869–1957). In his time he was recognized as a pioneer in the definition of sampling techniques and his methods and assumptions were the subject of much debate. In the event some of his approaches were found to be defective but his work focussed attention on the problem. In 1926 he summarized the theory of sampling, and a short paper of 1936 outlines the application of sampling to economic and social problems. He served on numerous official committees that investigated the economic state of the nation, the social effects of unemployment and so on, and worked directly on many surveys. Maunder (1972) has written a memoir that points up his contributions, contributions that were somewhat overshadowed by the work of his contemporaries, Pearson, Fisher, and Neyman. He was a calm and courteous man, enormously concerned with social issues, and he occupied, at the London School of Economics, the first Chair devoted to statistics in the social sciences.

Bowley (1936) defines the sampling problem simply,

We are here concerned, . . . with the investigation of the numerical structure of an actual and limited universe, or "population" which is the better word for our purpose. Our problems are quite definitely to infer the population from the sample. The problem is strictly analogous to that of estimating the proportion of the various colours of balls in a limited urn on the basis of one or more trial draws. (pp. 474–475)

In the early years of this century, Bowley began to examine both the practice and theory of survey sampling. His work helped to highlight the utility of probability sampling of one form or another. *Systematic selection* was adopted and advocated by A. N. Kiaer (1838–1919), Director of the Norwegian Bureau of Statistics, in his examinations of census data, but the majority of influential statisticians, represented by the International Statistical Institute, rejected sampling, pressing for complete enumeration. It took almost 30 years for the utility and benefits of the methods to be appreciated. Seng (1951) and Kruskal and Mosteller (1979) give accounts of this most interesting period in statistical history. The latter authors give a translation and paraphrase of the remarks of Georg von Mayer, Professor at the University of Munich, on Kiaer's work on the *representative method*, which was presented at a meeting of the Institute in Berne in 1895,

> I regard as most dangerous the point of view found in his work. I understand that representative samples can have some value, but it is a value restricted to terrain already illuminated by full coverage. One cannot replace by calculation the real observation of facts. A sample provides statistics for the units actually observed, but not true statistics for the entire terrain.
>
> It is especially dangerous to propose representative sampling in the midst of an assembly of statisticians. Perhaps for legislative or administrative goals sampling may have uses—but one must never forget that it cannot replace a complete survey. It is necessary to add that there is among us these days a current in the minds of mathematicians that would, in many ways, have us calculate rather than observe. We must remain firm and say: no calculations when observations can be made. (Quoted by Kruskal & Mosteller, 1979, pp. 174–175)

Oddly enough, Kiaer's work is not mathematical in the sense that modern methods of parameter estimation are mathematical. At the time those methods were not fully delineated nor understood. Kiaer aimed, by a variety of techniques, to produce a miniature of the population, although he noted as early as 1899 the necessity for the investigation of both the practical and theoretical aspects of his methods. At a meeting in 1901 (a report of which was published in 1903), Kiaer returned to the theme and it was in a discussion of his contribution that L. von Bortkiewicz suggested that the "calculus of probabilities" could be used to test the efficacy of sampling. By establishing how much of a difference between sample and population could be obtained accidentally and checking whether or not an observed difference lay outside those limits, the representativeness of the sample could be decided upon. Bortkiwiecz did not, apparently, formulate all the necessary tests and others had employed this method, but he seems to have been the first to draw the attention of practicing statisticians to the possibilities.

In 1903, Kiaer must have thought that the sampling argument was won, for a subcommittee of the International Statistical Institute proposed a resolution at the Berlin meeting:

> The Committee, considering that the correct application of the representative method, in a certain number of cases, can furnish exact and detailed observations from which the results can be generalized, within certain limits, recommends its use, provided that in the publication of the results the conditions under which the selection of the observation units is made are completely specified. The question will be kept on the agenda, so that a report may be presented in the next session on the application of the method in practice and on the value of the results arrived at. (Quoted by Seng, 1951, p. 220)

What is more, a discussant at the meeting, the French statistician, Lucien March, returned to the ideas that had been put forward by Bortkiewicz and outlined some of the basics of probability sampling. (See Kruskal & Mosteller, 1979, for a short summary of this presentation). The way ahead seemed clear.

In fact the question was, for all intents and purposes, shelved for over 20 years, and it was not until 1925, at the Rome session of the Institute, that the advantages of the sampling method were fully recognized. This was in no small way due to the theoretical work of Bowley. Bowley had suggested in his Presidential address to the Economic Science and Statistical Section of the British Association as early as 1906, that a systematic approach to the problem of sampling would bear fruit.

> In general, two lines of analysis are possible: we may find an empirical formula (with Professor Karl Pearson) which fits this class of observations, [Bowley is referring to data that may not be normally distributed] and by evaluating the constants determine an appropriate curve of frequency, and hence allot the chances of possible differences between our observation and the unknown true value; or we may accept Professor Edgeworth's analysis of the causes which would produce his generalised law of great numbers, and determine *a priori* or by experiment whether this universal law may be expected or is to be found in the case in question. (Bowley, 1906, pp. 549–550)

Edgeworth's method is based on the *Central Limit Theorem* and Bowley explains its utility clearly and simply:

> If quantities are distributed according to almost any curve of frequency, . . . the average of successive groups of . . . these conform to a normal curve (the more and more closely as *n* is increased) whose standard deviation diminishes in inverse ratio to the number in each sample . . . If we can apply this method . . ., we are able to give not only a numerical average, but a reasoned estimate for the real physical quantity of which the average is a local or temporary instance. (Bowley, 1906, p. 550)

The procedure demands random sampling:

> . . . The *chances are the same for all the items of the groups to be sampled, and the way they are taken is absolutely independent of their magnitude.*
> . . . It is frequently impossible to cover a whole area as the census does, . . . but it is not necessary. We can obtain as good results as we please by sampling, and very often quite small samples are enough; the only difficulty is to ensure that every person or thing has the same chance of inclusion in the investigation. (Bowley, 1906, pp. 551–553)

THE THEORY OF ESTIMATION

Over the next 20 years Bowley and his associates completed a number of surveys and his theoretical researches produced *The Measurement of the Precision Attained in Sampling* in 1926. This paper formed part of the report of the International Statistical Institute, which recommended and drew attention to the methods of random selection and *purposive* selection, "A number of groups of units are selected which together yield nearly the same characteristics as the totality" (p. 2). The report does not directly address the method of *stratified* sampling even though the technique had been in general use. This procedure received close attention from Neyman in his paper of 1934. Bowley had attempted to present a theory of purposive sampling in his 1926 report.

> A distinctive feature of this method, according to Bowley, was that it was a case of cluster sampling. It was assumed that the quantity under investigation was correlated with a number of characters, called *controls*, and that the regression of the cluster means of the quantity on those of each control was linear. Clusters were to be selected in such a way that average of each control computed from the chosen clusters should (approximately) equal its population mean. It was hoped that, due to the assumed correlations between controls and the quantity under investigation, the above method of selection would result in a representative sample with respect to the quantity under investigation. (Chang, 1976, pp. 305–306)

Unfortunately, a practical test of the method (Gini, 1928) proved unsatisfactory and Neyman's analysis concluded that it was not a consistent nor an efficient procedure.

As Neyman pointed out, the problem of sampling is the problem of estimation. The first forays into the establishment of a theory of estimation had been made by Fisher (1921a, 1922b, 1925c) but the *manner* of sampling had received little attention from him. The method of maximum likelihood, which rested entirely on the properties of the distribution of observations, gave the most efficient estimate. Any appeal to the properties of the a priori distribution—the Bayesian approach—was rejected by Fisher. Neyman attempted to clarify the situation:

> We are interested in characteristics of a certain population, say, π, . . . it has been usually assumed that the accurate solution of such a problem requires the knowledge of probabilities a priori attached to different admissible hypotheses concerning the values of the collective characters [the parameters] of the population π. (Neyman, 1934, p. 561)

He then turns to Bowley's work, noting that when the population π is known then questions about the sort of samples that it could produce can be answered from "the safe ground of classical theory of probability" (p. 561). The second question involves the determination, when we know the sample, of the probabilities a posteriori to be ascribed to hypotheses concerning the populations. Bowley's conclusions are based,

> . . . on some quite arbitrary hypotheses concerning the probabilities *a priori*, and Professor Bowley accompanies his results with the following remark: "It is to be emphasized that the inference thus formulated is based on assumptions that are difficult to verify and which are not applicable in all cases." (Neyman, 1934, p. 562)

Neyman then suggests that Fisher's approach (that involving the notion of *fiducial* probability, although Neyman does not use the term), "removes the difficulties involved in the lack of knowledge of the *a priori* probability law" (p. 562). He further suggests that these approaches have been misunderstood, due, he thinks to Fisher's condensed form of explanation and difficult method of attacking the problem.

> The form of the solution consists in determining certain intervals which I propose to call confidence intervals . . ., in which we may assume are contained the values of the estimated characters of the population, the probability of the error in a statement of this sort being equal to or less than $1 - \epsilon$, where ϵ is any number $0 < \epsilon < 1$, chosen in advance. The number ϵ I call the confidence coefficient. (Neyman, 1934, p. 562)

Neyman's comments on Fisher's ability to explain his view produced, in the discussion of his paper, the first (mild) reaction from Fisher. Subsequent reactions to Neyman's work and that of his collaborator, Egon Pearson, became increasingly vitriolic. The report reads:

> Dr Fisher thought Dr Neyman must be mistaken in thinking the term fiducial probability [Neyman had used the term "confidence coefficient"] had led to any misunderstanding; he had not come upon any signs of it in the literature. When Dr Neyman said "it really cannot be distinguished from the ordinary concept of probability," Dr Fisher agreed with him . . . He qualified it from the first with the word *fiducial* . . . Dr Neyman qualified it with the word *confidence*. The meaning was evidently the same, and he did not wish to deny that confidence could be used adjectivally. They were all too familiar with it, as Professor Bowley had reminded them, in the phrase "confidence trick." (Discussion on Dr Neyman's paper, 1934, p. 617)

From the standpoint of the familiar statistical procedures found in our texts, this paper is important for its treatment of *confidence intervals* and its emphasis of the importance of random sampling. It extended estimation from so-called *point* estimation, the use of a sample value to infer a population value, to *interval* estimation, which assesses the probability of a range of values. Neyman demonstrates the use of the Markov[2] method for deriving the linear unbiased estimators. It also contains other important ideas, in particular, a discussion of the methods of *stratified* sampling and appropriate statistical models for it. Neyman's paper marks a new era in both the method and theory of sampling, although, at the time, it was its treatment of the problem of estimation that received the most attention. In a sense it complemented and supplemented the work of Ronald Fisher that was going on at Rothamsted, but it became evident that Fisher did not quite see it that way.

THE BATTLE FOR RANDOMIZATION

There is no doubt that the requirement that samples should be randomly drawn was thought of by the survey-makers as a protection against selection bias. And there is also no doubt that when sample size is large it affords such protection, but not, it must be stressed, a guarantee.

In agricultural research it had long been recognized that reduction of experimental error was of critical importance. At Rothamsted two methods were available: repeating the experiments over many years and multiplying the number of plots on a field. Mercer and Hall (1911) discuss the problem in considerable detail and give suggestions for arranging the plots so that they may be "scattered." This was the approach that was abandoned, though not immediately, when Fisher started his important work at the Station. Eventually, for Fisher and his coworkers the argument for randomization had a quite different motive from that of trying to obtain a representative sample, one that is crucial for an appre-

---

[2]Andrei Andreyevich Markov (or Markoff, 1856–1922) is best known for his studies of the probabilities of linked chains of events. Markov chains have been used in a variety of social and biological studies in the last 30 or 40 years. But Markov made many contributions to probability theory.

If we have a random variable X, then regardless of its distribution, for any positive number c (i.e. $c > 0$), the probability, $P_X\{X \geq c\mu\}$, that the random variable X is greater than c times its expected value $\mu_X = \mu$ does not exceed $1/c$. That is,

$$P_X\{X \geq c\mu\} \leq 1/c.$$

This is known as the *Markov Inequality*.

Markov was a student of Pafnuti L. Tchebycheff (sometimes spelled Chebychev or Chebichev, 1821–1894), who formulated the *Tchebycheff Inequality* which states that,

$$P_X\{X \leq \mu - d\sigma \text{ or } X \geq \mu + d\sigma\} \leq 1/d^2.$$

where X is a random variable with expected value μ and variance σ^2, and $d > 0$. This result was independently arrived at by the French mathematician I.J. Bienaymé (1796–1876). These inequalities are important in the development of the descriptions of the properties of probability distributions.

ciation of the use of statistics in psychology. Fisher, although a brilliant methematician, was a *practical* statistician and his approach to statistics can only be understood through his work on the *design* of experiments and the *analysis* of the resultant data. The core of Fisher's argument rests on the contention that the value of an experiment depends on the valid estimation of error, an argument that everyone would agree with. But how was the estimate to be made?

> In nearly all systematic arrangements of replicated plots care is taken to put the unlike plots as close together as possible, thus introducing a flagrant violation of the conditions upon which a valid estimate is possible.
>
> One way of making sure that a valid estimate of error will be obtained is to arrange the plots deliberately at random.
>
> The estimate of error is valid, because, if we imagine a large number of different results obtained by different random arrangements, the ratio of the real to the estimated error, calculated afresh for each of these arrangements, will be actually distributed in the theoretical distribution by which the significance of the result is tested. Whereas if a group of arrangements is chosen such that the real errors in this group are on the whole less than those appropriate to random arrangements, it has now been demonstrated that the errors, as estimated, will, in such a group, be higher than is usual in random arrangements, and that, in consequence, within such a group, the test of significance is vitiated. (Fisher, 1926b, pp. 506–507)

The contribution of Fisher that is overwhelmingly important is the development of the t and z tests and the general technique of *analysis of variance*. The essence of these procedures is that they provide estimates of error in the observations and the application of tests of statistical significance. These methods were not immediately recognized as being useful for larger-scale sample surveys and it was partly the work of Neyman (mentioned earlier) and others in the mid-1930s that, ironically, introduced them to this area.

Arguments about randomized versus systematic designs began in the middle 1920s. Mostly they revolved around the issue of what to do when there was an unwanted assignment of treatments to experimental units, that is to say when the assignment had a pattern that the researcher either knew or suspected might confound the treatments. Fisher argued very strongly against the use of systematic designs, on the basis of theory, but his argument was not wholly consistent. Some had suggested that if a random design produced a pattern then it should be discarded and another random assignment drawn. Of course the subjectivity introduced by this sort of procedure is precisely that of the deliberate balancing of the design. And how many draws might one be allowed?

> Most experimenters on carrying out a random assignment of plots will be shocked to find out how far from equally the plots distribute themselves . . . if the experimenter rejects the arrangement arrived at by chance as altogether "too bad," or in

other ways "cooks" the arrangement to suit his preconceived ideas, he will either (and most probably) increase the standard error as estimated from the yields; or, if his luck or his judgment is bad, he will increase the real errors while diminishing his estimate of them. (Fisher, 1926b, p. 509–510)

But even Fisher never quite escaped the difficulty. Savage (1962) talked with him.

"What would you do," I had asked, if, drawing a Latin Square at random for an experiment, you happened to draw a Knut Vik square?" Sir Ronald said he thought he would draw again and that, ideally, a theory explicitly excluding regular squares should be developed. (Savage, 1962, p. 88)

Students and teachers cursing their way through statistical theory and practice should take some comfort from the inconsistencies expressed by the master.

The debate reached its height in argument between "Student" and Fisher. "Student" consistently advocated systematic arrangements. In a letter to Egon Pearson (Pearson, 1939a) written shortly before his death in 1937, "Student" comments on work by Tedin (1931) which had examined the outcomes when systematic, as opposed to random, Latin squares were used in experimental designs. The "Knight's move" Latin square he prefers above all others: "It is interesting as an illustration of what actually happens when we depart from artificial randomisation: I would Knight's move every time!" (Quoted by E.S. Pearson, 1939a). p. 248[3]

Over the previous year a series of papers, letters, and letters of rebuttal had come forth from "Student" and Fisher. "Student" was adamant to the end and Fisher reiterated his claim that valid error estimates cannot be computed in arranged designs and that in such cases the test of significance is made ineffective. Picard (1980) describes and discusses the argument and also examines the contributions of Pearson and Yates, who had succeeded Fisher at Rothamsted. Others entered the debate. Jeffreys (1939) is puzzled.

Reading "Student's" paper [of 1937] and Fisher's *Design of Experiments* I find myself in almost complete agreement with both; and I should therefore have expected them to agree with each other.

---

[3]An illustration of "Two Knight's moves" would be,
    D E A B C
    B C D E A
    E A B C D
    C D E A B
    A B C D E

But it seems to me that "Student" is wrong in regarding Fisher as an advocate of extreme randomness, and possibly Fisher has not sufficiently emphasized the amount of system in his methods. (Jeffreys, 1939, p. 5)

Jeffreys makes the point that omitting to take account of relevant information makes avoidable errors,

The best procedure is to design the work so as to determine it [the error] as accurately as possible and not to leave it to chance whether it can be determined at all. . . . The hypothesis is a considered proposition . . . The argument is inductive and not deductive; it is not dealt with by considering an estimable error that has nothing to do with it. (Jeffreys, 1939, p. 5)

As ever, Jeffrey's argument is a paragon of logic and it notes that Fisher's advice to balance or eliminate the larger systematic effects as accurately as possible and randomize the rest, "sums up the situation very well" (p. 7). This is the prescription that the design of experiments follows today.

E.S. Pearson (1938b) attempted to expand on and to clarify "Student's" stand but he clearly understood the view of the opposition. Nevertheless he concluded that balanced layouts could give some slight advantage. Yates (1939), in a lengthy paper also goes over the whole of "Student's" views on the matter but his conclusion supports the essence of Fisher's views:

The conclusion is reached that in cases where Latin square designs can be used, and in many cases where randomized blocks have to be employed, the gain in accuracy with systematic arrangements is not likely to be sufficiently great to outweigh the disadvantages to which systematic designs are subject.

On the other hand, systematic arrangements may in certain cases give decidedly greater accuracy than randomized blocks, but it appears that in such cases the use of the modern devices of confounding, quasi-factorial designs, or split-plot Latin squares which are much more satisfactory statistically, are likely to give a similar gain in accuracy. (Yates, 1939, p. 464)

which brings us to the approaches of the present day.

The realization that sampling was important in psychological research, and that its techniques had been much neglected, was presented to the discipline by McNemar (1940). In an extensive discussion he points out situations that are still with us.

One wonders, for instance, how many psychometric test scores for policeman, firemen, truck drivers *et al.* have been interpreted by the clinician in terms of college sophomore norms.

In psychological research we are more frequently interested in making an inference regarding the likeness or difference of two differentially defined universes, such as two racial groups, or an experimental *vs.* a control group. The writer ventures the guess that at least 90% of the research in psychology involves such comparisons. It is not only necessary to consider the problem of sampling in the case of experimental and control groups, but also convenient from the viewpoint of both good experimentation and sound statistics to do so. (McNemar, 1940, p. 335)

This paper, which, regrettably, is not among those most widely cited in the psychological literature, should be required reading for all those embarking on research in any aspect of the social sciences. Its closing remarks contain a prediction that has been most certainly fulfilled and whose content will be dealt with shortly.

The applicability in psychology of certain of Professor R.A. Fisher's designs should be examined. Eventually, the analysis of variance will come into use in psychological research. (McNemar, 1940, p. 363)

For the moment no more needs to be said.

9

Sampling Distributions

Large sets of elementary events are commonly called *populations* or *universes* in statistics, but the set theory term, *sample space*, is perhaps more descriptive. The term *population distribution* refers to the distribution of the values of the possible observations in the sample space. Although the characteristics or *parameters* of the population (e.g., the mean, μ, or the standard deviation, σ) are of both practical and theoretical interest, these values are rarely, if ever, known precisely. Estimates of the values are obtained from corresponding sample values, the *statistics*. Clearly, for a sample of a given size drawn randomly from a sample space, a distribution of values of a particular summary statistic exists. This simple statement defines a *sampling distribution*. In statistical practice it is the properties of these distributions that guides our inferences about properties of populations of actual or potential observations. In chapter 6 the *binomial*, the *Poisson*, and the *normal* distributions were discussed. Now that sampling has been examined in some detail, three other distributions and the *statistical tests* associated with them will be reviewed.

CHI SQUARE

The development of the χ^2 (chi-square) test of "goodness-of-fit" represents one of the most important breakthroughs in the history of statistics, certainly as important as the development of the mathematical foundations of regression. The fact that both creations are attributable to the work of one man, Karl Pearson, is impressive attestation of his role in the discipline. There are a number of routes by which the test can be approached, but the path that has been followed thus far

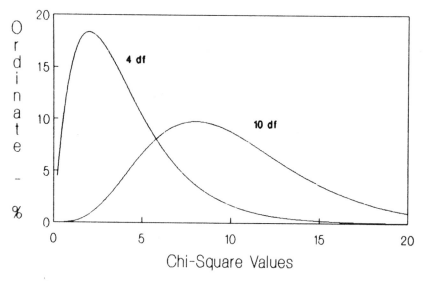

FIG. 9.1. Chi-square for 4 and 10 Degrees of Freedom.

will be continued here.[1] This path leads directly to the work of Pearson and Fisher who did not make use, and, it seems, were in general unaware, of the earlier work on goodness-of-fit by mathematicians in Europe. Before looking at the development of the test of goodness-of-fit the structure of the chi-square distribution itself is worth examining. Figure 9.1 shows 2 chi-square distributions. Given a normally distributed population of scores Y with a mean μ, and a variance σ^2, suppose that samples of size $n = 1$ are drawn from the distribution and each score converted to its corresponding standard score z.

$z = (Y - \mu)/\sigma$ and $\chi^2 = (Y - \mu)^2/\sigma^2$ defines the chi-square distribution with one degree of freedom. If samples of $n = 2$ are drawn, then χ^2 is given by $(Y_1 - \mu)^2/\sigma^2 + (Y_2 - \mu)^2/\sigma^2$. In fact if n independent measures are taken randomly from a distribution with mean μ, and variance σ^2, χ^2 is defined as the sum of the squared standardized scores:

$$\chi^2 = \frac{\sum_{i}^{n}(Y_i - \mu)^2}{\sigma^2}$$

---

[1]MacKenzie (1981) gives a brief account of Arthur Black (1851–1893), a tragic figure who, on his death, left a lengthy, and now lost, manuscript, *Algebra of Animal Evolution*, which was sent to Karl Pearson. "Pearson started to read it, but realized immediately that it discussed topics very similar to those he was working on, and decided not to read it himself but to send it to Francis Galton for his advice" (p. 99). Of great interest is that buried among Black's notebooks, which have survived, is a derivation of the chi-square approximation to the multi-nomial distribution.

This is the essence of the distribution that Pearson used in his formulation of the test of goodness-of-fit. Why was such a test so necessary? Games of chance and observational errors in astronomy and surveying were subject to the random processes that led scientists in the 18th and early 19th centuries to the examination of error distributions. The quest was for a sound mathematical basis for the exercise of estimating true values. Simpson introduced a triangular distribution and Daniel Bernoulli in 1777 suggested a semicircular one. In the absence of empirical data these distributions, established on a priori grounds, were somewhat arbitrarily regarded as having no more and no less claim to accuracy and utility. But the 19th century saw the normal law established. It had powerful credentials because of the fame of its two main developers, Gauss and Laplace. Starting from the assumption that the arithmetic mean represented the true value, Gauss showed that the error distribution was normal. Laplace, starting from the view that every individual observation arises from a very great number of independently acting random factors (the essence of the *central limit theorem*), came to the same result. Gauss's proof of the method of least squares further established the importance of the normal distribution, and when, in 1801, he used the initial data collected from observations on a new planet, *Ceres*,[3] to accurately predict where it would be observed later in the year these procedures, as well as Gauss's reputation, were firmly established in astronomy.

In astronomy as well as in biology and social science the Laplace-Gassian distribution was indeed *law*, it was indeed regarded as *normal*. This prescription led to Quetelet's use of it as a "double-edged sword" (see chap. 1) and led to many astronomers using it as a reason to reject observations that were considered to be doubtful, for example Peirce (1852). Quetelet's procedure for establishing the "fit" of the normal curve was the same as that of the early astronomers. The tabulation, and later the graphing, of observed and expected frequencies led to their being compared by nothing more than visual inspection (see, e.g., Airy, 1879).

There was some dissent. Egon Pearson (1965) notes,

As a reaction to this view among astronomers I remember how Sir Arthur Eddington in his Cambridge lectures about 1920 on the Combination of Observations

---

[2]A history of the mathematics of the χ^2 distribution would include the development of the gamma function by the French mathematician, I.J. Bienaymé (1796–1876) who, in the 1850s, found a statistic that is equivalent to the Pearson χ^2 in the context of least squares theory. Pearson was apparently not aware of his work, and nor was F.R. Helmert and E. Abbé who, in the 1860s and 70s also arrived at the χ^2 distribution for the sum of squares of independent normal variates. Long after the test had become commonly used Von Mises (1919) linked Bienaymé's work to the Pearson χ^2. Many of the details of this aspect of the test and distribution's history are given by Lancaster (1966), Sheynin (1966), and Chang (1973).

[3]*Ceres* was the first discovered "planetoid" in the asteroid belt. Gauss also determined the orbit of *Pallas*, another planetoid.

used to quote the remark that 'to say that errors must obey the normal law means taking away the right of the free-born Englishman to make any error he darn well pleases!' (1965, p. 6)

Karl Pearson's first statistical paper (1894) was on the problem of interpreting a bimodal distribution as two normal distributions, the problem that had arisen as a result of Weldon's discovery that the distribution of the relative frontal breadths of his sample of Naples crabs was a double humped curve. This paper introduced the *method of moments* as a means of fitting a theoretical curve to a set of observations. As Egon Pearson (1965) states it,

The question "does a Normal curve fit this distribution and what does this mean if it does not?" was clearly prominent in their discussions. There were three obvious alternatives;
(a) The discrepancy between theory and observation is no more than might be expected to arise in random sampling.
(b) The data are heterogeneous, composed of two or more Normal distributions.
(c) The data are homogeneous, but there is real asymmetry in the distribution of the variable measured.
The conclusion (c) may have been hard to accept, such was the prestige surrounding the Normal law. (1965, p. 9)

It appears from Yule's lecture notes[4] that Karl Pearson probably was employing a procedure which used the ratio of an absolute deviation from expectation to its standard error to examine the record of 7,000 (actually 7,006) tosses of 12 dice made by Mr Hull, a clerk at University College. This was the record (see chap. 1) that Weldon said Karl Pearson had rejected as "intrinsically incredible." Yule's notes also contain an empirical measure of goodness of fit that Egon Pearson says may be set down roughly as, $R = \Sigma|O - T|/\Sigma T$, where $|O - T|$ is the absolute value of the difference between the observed and theoretical frequency and ΣT the total theoretical frequency, though it should be mentioned that the actual notes do not contain the formula in this form. This expression, the *mean absolute error*, was in use during the latter years of the 19th century, and Bowley used it in the first edition of his textbook in 1902.

Karl Pearson's second statistical paper (1895) on asymmetrical frequency curves occupied the attention of the biologists but the question of the *biological* meaning of skewed distributions was not one that, at the time, was in the forefront of Pearson's thoughts. Interestingly enough, Pearson did not use the mean absolute error as a test of fit in any of his work. His preoccupation was with the development of a theory of correlation and it was in this context that he solved the goodness-of-fit problem. The 1895 paper and two supplements that

---

[4]These notes are reproduced in *Biometrika's* Miscellanea (Yule, 1938a).

followed in 1901 and 1916(b) introduced a comprehensive system of frequency curves that pointed a way to sampling distributions that are central to the use of statistical tests, but it was a way that Pearson himself did not fully develop.

Pearson's (1900a) seminal paper begins, *"The object of this paper is to investigate a criterion of the probability on any theory of an observed system of errors, and to apply it to the determination of goodness of fit in the case of frequency curves"* (p. 157).

Pearson takes a system of deviations x_1, x_2 . . . x_n from the means of n variables with standard deviations σ_1, σ_2, . . . σ_n and with correlations r_{12}, r_{13}, r_{23}, . . . $r_{n-1,n}$ and derives χ^2 as "the equation to a generalized 'ellipsoid,' all over the surface of which the frequency of the system of errors or deviations x_1, x_2 . . . x_n is constant" (p. 157).

It was Pearson's derivation of the multivariate normal distribution that formed the basis of the χ^2 test. Large x_i's represent large discrepancies between theory and observation and in turn would give large values of χ^2. But χ^2 can be made to become a test statistic by examining the probability of a system of errors occurring with a frequency as great or greater than the observed system. Pearson had already obtained an expression for the multivariate normal surface and he here gives the probability of n errors when the ellipsoid is squeezed to become a sphere, which is the geometric representation of zero correlation in the multivariate space, and shows how one arrives at the probability for a given value of χ^2. When we compare Pearson's mathematics with Hamilton Dickson's examination of Galton's elliptic contours, seen in the scatterplot of two correlated variables while Galton was waiting for a train, we see how far mathematical statistics had advanced in just 15 years.

Pearson considers an $(n + 1)$-fold grouping with observed frequencies, m'_1, m'_2, m'_3, . . . m'_n, m'_{n+1}, and theoretical frequencies known a priori, m_1, m_2, m_3, . . . m_n, m_{n+1}. $\Sigma m = \Sigma m' = N$, the total frequency, and $e = m' - m$ is the error. The total error Σe (i.e., $e_1 + e_2 + e_3 + . . . + e_{n+1}$) is zero. The degrees of freedom, as they are now known, follow; "Hence only n of the $n + 1$ errors are variables; the $n + 1$th is determined when the first n are known, and in using formula (ii) [Pearson's basic χ^2 formula] we treat only of n variables" (Pearson, 1900a, pp. 160–161).

Starting with the standard deviation for the random variation of error and the correlation between random errors, Pearson uses a rather complex trigonometric transformation to arrive at a result "of very great simplicity":

$$\chi^2 = \Sigma(e^2/m)$$

Chi-square (the statistic) is the weighted sum of squared deviations.

Pearson (1904, 1911) extended the use of the test to contingency tables and to the two sample case and in 1916(a) presented a somewhat simpler derivation than the one given in 1900a, a derivation that acknowledges the work of Soper (1914). The first 20 years of this century brought increasing recognition that the test was of the greatest importance. Starting with Edgeworth (who wrote to Pearson); "I have to thank you for your splendid method of testing my mathematical curves of frequency. That χ^2 of yours is one of the most beautiful of the instruments that you have added to the Calculus" (quoted by Kendall, 1968, p. 262).

And even Fisher, who by that time had become a fierce critic: "The test of goodness of fit was devised by Pearson, to whose labours principally we now owe it, that the test may readily be applied to great variety of questions of frequency distribution" (Fisher, 1922b, p. 597).

In the next chapter the argument that arose between Pearson and Yule on the assumption of continuous variation underlying the categories in contingency tables will be discussed. When Fisher's modifications and corrections to Pearson's theory were accepted, it was Yule who helped to spread the word on the interpretation of the new idea of *degrees of freedom*.

The goodness-of-fit test is readily applied when the expected frequencies based on some hypothesis are known. For example, hypothesizing that the expected distribution is normal with a particular mean and standard deviation enables the expected frequency of any value to be quickly calculated. Today χ^2 is perhaps more often applied to *contingency tables* where the expected values are computed from the observed frequencies.

This, now routine, procedure forms the basis of one of the most bitter disputes in statistics in the 1920s. In 1916 Pearson examined the question of partial contingency. The fixed n in a goodness-of-fit test imposes a constraint on the frequencies in the categories; only $k - 1$ categories are free to vary. Pearson realized that in the case of contingency tables additional linear constraints were placed on the group frequencies, but he argued that these constraints did not allow for a reduction in the number of variables in the case where the theoretical distribution was estimated from the observed frequencies. Other questions had also been raised.

Raymond Pearl (1879–1940), an American researcher who was at the Biometric Laboratory in the mid-1910s pointed out some problems in the application of χ^2 in 1912, noting that some hypothetical data he presents clearly show an excellent "fit" between observed and expected frequency but that the value of χ^2 was infinite! Pearson, of course, replied but Pearl was unmoved.

> I have earlier pointed out other objections to the χ^2 test . . . I have never thought it necessary to make any rejoinder to Pearson's characteristically bitter reply to my criticism, nor do I yet. The χ^2 test leads to this absurdity. (Pearl, 1917, p. 145)

Pearl repeats the argument that essentially notes that in cases where there are small expected frequencies in the cells of the table that the value of χ^2 can be grossly inflated.

Karl Pearson (1917), in a reproof that illustrates his disdain for those he believed had betrayed the Biometric school, responds to Pearl; "Pearl . . . provides a striking illustration of how the capable biologist needs a long continued training in the logic of mathematics before he ventures into the field of probability" (p. 429).

Pearl had in fact raised quite legitimate questions about the application of the χ^2 test, but in the context of Mendelian theory to which Pearson was steadfastly opposed. A close reading of Pearl's papers perhaps reveals that he had not followed all Pearson's mathematics, but the questions he had raised were germane. Pearson's response is the apotheosis of mathematical arrogance that, on occasion, frightens biologists and social scientists today.

> Shortly Dr Pearl's method is entirely fallacious, as any trained mathematician would have informed Dr Pearl had he sought advice before publication. It is most regrettable that such extensions of biometric theory should be lightly published, without any due sense of responsibility, not solely in biological but in psychological journals. It can only bring biometry into contempt as a science if, professing a mathematical foundation, it yet shows in its manifestations most inadequate mathematical reasoning. (Pearson, 1917, p. 432)

Social scientists beware!

In 1916 Ronald Fisher, then a schoolmaster, raised his standard and made his first foray into what was to become a war. The following correspondence is to be found in E.S. Pearson (1968):

> Dear Professor Pearson,
> There is an article by Miss Kirstine Smith in the current issue of *Biometrika* which, I think, ought not to pass without comment. I enclose a short note upon it.
>
> Miss Kirstine Smith proposes to use the minimum value of χ^2 as a criterion to determine the best form of a frequency curve; . . . It should be observed that χ^2 can only be determined when the material is grouped into arrays, and that its value depends upon the manner in which it is grouped.
>
> There is . . . something exceedingly arbitrary in a criterion which depends entirely upon the manner in which the data happens to be grouped. (pp. 454–455)

Pearson replied:

> Dear Mr Fisher,
> I am afraid that I don't agree with your criticism of Frøken K. Smith (she is a pupil of Thiele's and one of the most brilliant of the younger Danish statisticians). . . .
> your argument that χ^2 varies with the grouping is of course well known . . . What we have to determine, however, is with *given* grouping which method gives the lowest χ^2. (p. 455)

Pearson asks for a defense of Fisher's argument before considering its publication. Fisher's expanded criticism received short shrift. After thanking Fisher for a copy of his paper on Mendelian inheritance (Fisher, 1918), he hopes to find time for it,[5] but points out that he is "not a believer in cumulative Mendelian factors as being the solution of the heredity puzzle" (p. 456). He then rejects Fisher's paper.

> Also I fear that I do not agree with your criticism of Dr Kirstine Smith's paper and under present pressure of circumstances must keep the little space I have in *Biometrika* free from controversy which can only waste what power I have for publishing original work. (p. 456)

Egon Pearson thinks that we can accept his father's reasons for these rejections; the pressure of war work, the suspension of many of his projects, the fact that he was over 60 years old with much work unfinished, and his memory of the strain that had been placed on Weldon in the row with Bateson. But if he really was trying to shun controversy by refusing to publish controversial views, then he most certainly did not succeed. Egon Pearson's defense is entirely understandable but far too charitable. Pearson had censored Fisher's work before and appears to have been trying to establish his authority over the younger man and over statistics. Even his offer to Fisher of an appointment at the Galton Laboratory might be viewed in this light. Fisher Box (1978) notes that these experiences influenced Fisher in his refusal of the offer, in the summer of 1919, recognizing that, "nothing would be taught or published at the Galton laboratory without the approval of Pearson" (p. 82).

The last straw for Fisher came in 1920 when he sent a paper on the probable error of the correlation coefficient to *Biometrika*.

> Dear Mr Fisher,
> Only in passing through Town today did I find your communication of August 3rd. I am very sorry for the delay in answering . . .
>   As there has been a delay of three weeks already, and as I fear if I could give full attention to your paper, which I cannot at the present time, I should be unlikely to publish it in its present form . . . I would prefer you published elsewhere . . . I am regretfully compelled to exclude all that I think erroneous on my own judgment, because I cannot afford controversy. (Quoted by E.S. Pearson, 1968, p. 453)

Fisher never again submitted a paper to *Biometrika*, and in 1922(a) tackled the χ^2 problem.

---

[5]Here Pearson is dissembling. Fisher's paper was originally submitted to the Royal Society and, although it was not rejected outright, the Chairman of the Sectional Committee for Zoology "had been in communication with the communicator of the paper, who proposed to withdraw it." Karl Pearson was one of the two referees. Norton and Pearson (1976) describe the event and publish the referees' reports.

This short paper with all its juvenile inadequacies, yet did something to break the ice. Any reader who feels exasperated by its tentative and piecemeal character should remember that it had to find its way to publication past critics who, in the first place, could not believe that Pearson's work stood in need of correction, and who, if this had to be admitted, were sure that they themselves had corrected it. (Fisher's note preceding the paper's reprint, 1950, p. 5.86a, and in Bennett, 1971, p. 336)

Fisher notes that he is not criticizing the general adequacy of the χ^2 test but that he intends to show that,

. . . the value of n' with which the table should be entered is not now equal to the number of cells but to *one more than the number of degrees of freedom in the distribution*. Thus for a contingency table of r rows and c columns we should take $n' = (c - 1)(r - 1) + 1$ instead of $n' = cr$. This modification often makes a very great difference to the probability (P) that a given value of χ^2 should have been obtained by chance. (Fisher, 1922a, p. 88)

It should be noted in passing that Pearson entered the tables using $n' = v + 1$, where n' is the number of variables (i.e. categories) and v is what we now call degrees of freedom. The modern tables are entered using $v = (c - 1)(r - 1)$. The use of n' to denote sample size and n to denote degrees of freedom, even though in many writings n was also used for sample size, sometimes leads to frustrating reading in these early papers.

It is clear that Pearson did not recognise that in all cases linear restrictions imposed upon the frequencies of the sampled population, by our methods of reconstructing that population, have exactly the same effect upon the distribution of χ^2 as have restrictions placed upon the cell contents of the sample. (Fisher, 1922a, p. 92)

Pearson was angered and contemptuously replied in the pages of *Biometrika*. He reiterates the fundamentals of his 1900 paper and then says,

The process of substituting sample constants for sampled population constants does *not* mean that we select out of possible samples of size n, those which have precisely the same values of the constants as the individual sample under discussion. . . . In using the constants of the given sample to replace the constants of the sampled population, we in no wise restrict the original hypothesis of free random samples tied down only by their definite size. We certainly do not by using sample constants reduce in any way the random sampling degrees of freedom.

The above re-description of what seem to me very elementary considerations would be unnecessary had not a recent writer in the *Journal of the Royal Statistical Society* appeared to have wholly ignored them . . . the writer has done no service to the science of statistics by giving it broad-cast circulation in the pages of the *Journal of the Royal Statistical Society*. (K. Pearson, 1922, p. 187)

And on and on, never referring to Fisher by name but only as "my critic" or "the writer in the *Journal of the Royal Statistical Society*," until the final assault when he accuses Fisher of a disregard for the nature of the probable error.

> I trust my critic will pardon me for comparing him with Don Quixote tilting at the windmill; he must either destroy himself, or the whole theory of probable errors, for they are invariably based on using sample values for those of the sampled population unknown to us. For example here is an argument for Don Quixote of the simplest nature . . . (K. Pearson, 1922, p. 191)

The editors of the *Journal of the Royal Statistical Society* turned tail and ran, refusing to publish Fisher's rejoinder. Fisher vigorously protested, but to no avail and he resigned from the Society. There were other questions about Pearson's paper that he dealt with in Bowley's journal *Economica* in 1923 and in the *Journal of the Royal Statistical Society* (Fisher, 1924a), but the end came in 1926 when, using data tables that had been published in *Biometrika*, Fisher "calculated the actual average value of χ^2 which he had proved earlier should theoretically be unity and which Pearson still maintained should be 3. In every case the average was close to unity, in no case near to 3. . . . There was no reply" (Fisher Box, 1978, p. 88, commenting on Fisher 1926a).

THE *t* DISTRIBUTION

W.S. Gosset was a remarkable man not the least because he managed to maintain reasonably cordial relations with both Pearson and Fisher, and at the same time. Nor did he avoid disagreeing with them on various statistical issues. He was born in 1876 at Canterbury in England, and from 1895 to 1899 was at New College, Oxford where he took a degree in chemistry and mathematics. In 1899 Gosset became an employee of Arthur Guinness, Son and Company Ltd., the famous manufacturers of stout. He was one of the first of the scientists, trained either at Oxford or Cambridge, that the firm had begun hiring (E.S. Pearson, 1939a). His correspondence with Pearson, Fisher, and others shows him to have been a witty and generous man with a tendency to downplay his role in the development of statistics. Compared with the giants of his day he published very little, but his contribution is of critical importance. As Fisher puts it in his *Statistical Methods for Research Workers*:

> The study of the exact distributions of statistics commences in 1908 with "Student's" paper *The Probable Error of the Mean*. Once the true nature of the problem was indicated, a large number of sampling problems were within reach of mathematical solution. (Fisher, 1970, 14th Ed., p. 23)

The brewery had a policy on publishing by its employees that obliged Gosset to publish his work under the nom de plume "Student." In essence the problem that "Student" tackled was the development of a statistical test that could be applied to small samples. The nature of the process of brewing, with its variability in temperature and ingredients, means that it is not possible to take large samples over a long run. In a letter to Fisher in 1915, in which he thanks Fisher for the *Biometrika* paper that begins the mathematical solution to the small sample problem he says,

> The agricultural (and indeed almost any) Experiments naturally required a solution of the mean/S.D. problem, and the Experimental Brewery which concerns such things as the connection between analysis of malt or hops, and the behaviour of the beer, and which takes a day to each unit of the experiment, thus limiting the numbers, demanded an answer to such questions as, "If with a small number of cases I get a value *r*, what is the probability that there is really a positive correlation of greater value than (say) .25?" (Quoted by E.S. Pearson, 1968, p. 447)

Pearson (1939a) notes that, in his first few years at Guinness, Gosset was making use of Airy's *Theory of Errors* (1879), Lupton's *Notes on Observations* (1898), and Merriman's *The Method of Least Squares* (1884). In 1904 he presented a report to his firm that stated clearly the utility of the application of statistics to the work of the brewery and pointed up the particular difficulties that might be encountered. The *Report* concludes,

> We have been met with the difficulty that none of our books mentions the odds, which are conveniently accepted as being sufficient to establish any conclusion, and it might be of assistance to us to consult some mathematical physicist on the matter. (Quoted by Pearson, 1939a, p. 215)

A meeting was in fact arranged with Pearson and this took place in the summer of 1905. Not all of Gosset's problems were solved but a supplement to his *Report* and a second report in late August 1905 produced many changes in the statistics used in the brewery. The *standard deviation* replaced the mean error and Pearson's *correlation coefficient* became an almost routine procedure in examining relationships among the many factors involved with brewing. But one feature of the work concerned Gosset: "Correlation coefficients are usually calculated from large numbers of cases, in fact I have found only one paper in *Biometrika* of which the cases are as few in number as those at which I have been working lately" (quoted by Pearson, 1939a, p. 217).

He expressed doubt about the reliability of the probable error formula for the correlation coefficient when it was applied to small samples.

Gosset went to London in September 1906 to spend a year at the Biometric Laboratory. His first paper, published in 1907, derives Poisson's limit of the binomial distribution and applies it to the error in sampling when yeast cells are counted in a haemacytometer. But his most important work during that year was the preparation of his two papers on the probable error of the mean and of the correlation coefficient, both of which were published in 1908.

> The usual method of determining that the mean of the population lies within a given distance of the mean of the sample, is to assume a normal distribution about the mean of the sample with a standard deviation equal to $s/\sqrt{n}$, where s is the standard deviation of the sample, and to use the tables of the probability integral.
>
> But, as we decrease the number of experiments, the value of the standard deviation found from the sample of experiments becomes itself subject to increasing error, until judgments reached in this way become altogether misleading. ("Student," 1908a, pp. 1–2)

"Student" sets out what the paper intends to do.

> I. The equation is determined of the curve which represents the frequency distribution of standard deviations of samples drawn from a normal population.
> II. There is shown to be no kind of correlation between the mean and the standard deviation of such a sample.
> III. The equation is determined of the curve representing the frequency distribution of a quantity z, which is obtained by dividing the distance between the mean of the sample and the mean of the population by the standard deviation of the sample.
> IV. The curve found in I. is discussed.
> V. The curve found in III. is discussed.
> VI. The two curves are compared with some actual distributions.
> VII. Tables of the curves found in III. are given for samples of different size.
> VIII and IX. The tables are explained and some instances are given of their use.
> X. Conclusions. ("Student," 1908a, p. 2)

"Student" did not provide a proof for the distribution of z. Indeed he first examined this distribution, and that of s, by actually drawing samples (of size 4) from measurements, made on 3,000 criminals, taken from data used in a paper by Macdonell (1901). The frequency distributions for s and z were thus directly obtained, and the mathematical work came later. There has been comment over the years on the fact that "Student's" mathematical approach was incomplete, but this should not detract from his achievements. Welch (1958) maintains that:

> The final verdict of mathematical statisticians will, I believe, be that they have lasting value. They have the rare quality of showing us how an exceptional man was able to make mathematical progress without paying too much regard to the rules. He fortified what he knew with some tentative guessing, but this was backed by subsequent careful testing of his results. (pp. 785–786)

In fact "Student" had given to future generations of scientists, in particular social and biological scientists, a new and powerful distribution. The *z* test, which was to become the *t* test,[6] led the way for all kinds of significance tests, and indeed influenced Fisher as he developed that most useful of tools, the *analysis of variance*. It is also the case that the 1908(a) paper on the probable error of the mean, clearly distinguished between what we now call sample *statistics* and population *parameters*, a distinction that is absolutely critical in modern-day statistical reasoning.

The overwhelming influence of the biometricians of Gower Street can perhaps partly account for the fact that "Student's" work was ignored. In 1939 Fisher said that "Student's" work was received with "weighty apathy," and, as late as 1922, Gosset, writing to Fisher, and sending a copy of his tables, said, "you are the only man that's ever likely to use them!" (quoted by Fisher Box, 1981, p. 63). Pearson was, to say the least, suspicious of work using small samples. It was the assumption of normality of the sampling distribution that led to problems, but the biometricians never used small samples, and "only naughty brewers take *n* so small that the difference is not of the order of the probable error!" (Pearson writing to Gosset, September 1912, quoted by Pearson, 1939a, p. 218).

Some of "Student's" ideas had been anticipated by Edgeworth as early as 1883 and, as Welch (1958) notes, one might speculate as to what Gosset's reaction would have been had he been aware of this work.

Gosset's paper on the probable error of the correlation coefficient ("Student," 1908b) dealt with the distribution of the *r*'s obtained when sampling from a population in which the two variables were uncorrelated, that is, $R = 0$.[7] This endeavor was again based on empirical sampling distributions constructed from the Macdonell data and a mathematical curve fitted afterwards. With characteristic flair he says that he attempted to fit a Pearson curve to the "no correlation" distribution and came up with a Type II curve. "Working from $y = y_0(1 - x^2)^0$ for samples of 4 I guessed the formula $y = y_0(1 - x^2)^{(n-4)/2}$ and proceeded to calculate the moments" ("Student," 1908b, p. 306).

He concludes his paper by hoping that his work "may serve as illustrations for the successful solver of the problem" (p. 310). And indeed they did, for Fisher's paper of 1915 showed that "Student" had guessed correctly. Fisher had been in correspondence with Gosset in 1912, sending him a proof that appealed to n-dimensional space of the frequency distribution of *z*. Gosset wanted Pearson to publish it.

---

[6]Eisenhart (1970) concludes that the shift from *z* to *t* was due to Fisher and that Gosset chose *t* for the new statistic. In their correspondence Gosset used *t* for his own calculations and *x* for those of Fisher.

[7]*R* was Gosset's symbol for the population correlation coefficient. ρ appears to have been first used for this value by Soper (1913). The important point is that a different symbol was used for sample statistic and population parameter.

Dear Pearson,
I am enclosing a letter which gives a proof of my formulae for the frequency
distribution of $z(=x/s)$, . . . Would you mind looking at it for me; I don't feel at
home in more than three dimensions even if I could understand it otherwise.

It seemed to me that if it's all right perhaps you might like to put the proof in a note.
It's so nice and mathematical that it might appeal to some people. (Quoted by E.S.
Pearson, 1968, p. 446)

In fact the proof was not published then, but again approaching the mathematics through a geometrical representation, Fisher derived the sampling distribution of the correlation coefficient and this, together with the derivation of the z
distribution, was published in the 1915 paper. The sampling distribution of r
was, of course, of interest to Pearson and his colleagues, after all, r was Pearson's statistic. Moreover, the distribution follows a remarkable system of curves,
with a variety of shapes that depart greatly from the *normal*, depending on n and
the value of the true unknown correlation coefficient R, or, as it is now generally
known, ρ. Pearson was anxious to translate theory into numbers and the computation of the distribution of r was commenced and published as the "co-
operative study" of Soper, Young, Cave, Lee, and K. Pearson in 1917. Although
Pearson had said that he would send Fisher the proofs of the paper (the letter is
quoted in E.S.Pearson, 1965) there is, apparently, no record that he in fact
received them. E.S. Pearson (1965) suggests that Fisher did not know "until late
in the day" of the criticism of his particular approach in a section of the study,
"On the Determination of the 'Most Likely' Value of the Correlation in the
Sampled Population." Pearson argues that his father's criticism, for presumably
the elder Pearson had taken a major role in the writing of the "co-operative
study," was a misunderstanding based on Fisher's failure to adequately define
what he meant by "likelihood" in 1912 and the failure to make clear that it was
not based on the Bayesian principle of inverse probability. Fisher Box (1978)
says, "their criticism was as unexpected as it was unjust, and it gave an impression of something less than scrupulous regard for a new and therefore vulnerable
reputation" (Fisher Box, 1978, p. 79).

Fisher's response, published in *Metron* in 1921(a), was the paper, mentioned
earlier, that Pearson summarily rejected because he could not afford controversy.
In this paper Fisher makes use of the $r = \tanh z$ transformation, a transformation
that had been introduced, a little tentatively, in the 1915 paper. Its immense
utility in transforming the complex system of distributions of r to a simple
function of z, which is almost normally distributed, made the laborious work of
the co-operative study redundant. In a paper published in 1919 Fisher examines
the data on resemblance in twins that had been studied by Edward L. Thorndike
in 1905. This is the earliest example of the application of Fisherian statistics to
psychological data, for the traits examined were both mental and physical. Fisher
looked at the question of whether there was any differences between the resemblances of twins in different traits and here uses the z transformation.

When the resemblances have been expressed in terms of the new variable, a correlation table may be constructed by picking out every pair of resemblances between the same twins in different traits. The values are now centered symmetrically about a mean at 1.28, and the correlation is found to be -.016 ± .048, negative but quite insignificant. The result entirely corroborates THORNDIKE'S conclusions as to the specialization of resemblance. (Fisher, 1919, p. 493)

These manipulations and the development of the same general approach to the distribution of the *intraclass* correlation coefficient in the 1921 paper are important for the fundamentals of *analysis of variance*.

From the point of view of the present-day student of statistics Fisher's (1925b) paper on the applications of the *t* distribution is undoubtedly the most comprehensible. Here we see, in familiar notation and most clearly stated, the utility of the *t* distribution, a proof of its "exactitude . . . for normal samples" (p. 92), and the formulae for testing the significance of a difference between means and the significance of regression coefficients.

Finally the probability integral with which we are concerned is of value in calculating the probability integral of a wider class of distributions which is related to "Student's" distribution in the same manner as that of χ^2 is related to the normal distribution. This wider class of distributions appears (i) in the study of intraclass correlations (ii) in the comparison of estimates of the variance, or of the standard deviation from normal samples (iii) in testing the goodness of fit of regression lines (iv) in testing the significance of a multiple correlation, or (v) of a correlation ratio. (Fisher, 1925b, pp. 102–103)

These monumental achievements were realized in less than 20 years after Gosset's mixture of mathematical conjecture, intuition, and the practical necessities of his work, led the way to the *t* distribution.

From 1912 Gosset and Fisher had been in correspondence (although there were some lengthy gaps), but they did not actually meet until September 1922 when Gosset visited Fisher at Harpenden. Fisher Box (1981) describes their relationship and reproduces excerpts from their letters. At the end of World War I, in 1918, Gosset did not even know how Fisher was employed, and when he learned that Fisher had been a schoolmaster for the duration of the war and was looking for a job wrote; "I hear that Russell [the head of the Rothamsted Experimental station] intends to get a statistician soon, when he gets the money I think, and it might be worth while to keep your ears open to news from Harpenden" (quoted by Fisher Box, 1981, p. 62).

In 1922 work began on the computation of a new set of *t* tables using values of $t = z\sqrt{(n - 1)}$ rather than *z*, and the tables being entered with the appropriate degrees of freedom rather than *n*. Fisher and Gosset both worked on the new tables and after delays, and fits and starts, and the checking of errors the tables were published by "Student" in *Metron* in 1925. Figure 9.2 compares two *t*

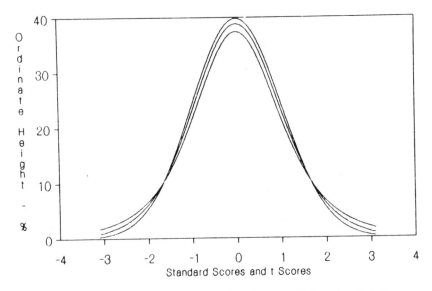

FIG. 9.2.   The Normal Distribution and the t Distributions for df = 10 and df = 4.

distributions to the normal distribution. Fisher's "Applications" paper, mentioned earlier, appeared in the same volume but it had, in fact, been written quite early in 1924. At that time Fisher was completing his 1925 book and needed tables. Gosset wanted to offer the tables to Pearson and expressed doubts about the copyright, because the first tables had been published in *Biometrika*. Fisher went ahead and computed all the tables himself, a task he completed later in the year (Fisher Box, 1981).

Fisher sent the "Applications" paper to Gosset in July 1924. He says that the note is,

> . . . larger than I had intended, and to make it at all complete should be larger still, but I shall not have time to make it so, as I am sailing for Canada on the 25th, and will not be back till September. (Quoted by Fisher Box, 1981, p. 66)

The visit to Canada was made to present a paper (Fisher, 1924b) at the International Congress of Mathematics, meeting that year in Toronto. This paper discusses the interrelationships of χ^2, z, and t. Fisher was only 35 years old and yet the foundations of his enormous influence on statistics were now securely laid.

THE *F* DISTRIBUTION

The Toronto paper did not, in fact, appear until almost 4 years after the meeting, by which time *Statistical Methods for Research Workers* (1925a) had been published. The first use of an analysis of variance technique was reported earlier (Fisher & Mackenzie, 1923) but this paper was not encountered by many outside the area of agricultural research. It is possible that if the mathematics of the Toronto paper had been included in Fisher's book then much of the difficulty that its first readers had with it would have been reduced or eliminated, a point that Fisher acknowledged.

After a general introduction on error curves and goodness-of-fit, Fisher examines the χ^2 statistic and briefly discusses his (correct) approach to degrees of freedom. He then points out that if a number of quantities $x_1 \ldots x_n$ are distributed independently in the normal distribution with unit standard deviation, then $\chi^2 = \Sigma x^2$ is distributed as "the Pearsonian measure of goodness of fit." In fact Fisher uses $S(x^2)$ to denote the latter expression, but here, and in what follows on the commentary on this paper, the more familiar modern notation will be employed. Fisher refers to "Student's" work on the error curve of the standard deviation of a small sample drawn from a normal distribution and shows its relation to χ^2. For,

$$\chi^2 = \frac{\Sigma(X - \bar{X})^2}{\sigma^2} = \frac{ns^2}{\sigma^2}$$

where n is the number of degrees of freedom (one less than the number in the sample) and s^2 is the best estimate from the sample of the true *variance* σ^2.

For the general z distribution Fisher first points out that s_1^2 and s_2^2 are misleading estimates of σ_1^2 and σ_2^2 when sample sizes, drawn from normal distributions, are small.

The only exact treatment is to eliminate the unknown quantities σ_1 and σ_2 from the distribution by replacing the distribution of s by that of log s, and so deriving the distribution of log s_1/s_2. Whereas the sampling errors in s_1 are proportional to σ_1, the sampling errors of log s_1 depend only upon the size of the sample from which s_1 was calculated. (Fisher, 1924b, p. 808)

Now, $n_1 s_1^2 = \sigma_1^2 \chi_1^2 = \sigma_1^2 \Sigma x_1^2$ and $n_2 s_2^2 = \sigma_2^2 \chi_2^2 = \sigma_2^2 \Sigma x_2^2$.

And,
$$e^{2z} = \frac{s_1^2}{s_2^2} = \frac{\sigma_1^2 \, n_2 \Sigma x_1^2}{\sigma_2^2 \, n_1 \Sigma x_2^2}$$

. . . then z will be distributed about log σ_1/σ_2 as mode, in a distribution which depends wholly upon the integers n_1 and n_2. Knowing this distribution we can tell at once if an observed value of z is or is not consistent with any hypothetical value of the ratio σ_1/σ_2. (Fisher, 1924b, p. 808)

The cases for infinite and unit degrees of freedom are then considered. In the latter case the "Student" distributions are generated.

In discussing the accuracy to be ascribed to the mean of a small sample, "Student" took the revolutionary step of allowing for the random sampling variation of his estimate of the standard error. If the standard error were known with accuracy the deviation of an observed value from expecation (say zero), divided by the standard error would be distributed normally with unit standard deviation; but if for the accurate standard deviation we substitute an estimate based on n degrees of freedom we have

$$t = \frac{x\sqrt{n}}{\sqrt{(\Sigma x^2)}}$$

$$t^2 = \frac{n\,x^2}{\Sigma x^2} = e^{2z} \text{ if } \begin{vmatrix} n_1 = 1 \\ n_2 = n \end{vmatrix}$$

consequently the distribution of t is given by putting n_1 [degrees of freedom] $= 1$ and substituting $z = \frac{1}{2}\log t^2$. (Fisher, 1924b, pp. 808–809)

For the case of an infinite number of degrees of freedom the t distribution becomes the normal distribution.

In the final sections of the paper the $r = \tanh z$ transformation is applied to the *intraclass* correlation, an analysis of variance summary table is shown, and $z = \log_e s_1/s_2$ is the value that may be used to test the significance of the *intraclass* correlation. These basic methods are also shown to lead to tests of significance for multiple correlation and η (eta), the correlation ratio.

The transition from z to F was not Fisher's work. In 1934, George W. Snedecor, in the first of a number of texts designed to make the technique of analysis of variance intelligible to a wider audience, defined F as the ratio of the *larger mean square* to the *smaller mean square* taken from the summary table, using the formula $z = \frac{1}{2}\log_e F$. Figure 9.3 shows two F distributions. Snedecor was Professor of Mathematics and Director of the Statistical Laboratory at Iowa State College in the United States. This institution was largely responsible for promoting the value of the modern statistical techniques in North America.

Fisher himself avoided the use of the symbol F because it was not used by P.C. Mahalonobis, an Indian statistician who had visited Fisher at Rothamsted in 1926, and who had tabulated the values of the variance ratio in 1932, and thus established priority. Snedecor did not know of the work of Mahalonobis, a clear-thinking and enthusiastic worker who became the first Director of the Indian Statistical Institute in 1932. Today it is still occasionally the case that the variance ratio is referred to as "Snedecor's F" in honor of both Snedecor and Fisher.

THE CENTRAL LIMIT THEOREM

The transformation of numerical data to statistics and the assessment of the probability of the outcome being a chance occurrence, or the assessment of a probable range of values within which the outcome will fall is a reasonable general description of the statistical inferential strategy. The mathematical foun-

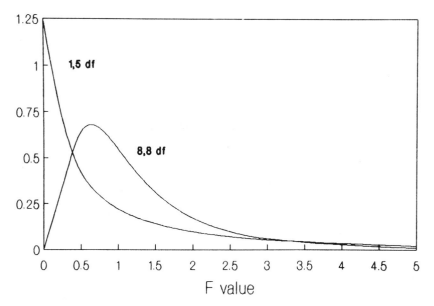

FIG. 9.3. The F Distributions for 1,5 and 8,8 Degrees of Freedom.

dations of these procedures rest on a remarkable theorem, or rather a set of theorems, that are grouped together as the *Central Limit Theorem*. Much of the work that led to this theorem has already been mentioned but it is appropriate to summarize it here.

In the most general terms the problem is to discover the probability distribution of the cumulative effect of many independently acting, and very small, random effects. The central limit theorem brings together the mathematical propositions that show that the required distribution is the *normal* distribution. In other words a summary of a subset of random observations $X_1, X_2, \ldots, X_n$, say their sum, $\Sigma X = X_1 + X_2 + \ldots + X_n$ or their mean, $(\Sigma X)/n$, has a sampling distribution that approaches the shape of the normal distribution. Figure 9.4 is an illustration of a sampling distribution of means. This chapter has described the distributions of other statistical summaries, but it will have been noted that, in one way or another, those distributions have links with the normal distribution.

The history of the development of the theorem has been brought together in a useful and eminently readable little book by Adams (1974). The story begins with the definition of probability as long-run relative frequency, the ratio of the number of ways an event can occur to the total number of possible events, given that the events are independent and equally likely. The most important contribution of James Bernoulli's *Ars Conjectandi* is the first limit theorem of probability theory. The logic of Bernouilli's approach has been the subject of some debate and we know that he himself wrestled with it. Hacking (1971) states:

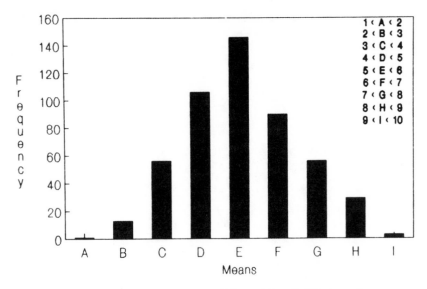

FIG. 9.4.   A Sampling Distribution of Means (N = 4). 500 draws from
the numbers 1 through 10.

No one writes dispassionately about Bernoulli. He has been fathered with the the
first subjective concept of probability, and with a completely objective concept of
probability as relative frequency determined by trials on a chance set-up. He has
been thought to favour an inductive theory of probability akin to Carnap's. Yet he
is said to anticipate Neyman's confidence interval technique of statistical inference,
which is quite opposed to inductive probabilities. In fact Bernoulli was, like so
many of us, attracted to many of these seemingly incompatible ideas, and he was
unsure where to rest his case. He left his book unpublished. (pp. 209–210)

But Bernoulli's mathematics are not in question. When the probability p of an
event E is unknown and a sequence of n trials is observed and the proportion of
occurrences of E is E_n then Bernoulli maintained that an "instinct of nature"
causes us to use E_n as an estimate of p. Bernoulli's *Law of Large Numbers* shows
that for any small assigned amount ϵ, $|p - E_n| < \epsilon$ increases to 1 as n increases
indefinitely.

It is concluded that in 25,550 trials it is more than one thousand times more likely
that the r/t [the ratio of what Bernoulli calls "fertile" events to the total, that is, the
event of interest here called E] will fall between 31/50 and 29/50 than that r/t will
fall outside these limits. (Bernoulli, 1713/1966, p. 65)

The above results hold for known p. If p is 3/5, then we can be morally certain that
. . . the deviation . . . will be less than 1/50. But Bernoulli's problem is the

inverse of this. When p is unknown, can his analysis tell when we can be morally certain that some estimate of p is right? That is the problem of statistical inference. (Hacking, 1971, p. 222)

The determination of p was of course the problem tackled by De Moivre. He used the integral e^{-x^2} to approximate it, but as Adams (1974) and others have noted there is no direct evidence that implies that De Moivre thought of what is now called the *normal distribution* as a *probability distribution* as such. Simpson introduced the notion of a probability distribution of observations and others, notably Joseph Lagrange (1736–1813) and Daniel Bernoulli (1700–1782, and James's nephew) elaborated laws of *error*. The late 18th century saw the culmination of this work in the development of the normal *law of frequency of error* and its application to astronomical observations by Gauss. It was Laplace's memoir of 1810 that introduced the central limit theorem, but the nub of his discovery was described in nonmathematical language in his famous *Essai* published as the introduction to the third edition of *Théorie Analytique des Probabilités* in 1820.

The general problem consists in determining the probabilities that the values of one or several linear functions of the errors of a very great number of observations are contained within any limits. The law of the possibility of the errors of observations introduces into the expressions of these probabilities a constant, whose value seems to require the knowledge of this law, which is almost always unknown. Happily this constant can be determined from the observations.

There often exists in the observations many sources of errors: . . . The analysis which I have used leads easily, whatever the number of the sources of error may be, to the system of factors which gives the most advantageous results, or those in which the same error is less probable than in any other system.

I ought to make here an important remark. The small uncertainty that the observations, when they are not numerous, leave in regard to the values of the constants . . . renders a little uncertain the probabilities determined by analysis. But it almost always suffices to know if the probability, that the errors of the results obtained are comprised within narrow limits, approaches closely to unity; and when it is not, it suffices to know up to what point the observations should be multiplied, in order to obtain a probability such that no reasonable doubt remains . . . The analytic formulae of probabilities satisfy perfectly this requirement; . . . They are likewise indispensable in solving a great number of problems in the natural and moral sciences. (Laplace, 1820, pp. 192–195 in the translation by Truscott & Emory, 1951)

These are elegant and clear remarks by a genius who succeeded in making the labors of many years intelligible to a wide readership.

Adams (1974) gives a brief account of the final formal development of the abstract *central limit theorem*. The Russian mathematician Alexander Lyapunoff (1857–1918), a pupil of Tchebycheff, provided a rigorous mathematical proof of the theorem. His attention was drawn to the problem when he was preparing lectures for a course in probability theory and his approach was a triumph. His methods and insights led, in the 1920s, to many valuable contributions and even more powerful theorems in probability mathematics.

10

Comparisons, Correlations,
and Predictions

COMPARING MEASUREMENTS

Since the time of De Moivre the variables that have been examined by workers in the field of probability have expressed measurements as multiples of a variety of basic units that reflect the dispersion of the range of possible scores. Today the chosen units are units of *standard deviation* and the scores obtained are called *standard scores* or *z* scores. Karl Pearson used the term *standard deviation* and gave it the symbol σ (the small Greek letter sigma) in 1894, but the unit was known (though not in its present-day form) to De Moivre. It corresponds to that point on the abscissa of a normal distribution such that an ordinate erected from it would cut the curve at its *point of inflection*, or, in simple terms, the point where the curvature of the function changes from concave to convex. Sir George Airy (1801–1892) named $\sigma\sqrt{2}$ the *modulus*, (although this term had been used, in passing, for $\sqrt{n}$ by De Moivre as early as 1733) and described a variety of other possible measures including the *probable error* in 1875.[1] This latter was the unit chosen by Galton, (whose work is discussed later), although he objected strongly to the name,

---

[1] The probable error is defined as one half of the quantity which encompasses the middle 50% of a normal distribution of measurements. It is equivalent to what is sometimes called the semi-interquartile range (that portion of the distribution between the first quartile or the twenty-fifth percentile, and the third quartile or the seventy-fifth percentile, divided by two). The probable error is 0.67449 times the standard deviation. Nowadays, everyone follows Pearson who wrote, "I have always found it more convenient to work with the standard deviation than with the probable error or the modulus, in terms of which the error function is usually tabulated" (1894, p. 88).

It is astonishing that mathematicians, who are the most precise and perspicacious of men, have not long since revolted against this cumbrous, slip-shod, and misleading phrase. . . . Moreover the term Probable Error is absurd when applied to the subjects now in hand, such as Stature, Eye-colour, Artistic Faculty, or Disease. I shall therefore usually speak of Prob. Deviation. (Galton, 1889, p. 58)

This objection reflects Galton's determination, and that of his followers, to avoid the use of the concept of error in describing the variation of human characteristics. It also foreshadows the well-nigh complete replacement of *probable error* with *standard deviation*, and *law of frequency of error* with *normal distribution*, developments that reflect philosophical dispositions rather than mathematical advance. Figure 10.1 shows the relationship between standard scores and probable error.

Perhaps a word or two of elaboration and example will illustrate the utility of measurements made in units of variability. It may seem trite to make the statement that individual measurements and quantitative descriptions are made for the purpose of making comparisons. Someone who pays $1,000 for a suit has bought an expensive suit, as well as having paid a great deal more than the individual who has picked up a cheap outfit for only $50. The labels "expensive" and

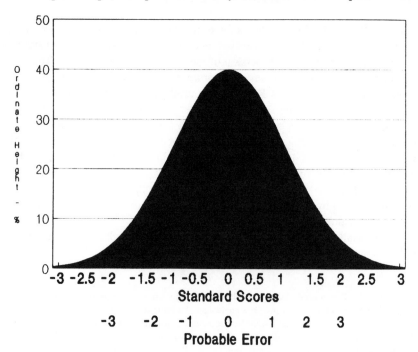

FIG. 10.1.   The Normal Distribution – Standard Scores and the Probable Error.

"cheap" are applied because the suit-buying population carries around with it some notion of the average price of suits and some notion of the range of prices of suits. This obvious fact would be made even more obvious by the reaction to an announcement that someone had just purchased a new car for $1,000. What is a lot of money for a suit suddenly becomes almost trifling for a brand new car. Again this judgment depends on a knowledge, which may not be at all precise, of the average price, and the price range, of automobiles. One can own an expensive suit and a cheap car and have paid the same absolute amount for both, though it must be admitted that such a juxtaposition of purchases is unlikely! The point is that these examples illustrate the fundamental objective of *standard scores*, the comparison of measurements.

If the mean price of cars is $9,000 and the standard deviation is $2,500 then our $1,000 car has an equivalent z score of ($1,000 − $9,000)/$2,500 or −3.20.

If suit prices have a mean of $350 and a standard deviation of $150, then the $1,000.00 suit has an equivalent z score of ($1,000 − $350)/$150 or +4.33.

We have a very cheap car and a very, very expensive suit. It might be added that, at the time of writing, these figures were entirely hypothetical.

These simple manipulations are well-known to users of statistics and, of course, when they are applied in conjunction with the probability distributions of the measurements, they enable us to obtain the probability of occurrence of particular scores or particular ranges of scores. They are intuitively sensible. A more challenging problem is that of the comparison of *sets* of pairs of scores and of determining a quantitative description of the relationship between them. It is a problem that was solved during the second half of the 19th century.

GALTON'S DISCOVERY OF "REGRESSION"

Sir Francis Galton (his work was recognized by the award of a knighthood in 1909) has been described as a Victorian genius. If we follow Edison's oft-quoted definition of this condition[2] then there can be no quarrel with the designation, but Galton was a man of great flair as well as great energy and his ideas and innovations were many and varied. In a long life he produced over 300 publications, including 17 books. But, in one of those odd happenings in the history of human invention, it was Galton's discovery and subsequent misinterpretation of a statistical artifact that marks the beginning of the technique of correlation as we now know it.

1860 was the year of the famous debate on Darwin's work between Thomas Huxley (1825–1895) and Bishop Samuel Wilberforce (1805–1873). This encounter, which held the attention of the nation, took place at the meeting of the

---

[2]In 1932, Thomas Alva Edison said that, "Genius is one percent inspiration and ninety-nine per cent perspiration."

British Association (for the Advancement of Science) held that year at Oxford. Galton attended the meeting, and although we do not know what role he had at it, we do know that he later became an ardent supporter of his cousin's theories. *The Origin of Species*, he said, "made a marked epoch on my development, as it did in that of human thought generally" (Galton, 1908, p. 287).

Cowan (1977) notes that, although Galton had made similar assertions before, the impact of *The Origin* must have been retrospective, describing his initial reaction to the book as, "pedestrian in the extreme." She also asserts that, "Galton never really understood the argument for evolution by natural selection, nor was he interested in the problem of the creation of new species" (Cowan, 1977, p. 165).

In fact it is apparent that Galton was quite selective in using his cousin's work to support his own view of the mechanisms of heredity.

The Oxford debate was not just a debate about evolution. MacKenzie (1981) describes Darwin's book as the "basic work of Victorian scientific naturalism" (p. 54), the notion of the world, and the human species and its works, as part of rational scientific nature, needing no recourse to the supernatural to explain the mysteries of existence. *Naturalism* has its origins in the rise of science in the 17th and 18th centuries and its opponents expressed their concern, because of its attack, implicit and overt, on traditional authority. As one 19th-century writer notes, for example:

> Wider speculations as to morality inevitably occur as soon as the vision of God becomes faint; when the Almighty retires behind second causes, instead of being felt as an immediate presence, and his existence becomes the subject of logical proof, (Stephen, 1876, Vol II, p. 2).

The return to nature espoused by writers such as Jean Jacques Rousseau (1712–1778) and his followers would have rid the world of kings and priests and aristocrats whose authority rested on tradition and instinct rather than reason, and thus, they insisted, have brought about a simple "natural" state of society. MacKenzie (1981), citing Turner (1978) adds a very practical note to this philosophy. The battle was not just about intellectual abstractions but about *who* should have authority and control and *who* should enjoy the material advantages that flow from the possession of that authority. Scientific naturalism was the weapon of the middle class in its struggle for power and authority based on intellect and merit and professional elitism, and not on patronage or nobility or religious affiliation.

These ideas, and the new biology, certainly turned Galton away from religion, as well as providing him with an abiding interest in heredity. Forrest (1974) suggests that his fascination for, and work on, heredity coincided with the realization that his own marriage would be infertile. This also may have been a factor in the mental breakdown that he suffered in 1866. "Another possible precipitating factor was the loss of his religious faith which left him with no compensatory philosophy until his programme for the eugenic improvement of mankind became a future article of faith" (Forrest, 1974, p. 85). During the years 1866 to 1869 Galton was in generally poor health but he collected the material for, and wrote one of his most famous books, *Hereditary Genius*, which was published in 1869. In this book and in *English Men of Science*, published in 1874, Galton expounds and expands upon his view that ability, talent, intellectual power, and accompanying eminence are innately rather than environmentally determined. The corollary of this view was, of course, that agencies of social control should be established that would encourage the "best stock" to have children, and to discourage those whom Galton described as having the smallest quantities of "civic worth" from breeding. It has been mentioned that Galton was a collector of measurements to a degree that was almost compulsive and it is certain that he was not happy with the fact that he had had to use qualitative rather than quantitative data in support of his arguments in the two books just cited.

MacKenzie (1981) maintains that,

> . . . the needs of eugenics in large part determined the content of Galton's statistical theory. . . . If the immediate problems of eugenics research were to be solved, a new theory of statistics, different from that of the previously dominant error theorists had to be constructed. (MacKenzie, 1981, p. 52)

Galton embarked on a comparative study of the size and weight of sweet pea seeds over two generations,[3] but, as he later remarked, "It was anthropological evidence that I desired, caring only for the seeds as means of throwing light on heredity in man. I tried in vain for a long and weary time to obtain it in sufficient abundance" (Galton, 1885a, p. 247).

Galton began by weighing, and measuring the diameters of, thousands of sweet pea seeds. He computed the mean and the probable error of the weights of these seeds and made up packets of 10 seeds, each of the seeds being exactly the same weight. The smallest packet contained seeds weighing the mean minus three times the probable error, the next the mean minus twice the probable error, and so on up to packets containing the largest seeds weighing the mean plus three times the probable error. Sets of the seven packets were sent to friends across the length and breadth of Britain with detailed instructions on how they were to be planted and nurtured. There were two crop failures but the produce of seven harvests provided Galton with the data for a Royal Institution lecture, "Typical

---

[3]In *Memories of my Life* (1908) Galton says that he determined on experimenting with sweet peas in 1885 and that the suggestion had come to him from Sir Joseph Hooker (the botanist, 1817–1911) and Darwin. But Darwin had died in 1882 and the experiments must have been suggested and were begun in 1875. Assuming that this is not just a typographical error, perhaps Galton was recalling the date of his important paper on regression in hereditary stature.

Laws of Heredity," given in 1877. Complete data for Galton's experiment are not available but he observed what he stated to be a simple law that connected parent and offspring seeds. The offspring of each of the parental weight categories had weights that were what we would now call normally distributed, and, the probable error (we would now calculate the standard deviation) was the same. However, the mean weight of each group of offspring was not as extreme as the parental weight. Large parent seeds produced larger than average seeds but mean offspring weight was not as large as parental weight. At the other extreme small parental seeds produced, on average, smaller offspring seeds, but the mean of the offspring was found not to be as small as that of the parents. This phenomenon Galton termed *reversion*.

Seed diameters, Galton noted, are directly proportional to their weight, and show the same effect.

By family variability is meant the departure of the children of the same or similarly descended families, from the ideal mean type of all of them. Reversion is the tendency of that ideal mean filial type to depart from the parent type, "reverting" towards what may be roughly and perhaps fairly described as the average ancestral type. If family variability had been the only process in simple descent that affected the characteristics of a sample, the dispersion of the race from its mean ideal type would indefinitely increase with the number of generations; but reversion checks this increase, and brings it to a standstill. (Galton, 1877, p. 291)

In the 1877 paper, Galton gives a measure of *reversion* which he symbolized *r*, and arrives at a number of the basic properties of what we now call *regression*.

Some years passed before Galton returned to the topic, but during those years he devised ways of obtaining the anthropometric data he wanted. He offered prizes for the most detailed accounts of family histories of physical and mental characteristics, character and temperament, occupations and illnesses, height and appearance, and so on, and, in 1884 he opened, at his own expense, an anthropometric laboratory at the International Health Exhibition.

For a small sum of money members of the public were admitted to the laboratory. In return the visitors received a record of their various physical dimensions, measures of strength, sensory acuities, breathing capacity, color discrimination, and judgments of length. 9,337 persons were measured, of whom 4,726 were adult males and 1,657 adult females. At the end of the exhibition, Galton obtained a site for the laboratory at the South Kensington Museum where data continued to be collected for close to 8 more years. These data formed part of a number of papers. They were, of course, not entirely free from errors due to apparatus failure, the circumstances of the data recording, and other factors that are familiar enough to experimentalists of the present day. Some artifacts might have been introduced in other ways. Galton (1884) commented, "Hardly any trouble occurred with the visitors, though on some few occasions rough persons entered the laboratory who were apparently not altogether sober" (p. 206).

In 1885(b), Galton's Presidential Address to the Anthropological Section of the British Association, meeting that year in Aberdeen, Scotland, discussed the phenomenon of what he now termed *regression* toward mediocrity in human hereditary stature. An extended paper in the *Journal of the Anthropological Institute* of 1885(a) gives illustrations which are reproduced here.

First it may be noted that Galton used a measure of parental heights which he termed the height of the "mid-parent." He multiplied the mother's height by 1.08 and took the mean of the resulting value and the father's height to produce the mid-parent value.[4] He found that a deviation from mediocrity of one unit of height in the parents was accompanied by a deviation, on average, of about only two-thirds of a unit in the children (Fig. 10.2). This outcome paralleled what he had observed in the sweet pea data.

When the frequencies of the (adult) children's measurements were entered into a matrix against mid-parent heights, the data being "smoothed" by computing the means of four adjacent cells, Galton noticed that values of the same frequency fell on a line that constituted an ellipse. Indeed, the data produced a series of ellipses all centered on the mean of the measurements. Straight lines drawn from this center to points on the ellipse that were maximally distant (the points of contact of the horizontal and vertical tangents—the lines YN and XM in Fig. 10.3) produce the *regression lines* and the slopes of these lines give the regression values of $\frac{2}{3}$ and $\frac{1}{3}$.

The elliptic contours, which Galton said he noticed when he was pondering on his data while waiting for a train, are nothing more than the contour lines that are produced from the horizontal sections of the frequency surface generated by two normal distributions (Fig. 10.4).

The time had now come for some serious mathematics.

All the formulae for Conic Sections having long since gone out of my head, I went on my return to London to the Royal Institution to read them up. Professor, now Sir James, Dewar, came in, and probably noticing signs of despair on my face, asked me what I was about; then said, "Why do you bother over this? My brother-in-law, J. Hamilton Dickson of Peterhouse loves problems and wants new ones. Send it to him." I did so, under the form of a problem in mechanics, and he most cordially

---

[4]Galton maintains that this factor, "differs a very little from the factors employed by other anthropologists, who, moreover, differ a trifle between themselves; anyhow it suits my data better than 1.07 or 1.09" (p.247). Galton also maintained (and checked in his data), "that marriage selection takes little or no account of shortness or tallness . . . we may therefore regard the married folk as couples picked out of the general population at haphazard" (1885a, pp. 250–251)—a statement that is not only implausible to anyone who has casually observed married couples but is also not borne out by reasonably careful investigation.

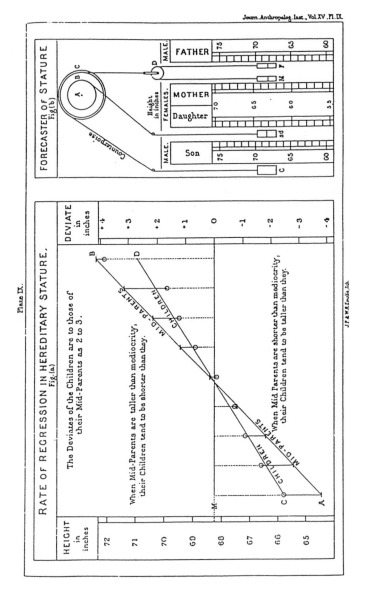

FIG. 10.2. Plate from Galton's 1885a Paper (Journal of the Anthropological Institute).

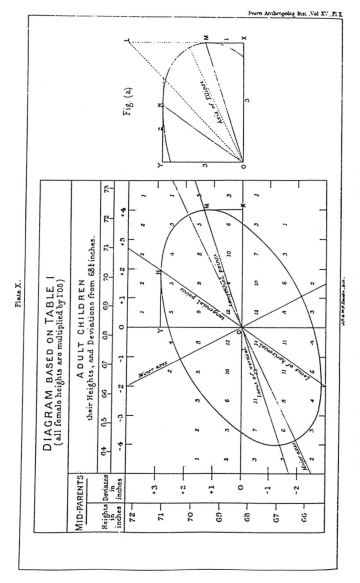

FIG. 10.3.   Plate from Galton's 1885a Paper (Journal of the Anthropological Institute).

129

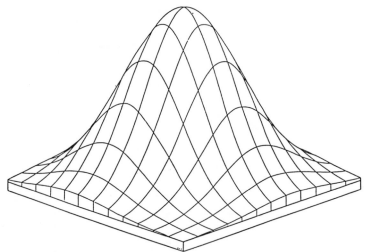

Fig. 9.1.—The ideal symmetrical (" normal ") frequency-surface, with the extremes truncated

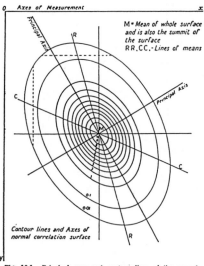

Fig. 10.1.—Principal axes and contour lines of the normal correlation surface

FIG. 10.4. Frequency Surfaces and Ellipses (From Yule & Kendall, 14th Ed., 1950).

helped me by working it out, as proposed, on the basis of the usually accepted and generally justifiable Gaussian Law of Error. (Galton, 1908, pp. 302–303)

I may be permitted to say that I never felt such a glow of loyalty and respect towards the sovereignty and magnificent sway of mathematical analysis as when his answer reached me, confirming, by purely mathematical reasoning, my various and laborious statistical conclusions with far more minuteness than I had dared to hope, for the original data ran somewhat roughly, and I had to smooth them with tender caution. (Galton, 1885b, p. 509)

Now Galton was certainly not a mathematical ignoramus but the fact that one of statistics' founding fathers sought help for the analysis of his momentous discovery may be of some small comfort to students of the social sciences who sometimes find mathematics such a trial. Another breakthrough was to come, and again, it was to culminate in a mathematical analysis, this time by Karl Pearson, and the development of the familiar formula for the *correlation coefficient*.

In 1886, a paper on "Family Likeness in Stature," published in the *Proceedings of the Royal Society*, presents Hamilton Dickson's contribution, as well as data collected by Galton from family records. Of passing interest is his use of the symbol *w* for "the ratio of regression" (short-lived as it turns out) as he details correlations between pairs of relatives.

Galton's work had led him to a method of describing the relationship between parents and offspring and between other relatives on a particular characteristic by using the regression slope. Now he applied himself to the task of quantifying the relationship between different characteristics, the sort of data collected at the anthropometric laboratory. It dawned on him in a flash of insight that if each characteristic was measured on a scale based on its own variability (in other words in what we now call *standard scores*) then the regression coefficient could be applied to these data. The incident was mentioned in chapter 1 where it was noted that the location of this illumination was perhaps not the place that Galton recalled in his memoirs (written when he was in his eighties) so that the commemorative tablet that Pearson said the discovery deserved will have to be sited carefully.

Before examining some of the consequences of Galton's inspiration, the phenomenon of regression is worth a further look. Arithmetically it is real enough, but, as Forrest (1974) puts it:

It is not that the offspring have been forced towards mediocrity by the pressure of their mediocre remote ancestry, but a consequence of a less than perfect correlation between the parents and their offspring. By restricting his analysis to the offspring of a *selected* parentage and attempting to understand their deviations from the mean Galton fails to account for the deviation of all offspring. . . . Galton's conclusion is that regression is perpetual and that the only way in which evolutionary change can occur is through the occurrence of sports. (p. 206)[5]

---

[5]In this context the term "sport" refers to an animal or a plant that differs strikingly from its species type. In modern parlance we would speak of "mutations." It is ironic that the Mendelians, led by William Bateson (1861–1926), used Galton's work in support of their argument that evolution was discontinuous and saltatory, and that the biometricians, led by Pearson and Weldon, who held fast to the notion that continuous variation was the fountain-head of evolution, took inspiration from the same source.

Wallis and Roberts (1956) present a delightful account of the fallacy and give examples of it in connection with company profits, family incomes, mid-term and final grades, and sales and political campaigns. As they say:

> Take any set of data, arrange them in groups according to some characteristic, and then for each group compute the average of some second characteristic. Then the variability of the second characteristic will usually appear to be less than that of the first characteristic. (Wallis & Roberts, 1956, p. 263)

In statistics the term *regression* now means *prediction*, a point of confusion for many students unfamiliar with its history. Yule and Kendall (1950) observe:

> The term "regression" is not a particularly happy one from the etymological point of view, but it is so firmly embedded in statistical literature that we make no attempt to replace it by an expression which would more suitably express its essential properties. (p. 213)

The word is now part of the statistical arsenal and it serves to remind those of us who are involved in its application of an important episode in the history of the discipline.

GALTON'S MEASURE OF CO-RELATION

On December 20th, 1888, Galton's paper, *Co-relations and Their Measurement, Chiefly from Anthropometric Data*, was read before the Royal Society of London. It begins,

> "Co-relation or correlation of structure" is a phrase much used in biology, and not least in that branch of it which refers to heredity, and the idea is even more frequently present than the phrase; but I am not aware of any previous attempt to define it clearly, to trace its mode of action in detail, or to show how to measure its degree. (Galton, 1888, p. 135)

He goes on to state that the co-relation between two variable organs must be due, in part, to common causes, that if variation was wholly due to common causes then co-relation would be perfect, and if variation "were in no respect due to common causes, the co-relation would be *nil*" (p. 135). His aim then is to show how this co-relation may be expressed as a simple number and he uses as an illustration the relationship between the left cubit (the distance between the elbow of the bent left arm and the tip of the middle finger) and stature, although he presents tables showing the relationships between a variety of other physical measurements. His data are drawn from measurements made on 350 adult males at the anthropometric laboratory, and then, as now, there were missing data.

"The exact number of 350 is not preserved throughout, as injury to some limb or other reduced the available number by 1, 2, or 3 in different cases" (Galton, 1888, p. 137).

After tabulating the data in order of magnitude, Galton noted the values at the first, second, and third quartiles. One half the value obtained by subtracting the value at the first from the value at the third quartile, gives him Q, which, he notes, is the probable error of any single measure in the series, and the value at the second quartile is the median. For stature he obtained a median of 67.2 inches, and a Q of 1.75 and for the left cubit, a median of 18.05 inches and a Q of 0.56. It should be noted that although Galton calculated the *median*, he refers to it as being practically the mean value, "because the series run with fair symmetry" (p. 137). Galton clearly recognized that these manipulations did not demand that the original units of measurement be the same:

> It will be understood that the Q value is a universal unit applicable to the most varied measurements, such as breathing capacity, strength, memory, keenness of eyesight, and enables them to be compared together on equal terms notwithstanding their intrinsic diversity. (Galton, 1888, p. 137)

and, perhaps in an unconscious anticipation of the inevitable universality of the metric system, he also records his data on physical dimensions in centimeters.

Figure 10.5 reproduces the data (Table III in Galton's paper) from which the closeness of the co-relation between stature and cubit was calculated.

A graph was plotted of stature, measured in deviations from M_s in units of Q_s, against the *mean* of the corresponding left cubits, again measured as deviations, this time from M_c, in units of Q_c (column A against column B in the table). Between the same axes, left cubit was plotted as a deviation from M_c measured in units of Q_c against the *mean* of corresponding statures measured as deviations from M_s in units of Q_s (columns C and D in the table). A line is then drawn to represent "the general run" of the plotted points.

> It is here seen to be a straight line, and it was similarly found to be straight in every other figure drawn from the different pairs of co-related variables that I have as yet tried. But the inclination of the line to the vertical differs considerably in different cases. In the present one the inclination is such that a deviation of 1 on the part of the subject [the ordinate values], whether it be stature or cubit, is accompanied by a mean deviation on the part of the relative [the values of the abscissa], whether it be cubit or stature, of 0.8. This decimal fraction is consequently the measure of the closeness of the co-relation. (Galton, 1888, p. 140)

Galton also calculates the predicted values from the regression line. He takes what he terms the "smoothed" (i.e., read from the regression line) value for a given deviation measure in units of Q_c or Q_s multiplies it by Q_c or Q_s, and adds the result to the mean M_c or M_s. For example, $+1.30(0.56) + 18.05 = 18.8$. In

134

Table III.—Stature M_s = 67·2 inches; Q_s = 1·75 inch; ... Left Cubit M_c = 18·05 inches; Q_c = 0·56 inch.

A / B

No. of cases.	Stature.	Deviation from M_s reckoned in		Mean of corresponding left cubit.	Deviation from M_c reckoned in			Smoothed values multiplied by Q_c.	Added to M_c.
		Inches.	Units of Q_c.		Inches.	Units of Q_c. Observed.	Smoothed.		
	inches.			inches.					
30	70·0	+2·8	+1·60	18·8	+0·8	+1·42	+1·30	+0·73	18·8
50	69·0	+1·8	+1·03	18·3	+0·3	+0·53	+0·84	+0·47	18·5
38	68·0	+0·8	+0·46	18·2	+0·2	+0·36	+0·38	+0·21	18·3
61	67·0	-0·2	-0·11	18·1	+0·1	+0·18	-0·08	-0·04	18·0
48	66·0	-1·2	-0·69	17·8	-0·2	-0·30	-0·54	-0·30	17·8
36	65·0	-2·2	-1·25	17·7	-0·3	-0·53	-1·00	-0·56	17·5
21	64·0	-3·2	-1·83	17·2	-0·8	-1·46	-1·46	-0·80	17·2

C / D

No. of cases.	Left cubit.	Deviation from M_c reckoned in		Mean of corresponding statures.	Deviation from M_s reckoned in			Smoothed values multiplied by Q_s.	Added to M_s.
		Inches.	Units of Q_c.		Inches.	Units of Q_s. Observed.	Smoothed.		
	inches.			inches.					
38	19·25	+1·20	+2·14	70·3	+3·1	+1·8	+1·70	+3·0	70·2
55	18·75	+0·70	+1·25	68·7	+1·5	+0·9	+1·00	+1·8	69·0
102	18·25	+0·20	+0·36	67·4	+0·2	+0·1	+0·28	+0·5	67·7
161	17·75	-0·30	-0·53	66·3	-0·9	-1·3	-0·43	-0·8	66·4
49	17·25	-0·80	-1·42	65·0	-2·2	-1·3	-1·16	-2·0	65·2
25	16·75	-1·30	-2·31	63·7	-3·5	-2·0	-1·85	-3·2	64·0

FIG. 10.5. Galton's Data 1888. Proceedings of the Royal Society.

modern terms, he computes $z'(s) + \bar{X} = X$. It is illuminating to recompute and to replot Galton's data and to follow his line of statistical reasoning.

Finally, Galton returns to his original symbol r, to represent degree of co-relation, the symbol which we use today, and redefines $f = \sqrt{(1 - r^2)}$ as "the Q value of the distribution of any system of x values, as x_1, x_2, x_3, &c., round the mean of all of them, which we may call X" (p. 144), which mirrors our modern-day calculation of the *standard error of estimate*, and which Galton had obtained in 1877.

This short paper is not a complete account of the measurement of correlation. Galton shows that he has not yet arrived at the notion of negative correlation nor of multiple correlation but his concluding sentences show just how far he did go.

> Let y = the deviation of the subject, whichever of the two variables may be taken in that capacity; and let x_1, x_2, x_3, &c., be the corresponding deviations of the relative, and let the mean of these be X. Then we find: (1) that $y = rX$ for all values of y; (2) that r is the same whichever of the two variables is taken for the subject; (3) that r is always less than 1; (4) that r measures the closeness of co-relation. (Galton, 1888, p. 145)

Chronologically Galton's final contribution to regression and heredity is his book, *Natural Inheritance*, published in 1889. This book was completed several months before the 1888 paper on correlation and contains none of its important findings. It was, however, an influential book which repeats a great deal of Galton's earlier work on the statistics of heredity, the sweet pea experiments, the data on stature, the records of family faculties, and so on. It was enthusiastically received by Walter Weldon (1860–1906) who was then a Fellow of St John's College, Cambridge, and University Lecturer in Invertebrate Morphology, and it pointed him toward quantitative solutions to problems in species variation which had been occupying his attention. This book linked Galton with Weldon, and Weldon with Pearson, and then Pearson with Galton, a concatenation that began the biometric movement.

THE COEFFICIENT OF CORRELATION

In June 1890 Weldon was elected a Fellow of the Royal Society and, later that year, became Jodrell Professor of Zoology at University College, London. In March of the same year the Royal Society had received the first of his biometric papers that describes the distribution of variations in a number of measurements made on shrimps. A Marine Biological Laboratory had been constructed at Plymouth 2 years earlier and since that time Weldon had spent part of the year there collecting measurements of the physical dimensions of these creatures and their organs. The Royal Society paper had been sent to Galton for review and with his help the statistical analyses had been reworked. This marked the beginning of Weldon's friendship with Galton and a concentration on biometric work that lasted for the rest of his life. In fact, the paper does not present the results of a correlational analysis although apparently one had been carried out.

> I have attempted to apply to the organs measured the test of *correlation* given by Mr. Galton . . . and the result seems to show that the degree of correlation between two organs is constant in all the races examined; Mr. Galton has, in a letter to myself, predicted this result. A result of this kind is, however, so important to the general theory of heredity, that I prefer to postpone a discussion of it until a larger body of evidence has been collected. (Weldon, 1890, p. 453)

The year 1892 saw these analyses published. Weldon begins his paper by summarizing Galton's methods. He then describes the measurements that he made, presents extensive tables of his calculations, the degree of correlation between the pairs of organs, and the probable error of the distributions ($Q\sqrt{(1 - r^2)}$). The actual calculation of the degree of correlation departs somewhat from Galton's method, although, because Galton was in close touch with Weldon, we can assume that it had his blessing. It is quite straightforward and it will be quoted in full.

> (1.). . . let all those individuals be chosen in which a certain organ, A, differs from its average size by a fixed amount, Y; then, in these individuals, let the deviations of a second organ, B, from its average be measured. The various individuals will exhibit deviations of B equal to $x_1, x_2, x_3, . . .$, whose mean may be called x_m. The ratio x_m/Y will be constant for all values of Y.
> In the same way, suppose those individuals are chosen in which the organ B has a constant deviation, X; then, in these individuals, y_m, the mean deviation of the organ A, will have the same ratio to X, whatever may be the value of X.
> (2.) The ratios x_m/Y and y_m/X are connected by an interesting relation. Let Q_a represent the probable error of distribution of the organ A about its average, and Q_b that of the organ B; then—
>
> $$\frac{y_m/X}{x_m/Y} = \frac{Q^2_a}{Q^2_b} \; ; \text{ or } \frac{x_m/Q_b}{Y/Q_a} = \frac{y_m/Q_a}{X/Q_b} = r,$$
>
> a constant.
> So that by taking a fixed deviation of *either* organ, expressed in terms of its probable error, and by expressing the mean associated deviation of the second organ in terms of its probable error, a ratio may be determined, whose value becomes ±1 when a change in either organ involves an equal change in the other, and 0 when the two organs are quite independent. This constant, therefore, measures the "degree of correlation" between the two organs. (Weldon, 1892, p. 3)

In 1893 more extensive calculations were reported on data collected from two large (each of 1,000 adult females) samples of crabs, one from the Bay of Naples and the other from Plymouth Sound. In this work Weldon (1893) computes the mean, the mean error, and the modulus. His greater mathematical sophistication in this work is evident. He states:

> The probable error is given below, instead of the mean error, because it is the constant which has the smallest numerical value of any in general use. This property renders the probable error more convenient than either the mean error, the modulus, or the error of mean squares, in the determination of the degree of correlation which will be described below. (Weldon, 1893, pp. 322–323)

Weldon found that in the Naples specimens the distribution of the "frontal breadth" produced what he terms an "asymmetrical result." This finding he hoped might arise from the presence in the sample of two races of individuals. He notes that Karl Pearson had tested this supposition and found that it was likely. Pearson (1906) states in his obituary of Weldon that it was this problem that led to his (Pearson's) first paper in the *Mathematical Contributions to the Theory of Evolution* series, received by the Royal Society in 1893.

Weldon defined r and attempted to name it for Galton,

> . . . a measure of the degree to which abnormality in one organ is accompanied by abnormality in a second. It becomes ± 1 when a change in one organ involves an equal change in the other, and 0 when the two organs are quite independent. The importance of this constant in all attempts to deal with the problems of animal variation was first pointed out by Mr. Galton . . . the constant . . . may fitly be known as "Galton's function." (Weldon, 1893, p. 325)

The statistics of heredity and a mutual interest in the plans for the reform of the University of London (which are described by Pearson in Weldon's obituary) drew Pearson and Weldon together and they were close friends and coworkers until Weldon's untimely death. Weldon's primary concern was to make his discipline, particularly as it related to evolution, a more rigorous science by introducing statistical methods. He realized that his own mathematical abilities were limited and he tried, unsuccessfully, to interest Cambridge mathematical colleagues in his endeavor. His appointment to the University College Chair brought him into contact with Pearson, but, in the meantime, he attempted to remedy his deficiencies by an extensive study of mathematical probability. Pearson (1906) writes,

> Of this the writer feels sure, that his earliest contributions to biometry were the direct results of Weldon's suggestions and would never have been carried out without his inspiration and enthusiasm. Both were drawn independently by Galton's *Natural Inheritance* to these problems. (p. 20)

Pearson's motivations were quite different from those of Weldon. MacKenzie (1981) has provided us with a fascinating account of Pearson's background, philosophy, and political outlook. He was allied with the Fabian socialists[6] ; he held strong views on women's rights; he was convinced of the necessity of adopting rational scientific approaches to a range of social issues; and his advocacy of the interests of the professional middle-class sustained his promotion of eugenics.

> His originality, his real transformation rather than re-ordering of knowledge, is to be found in his work in statistical biology, where he took Galton's insights and made out of them a new science. It was the work of his maturity—he started it only in his mid-thirties—and in it can be found the flowering of most of the major concerns of his youth. (MacKenzie, 1981, pp. 87–88)

> . . . it can be clearly seen that Pearson was not merely providing a mathematical apparatus for others to use . . . Pearson's point was essentially a political one: the viability, and indeed superiority to capitalism, of a socialist state with eugenically-planned reproduction. The quantitative statistical form of his argument provided him with convincing rhetorical resources, (MacKenzie, 1981, p. 91)

MacKenzie is at pains to point out that Pearson did not consciously set out to found a professional middle-class ideology. His analysis confines itself to the view that here was a match of beliefs and social interests that fostered Pearson's unique contribution, and that this sort of sociological approach may be used to assess the work of such exceptional individuals. Pearson did not seek to become the leader of a movement, indeed the compromises necessary for such an aspiration would have been anathema to what he saw as the role of the scientist and the intellectual.

However one assesses the operation of the forces that molded Pearson's work, it is clear that, from a purely technical standpoint, the introduction, at this juncture, of an able, professional mathematician to the field of statistical methods brought about a rapid advance and a greatly elevated sophistication.[7] The third paper in the *Mathematical Contributions* series was read before the Royal Society in November, 1895. It is an extensive paper which deals with, among other things, the general theory of correlation. It contains a number of historical misinterpretations and inaccuracies, that Pearson (1920) later attempted to rectify, but for today's users of statistical methods it is of crucial importance, for it presents the familiar deviation score formula for the *coefficient of correlation*.

---

[6]The Fabian Society (the Webbs and George Bernard Shaw were leading members) took its name from Fabius, the Roman Emperor who adopted a strategy of defence and harrassment in Rome's war with Hannibal and avoided direct confrontations. The Fabians advocated gradual advance and reform of society rather than revolution.

[7]Pearson placed Third Wrangler in the Mathematical Tripos at Cambridge in 1879. The "Wranglers" were the mathematics students at Cambridge who obtained First Class Honors—the ones who most successfully "wrangle" with maths problems. This method of classification was abandoned in the early years of this century.

It might be mentioned here that the latter term had been introduced for r by F.Y. Edgeworth (1845–1926) in an impossibly difficult-to-follow paper published in 1892. Edgeworth was Drummond Professor of Political Economy at Oxford from 1891 until his retirement in 1922 and it is of some interest to note that he had tried to attract Pearson to mathematical economics, but without success. Pearson (1920) says that Edgeworth was also recruited to correlation by Galton's *Natural Inheritance* and he remained in close touch with the biometricians over many years.

Pearson's important paper (published in the *Proceedings of the Royal Society* in 1896) warrants close examination. He begins with an introduction that states the advantages and limitations of the statistical approach pointing out that it cannot give us precise information about relationships between individuals and that nothing but means and averages and probabilities with regard to large classes can be dealt with.

On the other hand, the mathematical theory will be of assistance to the medical man by answering, *inter alia*, in its discussion of regression the problem as to the average effect upon the offspring of given degrees of morbid variation in the parents. It may enable the physician, in many cases, to state a belief based on a high degree of probability, if it offers no ground for dogma in individual cases. (Pearson, 1896, p. 255)

Pearson goes on to define the mean, median, and mode, the normal probability distribution, correlation, and regression, as well as various terms employed in selection and heredity. Next comes a historical section which will be examined further below. Section 4 of the paper examines the "special case of two correlated organs." He derives what he terms the "well-known Galtonian form of the frequency for two correlated variables," and says that r is the "GALTON function or coefficient of correlation" (p. 264). However, he is not satisfied that the methods used by Galton and Weldon give *practically* the best method of determining r and he goes on to show by what we would now call the *maximum likelihood* method that $S(xy)/(n\sigma_1\sigma_2)$ is the best value (today we replace S by Σ for summation). This expression is familiar to every beginning student in statistics. As Pearson (1896) puts it, "This value presents no practical difficulty in calculation, and therefore we shall adopt it" (p. 265). It is now well-known that we have done precisely that.[8]

There follows the derivation of the standard deviation of the coefficient of correlation, $(1 - r^2)/\sqrt{[n(1 + r^2)]}$ which Pearson translates to the *probable error*, $0.674506(1 - r^2)/\sqrt{[(n(1 + r^2)]}$. These statistics are then used to rework Weldon's shrimp and crab data and the results show that Weldon was mistaken in

---

[8]Pearson (p. 265) notes " . . . that S(xy) corresponds to the product-moment of dynamics, as $S(x^2)$ to the moment of inertia." This is why r is often referred to as the "product-moment coefficient of correlation."

assuming constancy of correlation in local races of the same species. Pearson's exhaustive re-examination of Galton's data on family stature also shows that some of the earlier conclusions were in error. The details of these analyses are now of narrow historical interest only, but Pearson's general approach is a model for all experimenters and users of statistics. He emphasizes the importance of sample size in reducing the probable error, mentions the importance of precision in measurement, cautions against general conclusions from biased samples, and treats his findings with admirable scientific caution.

Pearson introduces $V = (\sigma/m)100$, the coefficient of variation, as a way of comparing variation, and shows that "the significance of the mutual regressions of . . . two organs are as the squares of their coefficients of variation" (p. 277). It should also be noted that, in this paper, Pearson pushes much closer to the solution of problems associated with multiple correlation.

This almost completes the account of a historical perspective of the development of the Pearson *coefficient of correlation* as it is widely known and used. However, the record demands that Pearson's account be looked at in more detail and the interpretation of measures of association as they were seen by others, most notably George Udny Yule (1871–1951), who made valuable contributions to the topic, be examined.

CORRELATION—CONTROVERSIES AND CHARACTER

Pearson's (1896) paper includes a section on the history of the mathematical foundations of correlation. He says that the fundamental theorems were "exhaustively discussed" by Bravais in 1846. Indeed, he attributes to Bravais the invention of the *GALTON function* while admitting that, "a single symbol is not used for it" (p. 261). He also states that $S(xy)/(n\sigma_1\sigma_2)$ "is the value given by Bravais, but he does not show that it is the best" (p. 265). In examining the general theorem of a multiple correlation surface Pearson refers to it as *Edgeworth's Theorem*. Twenty-five years later he repudiates these statements and attempts to set his record straight. He avers that:

> They have been accepted by later writers, notably Mr Yule in his manual of statistics, who writes (p. 188):
> "Bravais introduced the product-sum, but not a single symbol for a coefficient of correlation. Sir Francis Galton developed the practical method, determining his coefficient (Galton's function as it was termed at first) graphically. Edgeworth developed the theoretical side further and Pearson introduced the product-sum formula."
>
> Now I regret to say that nearly the whole of the above statements are hopelessly incorrect. (Pearson, 1920, p. 28)

Now clearly, it is just not the case "that nearly the whole of the above statements are hopelessly incorrect." In fact, what Pearson is trying to do is to emphasize the importance of his own and Galton's contribution and to shift the blame for the maintenance of historical inaccuracies to Yule, with whom he had come to have some serious disagreement. The nature of this disagreement is of interest and can be examined from at least three perspectives. The first is that of eugenics, the second is that of the personalities of the antagonists, and the third is that of the *fundamental* utility of, and the assumptions underlying, measures of association. However, before these matters are examined, some brief comment on the contributions of earlier scholars to the mathematics of correlation is in order.

The final years of the 18th century and the first 20 years of the 19th was the period in which the theoretical foundations of the mathematics of errors of observation were laid. Laplace (1749–1827) and Gauss (1777–1855) are the best-known of the mathematicians who derived the law of frequency of error and described its application, but a number of other writers also made significant contributions (see Walker, 1929, for an account of these developments). These scholars all examined the question of the probability of the *joint* occurrence of two errors but, "None of them conceived of this as a matter which could have application outside the fields of astronomy, physics, and geodesy or gambling" (Walker, 1929, p. 94).

In fact, put simply, these workers were interested *solely* in the mathematics associated with the probability of the simultaneous occurrence of two errors in, say, the measurement of the position of a point in a plane or in three dimensions. They were clearly not looking for a measure of a possible *relationship* between the errors and certainly not considering the notion of organic relationships among directly measured variables. Indeed, astronomers and surveyors sought to make their basic measurements independent. Having said this, it is apparent that the mathematical formulations that were produced by these earlier scientists are strikingly similar to those deduced by Galton and Hamilton Dickson.

Auguste Bravais (1811–1863), who had careers as a naval officer, an astronomer, and physicist perhaps came closest to anticipating correlation coefficient, indeed he even uses the term *correlation*, in his paper of 1846. Bravais derived the formula for the frequency surface of the bivariate normal distribution and showed that it was a series of concentric ellipses, as did Galton and Hamilton Dickson 40 years later. Pearson's acknowledgment of the work of Bravais led to the correlation coefficient sometimes being called the *Bravais-Pearson coefficient*.

When Pearson came, in 1920, to revise his estimation of Bravais' role, he describes his own early investigations of correlation and mentions his lectures on the topic to research students at University College. He says:

I was far too excited to stop to investigate properly what other people had done. I wanted to reach new results and apply them. Accordingly I did not examine carefully either Bravais or Edgeworth, and when I came to put my lecture notes on correlation into written form, probably asked someone who attended the lectures to examine the papers and say what was in them. Only when I now come back to the papers of Bravais and Edgeworth do I realise not only that I did grave injustice to others, but made most misleading statements which have been spread broadcast by the text-book writers. (Pearson, 1920, p. 29)

The "Theory of Normal Correlation" was one of the topics dealt with by Pearson when he started his lectures on the "Theory of Statistics" at University College in the 1894–1895 session, "giving two hours a week to a small but enthusiastic class of two students—Miss Alice Lee, Demonstrator in Physics at the Bedford College, and myself" (Yule, 1897a, p. 457).

One of these enthusiastic students, Yule, published his famous text-book, *An Introduction to the Theory of Statistics*, in 1911, a book, which by 1920, was in its fifth edition. Later in the 1920 paper, Pearson again deals curtly with Yule. He is discussing the utility of a theory of correlation which is not dependent on the assumptions of the bivariate normal distribution and says, "As early as 1897 Mr G.U. Yule, then my assistant, made an attempt in this direction" (Pearson, 1920, p. 45).

In fact, Yule, in a paper in the *Journal of the Royal Statistical Society*, published in 1897(b), had derived least squares solutions to the correlation of two, three, and four variables. This method is a compelling demonstration of appropriateness of Pearson's formula for r under the least squares criterion. But Pearson is not impressed, or at least in 1920 he is not impressed:

Are we not making a fetish of the method of least squares as others made a fetish of the normal distribution? . . . It is by no means clear therefore that Mr Yule's generalisation indicates the real line of future advance. (Pearson, 1920, p. 45)

This, to say the least, cold approach to Yule's work (and there are many other examples of Pearson's overt invective) was certainly not evident over the 10 years that span the turn of the 19th to the 20th centuries. During what Yule described as "the old days" he spent several holidays with Pearson, and, even when their personal relationship had soured, Yule states that in nonintellectual matters Pearson remained courteous and friendly (Yule, 1936), although one cannot but help feel that here we have the words of an essentially kind and gentle man writing an obituary notice of one of the fathers of his chosen discipline. What was the nature of this disagreement that so aroused Pearson's wrath?

In 1900, Yule developed a measure of association for nominal variables, the frequencies of which are entered into the cells of a contingency table. Yule presents very simple criteria for such measures of association, namely, that they should be zero when there is no relationship (i.e., the variables are independent), +1 when there is complete dependence or association, and -1 when there is a complete negative relationship. The illustrative example chosen is that of a matrix formed from cells labeled as follows:

	vaccinated B	---------------------------- unvaccinated
survived A	AB	Aβ
died	αB	αβ

and Yule devised a measure, Q (named, it appears, for Quetelet), that satisfies the stated criteria, and is given by,

$$Q = \frac{[(AB)(\alpha\beta) - (A\beta)(\alpha B)]}{[(AB)(\alpha\beta) + (A\beta)(\alpha B)]}$$

Yule's paper had been "received" by the Royal Society in October of 1899, and "read" in December of the same year. It was described by Pearson (1900b), in a paper that examines the same problem, as, "Mr Yule's valuable memoir" (p. 1). In his paper, Pearson undertakes to investigate "the theory of the whole subject" (p. 1) and arrives at his measure of association for two-by-two contingency table frequencies, an index which he called the *tetrachoric coefficient of correlation*. He examines other possible measures of association, including Yule's Q, but he considers them to be merely approximations to the tetrachoric coefficient. The crucial difference between Yule's approach and that of Pearson is that Yule's criteria for a measure of association are empirical and arithmetical, whereas the fundamental assumption for Pearson was that the attributes whose frequencies were counted, in fact arose from an underlying continuous bivariate normal distribution. The details of Pearson's method are somewhat complex and will not be examined here. There were a number of developments from this work, including Pearson's derivation, in 1904, of the *mean square contingency* and the *contingency coefficient*. All these measures demanded the assumption of an underlying continuous distribution, even though the variables, as they were considered, were categorical. Battle commenced late in 1905 when Yule criticized Pearson's assumptions in a paper read to the Royal Society (Yule, 1906). *Biometrika*'s readers were soon to see, "Reply to Certain Criticisms of Mr. G.U. Yule" (Pearson, 1907) and, after Yule's discussion of his indices appeared in the first edition of his textbook, were treated to David Heron's exhortation, "The Danger of Certain Formulae Suggested as Substitutes for the Correlation Coefficient" (Heron, 1911). These were stirring statistical times, marked by swingeing attacks as the biometricians defended their position:

> If Mr Yule's views are accepted, irreparable damage will be done to the growth of modern statistical theory . . . we shall term Mr Yule's latest method of approaching the problem of relationship of attributes the *method of pseudo-ranks*. . . . we . . . reply to certain criticisms, not to say charges, Mr Yule has made against the work of one or both of us. (Pearson and Heron, 1913, pp. 159–160)

Articulate sniping and mathematical bombardment were the methods of attack used by the biometricians. Yule was more temperate but nevertheless, quite firm, in his views:

All those who have died of small-pox are all equally dead: no one of them is more dead or less dead than another, and the dead are quite distinct from the survivors.

The introduction of needless and unverifiable hypotheses does not appear to me to be a desirable proceeding in scientific work. (Yule, 1912, pp. 611–612)

Yule and his great friend, Major Greenwood, poked private fun at the opposition. Parts of a fantasy sent to Yule by Greenwood in November, 1913, are reproduced here.

Extracts from *The Times*, April 1925
G. Udny Yule, who had been convicted of high treason on the 7th ult., was executed this morning on a scaffold outside Gower St. Station. A short but painful scene occurred on the scaffold. As the rope was being adjusted, the criminal made some observation, imperfectly heard in the press enclosure, the only audible words being 'the normal coefficient is ---'. Yule was immediately seized by the Imperial guard and gagged.

Up to the time of going to press the warrant for the apprehension of Greenwood had not been executed, but the police have what they regard to be an important clue. During the usual morning service at St. Paul's Cathedral, which was well attended, the carlovingian creed was, in accordance with an imperial rescript, chanted by the choir. When the solemn words, 'I believe in one holy and absolute coefficient of four-fold correlation' were uttered a shabbily dressed man near the North door shouted 'balls'. Amid a scene of indescribable excitement, the vergers armed with several volumes of *Biometrika* made their way to the spot, . . . (Greenwood, quoted by MacKenzie, 1981, pp. 176–177)

The logical positions of the two sides were quite different. For Pearson it was absolutely necessary to preserve the link with interval-level measurement where the mathematics of correlation had been fully specified.

Mr Yule . . . does not stop to discuss whether his attributes are really continuous or discrete, or hide under discrete terminology true continuous variates. We see under such class indices as "death" or "recovery", "employment" or "non-employment" of mother, only measures of continuous variates . . . (p. 162)

The fog in Mr Yule's mind is well illustrated by his table . . . (p. 226)
Mr Yule is juggling with class-names as if they represented real entities, and his statistics only a form of symbolic logic. No knowledge of a practical kind ever came out of these logical theories. (p. 301) (Pearson and Heron, 1913)

Yule is attacked on almost every one of this paper's 157 pages, but for him the issue was quite straightforward. Techniques of correlation were nothing more and nothing less than descriptions of dependence in nominal data. If different techniques gave different answers, a point which Pearson and his followers frequently raised, then so be it. The mean, median, and mode give different answers to questions about the central tendency of a distribution, but each has its utility.

Of course the controversy was never resolved. The controversy can never be resolved, for there is no absolute, "right" answer. Each camp started with certain basic assumptions and a reconciliation of their views was not possible unless one or both sides were to have abrogated those assumptions, or unless it could have been shown with scientific certainty that only one side's assumptions were viable. For Yule it was a situation that he accepted. In his obituary notice of Pearson he says, "Time will settle the question in due course" (p. 84). In this he was wrong because there is no longer a question. The pragmatic practitioners of statistics in the present day are largely unaware that there ever even *was* a question.

The disagreement highlights the personality differences of the protagonists. Pearson could be described as a difficult man. He held very strong views on a variety of subjects and he was always ready to take up his pen and write scathing attacks on those whom he perceived to be misguided or misinformed. He was not ungenerous and he devoted immense amounts of time and energy to the work of his students and fellow researchers, but it is likely that tact was not one of his strong points and any sort of compromise would be seen as defeat.

In 1939, Yule commented on Pearson's polemics noting that, in 1914, Pearson said that, "Writers rarely . . . understand the almost religious hatred which arises in the true man of science when he sees error propagated in high places" (p. 221).

> Surely neither in the best type of religion nor in the best type of science should *hatred* enter in at all. . . . In one respect only has scientific controversy perforce improved since the seventeenth century. If *A* disagrees with *B*'s arguments, dislikes his personality and is annoyed by the cock of his hat, he can no longer, failing all else, resort to abuse of *B*'s latinity. (Yule, 1939, p. 221)

Yule had respect and affection for "K.P." even though he had distanced himself from the biometricians of Gower Street (where the Biometric Laboratory was located). He clearly disliked the way in which Pearson and his followers closed ranks and prepared for combat at the sniff of criticism. In some respects we can understand Pearson's attitudes. Perhaps he did feel isolated and beset. Weldon's death in 1906, and Galton's, in 1911, affected him greatly. He was the colossus of his field and yet Oxford had twice (in 1897 and 1899) turned down his applications for chairs, and in 1901 he applied, again unsuccessfully, for the chair of Natural Philosophy at Edinburgh. He felt the pressure of monumental amounts of work and longed for greater scope to carry out his research. This was indeed to come with grants from the Drapers' Company which supported the Biometric Laboratory, and Galton's bequest which made him Professor of Eugenics at University College in 1911. But more controversy, and more bitter battles, this time with Fisher, were just over the horizon.

Once more, we are indebted to MacKenzie, who so ably puts together the eugenic aspects of the controversy. It is his view that this provides a much more adequate explanation than one derived from the examination of a personality clash. It is certainly unreasonable to deny that this was an important factor.

Yule appears to have been largely apolitical. He came from a family of professional administrators and civil servants and he himself worked for the War Office and for the Ministry of Food during World War I, work for which he received the C.B.E. (*Commander of the British Empire*) in 1918. He was not a eugenist and his correspondence with Greenwood shows that his attitude toward the eugenics movement was far from favorable. He was an active member of the Royal Statistical Society, a body that awarded him its highest honor, the Guy Medal in gold, in 1911. The Society attracted members who were interested in an ameliorative and environmental approach to social issues—debates on vaccination were a continuing fascination. Although Major Greenwood, Yule's close friend, was at first an enthusiastic member of the biometric school, his career, as a statistician in the field of public health and preventive medicine, drew him toward the realization that poverty and squalor were powerful factors in the status and condition of the lower classes, a view that hardly reflected eugenic philosophy.

For Pearson, eugenics and heredity shaped his approach to the question of correlation and the notion of continuous variation was of critical importance.

> His notion of correlation, as a function allowing direct prediction from one variable to another, is shown to have its roots in the task that correlation was supposed to perform in evolutionary and eugenic prediction. It was not adequate simply to know that offspring characteristics were dependent on ancestral characteristics: this dependence had to be measured in such a way as to allow the prediction of the effects of natural selection, or of conscious intervention in reproduction. To move in the direction indicated here, from prediction to potential control over evolutionary processes, required powerful and accurate predictive tools: mere statements of dependence would be inadequate. (MacKenzie, 1981, p. 169)

Now MacKenzie's sociohistorical analysis is both compelling and provocative, but at least two points, both of which are recognized by him, need to be made. The first is that this view of Pearson's motivations is contrary to his earlier expressed views of the positivistic nature of science (Pearson, 1892), and secondly that the controversy might be placed in the context of a tightly knit academic group defending its position. To the first MacKenzie says that practical considerations outweighed philosophical ones, and yet it is clear that practical demands did not lead the biometricians to form or to join political groups that might have made their aspirations reality. The second view is mundane and realistic. The discipline of psychology has seen a number of controversies in its short history. Notable among them is the connectionist (stimulus-response) versus cognitive argument in the field of learning theory. The phenomenological, the psychodynamic, the social-learning, and the trait theorists have arraigned themselves against each other in a variety of combinations in personality research. Arguments about the continuity/discontinuity of animals and humankind are exemplified perhaps by the controversy over language acquisition in the higher primates. All these debates are familiar enough to today's students of psychology, and it is not inconceivable to view the correlation debate as part of the system of academic "rows" that will remain as long as there is freedom for intellectual controversy and scientific discourse.

But the Yule-Pearson debate and its implications are not among those discussed in university classrooms across the globe. For a multitude of reasons, not the least of which was the horror of the negative eugenics espoused by the German Nazis, and the demands of the growing discipline of psychology for quantitative techniques that would help it deal with its subject matter, very few if any of today's practitioners and researchers in the social sciences think of biometrics when they think of statistics. They busily get on with their analyses and, if they give thanks to Pearson and Galton at all, they remember them for their statistical insights rather than for their eugenic philosophy.

11
The Design
of Experiments

THE PROBLEM OF CONTROL

When Ronald Fisher accepted the post of statistician at Rothamsted Experimental Station in 1919 the tasks that faced him were to make what he could of a large quantity of existing data from ongoing long-term agricultural studies (one had begun in 1843!) and to try to improve the effectiveness of future field trials. Fisher later described the first of these tasks as, "raking over the muck heap," the second he approached with great vigor and enthusiasm, laying as he did so the foundations of modern experimental design and statistical analysis.

The essential problem is the problem of *control*. For the chemist in the laboratory it is relatively easy to standardize and manipulate the conditions of a specific chemical reaction. Social scientists, biologists, and agricultural researchers have to contend with the fact that their experimental material (people, animals, plants) is subject to irregular variation that arises as a result of complex interactions of genetic factors and environmental conditions. These many variations, unknown and uncertain, make it very difficult to be confident that observed differences in experimental observations are due to the manipulations of the experimenter rather than to chance variation. The challenge of the psychological sciences is the *sensitivity* of behavior and experience to a multiplicity of factors. But in many respects the challenge has not been answered because the unexplained variation in our observations is generally regarded as a nuisance or as irrelevant.

It is useful to distinguish between *experimental control* and the *controlled experiment*. The former is the behaviorist's ideal, the state where some consistent behavior can be set off and/or terminated by manipulating precisely specified variables. On the other hand, the controlled experiment describes a procedure in which the effect of the manipulation of the independent variable or variables is, as it were, checked against observations undertaken in the absence of the manipulation. This is the method that is employed and supported by the followers of the Fisherian tradition. The uncontrolled variables that affect the observations are assumed to operate in a random fashion, changing individual behavior in all kinds of ways so that when the data are averaged their effects are cancelled out, allowing the effect of the manipulated variable to be seen. The assumption of randomness in the influence of uncontrolled variables is, of course, not one that is always easy to justify and the relegation of important influences on variability to error may lead to erroneous inferences and disastrous conclusions.

Malaria is a disease that has been known and feared for centuries. It decimated the Roman Empire in its final years, it was quite widespread in Britain during the 17th century, and indeed was still found there in the fen country in the 19th century. The names *malaria, marsh fever,* and *paludism* all reflect the view that the cause of the disease was the breathing of damp, noxious air in swamp lands. The relationship between swamp lands and the incidence of malaria is quite clear. The relationship between swamp lands and the presence of mosquitos is also clear. But it was not until the turn of the century that it was realized that the mosquito was responsible for the transmission of the malarial parasite and only 20 years earlier, in 1880, was the parasite actually observed. In 1879, Sir Patrick Manson (1844–1922), a physician whose work played a role in the discovery of the malarial cycle, presented a paper in which he suggested that the disease *elephantiasis* was transmitted through insect bites. The paper was received with scorn and disbelief. The evidence for the life cycle of the malarial parasite in mosquitos and human beings and its being established as the *cause* of the illness came in a number of ways—not the least of which was the healthy survival, throughout the malarial season, of three of Manson's assistants living in a mosquito-proof hut in the middle of the Roman Campagna (Guthrie, 1946, pp. 357–358). This episode is an interesting example of the control of a concomitant or *correlated* bias or effect that was the direct cause of the observations.

In psychological studies, some of the earliest work that used true experimental designs is that of Thorndike and Woodworth (1901) on transfer of training. They used "before-after" designs, control group designs, and correlational studies in their work. However, the now routine inclusion of control groups in experimental investigations in psychology does not appear to have been an accepted necessity until about 50 years ago. In fact, controlled experimentation in psychology more or less coincided with the introduction of Fisherian statistics and the two quite quickly became inseparable. Of course it would be both foolish and wrong to imply that early empirical investigations in psychology were completely lacking in rigor, and mistaken conclusions rife. The point is that it was not until the 1920s and 1930s that the "rules" of controlled experimentation were spelled out and appreciated in the psychological sciences. The basic rules had been in existence for many decades, having been codified by John Stuart Mill (1806–1873) in a book first published in 1843, that is usually referred to as the *Logic*. These formulations had been preceeded by an earlier British philosopher, Francis Bacon, who made recommendations for what he thought would be sound inductive procedures.

METHODS OF ENQUIRY

Mill proposed four basic methods of experimental inquiry, and the five *Canons*, the first of which is, "If two or more instances of the phenomenon under investigation have only one circumstance in common, the circumstance in which alone all the instances agree, is the cause (or effect) of the given phenomenon" (Mill, 1843 [1st Ed.], p. 390).

If observations a, b, and c are made in circumstances A, B, C, and observations a, d, e, in circumstances A, D, E, then, it may be concluded that A causes a. Mill (1872) commented, "As this method proceeds by comparing different instances to ascertain in what they agree, I have termed it the Method of Agreement" (p. 390).

As Mill points out, the difficulty with this method is that of the impossibility of ensuring that A is the *only* antecedent of a that is common to both instances. The second canon is the Method of Difference. The antecedent circumstances A, B, C are followed by a, b, and c. When A is absent only b and c are observed.

> If an instance in which the phenomenon under investigation occurs, and an instance in which it does not occur, have every circumstance in common save one, that one occurring only in the former; the circumstance in which alone the two instances differ, is the effect or the cause, or an indispensable part of the cause of the phenomenon. (p. 391)

This method contains the difficulty in practice of being unable to guarantee that it is *the* crucial difference that has been found. As part of the way around this difficulty Mill introduces a joint method in his third canon.

> If two or more instances in which the phenomenon occurs have only one circumstance in common, while two or more instances in which it does not occur have nothing in common save the absence of that circumstance; the circumstance in which alone the two sets of instances differ, is the effect, or the cause, or an indispensable part of the cause, of the phenomenon. (p. 396)

In 1881 Louis Pasteur (1822–1895) conducted a famous experiment that exemplifies the methods of agreement and difference. Some 30 farm animals were injected by Pasteur with a weak culture of anthrax virus. Later these animals and a similar number of others that had not been so "vaccinated" were given a fatal dose of anthrax virus. Within a few days the non-vaccinated animals were dead or dying, the vaccinated ones healthy. The conclusion which was enthusiastically drawn was that Pasteur's vaccination procedure had produced the immunity that was seen in the healthy animals. The effectiveness of vaccination is now regarded as an established fact. But it is necessary to guard against incautious logic. The health of the vaccinated animals could have been due to some other fortuitous circumstance. Because it is known that some animals infected with anthrax do recover, an experimental group composed of these resistant animals could have resulted in a spurious conclusion. It should be noted that Pasteur himself recognized this as a possibility.

Mill's Method of Residues proclaims that having identified by the methods of agreement and differences that certain observed phenomena are the effects of certain antecedent conditions, the phenomena that remain are due to the circumstances that remain. "Subduct from any phenomenon such part as is known by previous inductions to be the effect of certain antecedents, and the residue of the phenomenon is the effect of the remaining antecedents" (p. 398).

Mill here uses a very modern argument for the use of the method in providing evidence for the debate on racial and gender differences.

> Those who assert, what no one has shown any real ground for believing, that there is in one human individual, one sex, or one race of mankind over another, an inherent and inexplicable superiority in mental faculties, could only substantiate their proposition by subtracting from the differences of intellect which we in fact see, all that can be traced by known laws either to the ascertained differences of physical organization, or to the differences which have existed in the outward circumstances in which the subjects of the comparison have hitherto been placed. What these causes might fail to account for, would constitute a residual phenomenon, which and which alone would be evidence of an ulterior original distinction, and the measure of its amount. But the assertors of such supposed differences have not provided themselves with these necessary logical conditions in the establishment of their doctrine. (p. 429)

The final method and the fifth canon is the Method of Concomitant Variations. "Whatever phenomenon varies in any manner whenever another phenomenon varies in some particular manner, is either a cause or an effect of that phenomenon, or is connected with it through some fact of causation" (p. 401). This method is essentially that of the correlational study, the observation of covariation.

> Let us suppose the question to be, what influence the moon exerts on the surface of the earth. We cannot try an experiment in the absence of the moon, so as to observe what terrestrial phenomenon her annihilation would put an end to; but when we find that all the variations in the *positions* of the moon are followed by corresponding

variations in the time and place of high water, the place always being either the part of the earth which is nearest to, or that which is most remote from, the moon, we have ample evidence that the moon is, wholly or partially, the cause which determines the tides. (p. 400)

Mill maintained that these methods were in fact the rules for inductive logic, that they were both methods of discovery and methods of proof. His critics, then and now, argued against a *logic* of induction (see chap. 2) but it is clear that experimentalists will agree with Mill that his methods constitute the means by which they gather experimental *evidence* for their views of nature.

The general structure of all the experimental designs that are employed in the psychological sciences may be seen in Mill's methods. The application and withholding of experimental *treatments* across groups reflect the methods of agreement and differences. The use of *placebos* and the systematic attempts to eliminate sources of error is the method of residues, and the method of concomitant variation is, as already noted, a complete description of the correlational study. It is worth mentioning that Mill attempted to deal with the difficulties presented by the correlational study and, in doing so, outlined the basics of multiple regression analysis, the mathematics of which were not to come for many years.

Suppose, then, that when A changes in quantity, a also changes in quantity, and in such a manner that we can trace the numerical relation which the changes of the one bear to such changes of the other as take place within the limits of our observation. We may then safely conclude that the same numerical relation will hold beyond those limits. (p. 403)

Mill elaborates upon this proposition and goes on to discuss the case where *a* is not wholly the effect of *A* but nevertheless varies with it:

It is probably a mathematical function not of A alone, but of A and something else: its changes, for example, may be such as would occur if part of it remained constant, or varied on some other principle, and the remainder varied in some numerical relation to the variations of A. (p. 403)

Mill's *Logic* is his principal work and it may be fairly cast as the book that first describes both a justification for, and the methodology of, the social sciences. Throughout his works the influence of the philosophers who were, in fact, the early social scientists, is evident. David Hartley (1705–1757) published his *Observations on Man* in 1749. This book is a psychology rather than a philosophy. It systematically describes *associationism* in a psychological context and is the first text that deals with physiological psychology. James Mill (1773–1836), John Stuart's father, much admired Hartley and his major work became one of the main source books that Mill the elder introduced to his son when he started his formal education at the age of three (when he learned Ancient Greek), although he did not get to formal logic until he was twelve. Another important early influence was Jeremy Bentham (1748–1832), a reformer who preached the doctrine of *Utilitarianism*, the essential feature of which is the notion that the several and joint effects of *pleasure* and *pain* govern all our thoughts and actions. Later Mill rejected strict Benthamism and questioned the work of a famous and influential contemporary, Auguste Comte (1798–1857), whose work marks the foundation of *positivism* and of sociology. The influence of the ideas of these thinkers on early experimental psychology is strong and clear but they will not be explored here. The main point to be made is that John Stuart Mill was an experimental psychologist's philosopher. More, he was *the* methodologist's philosopher. In a letter to a friend he said:

> If there is any science which I am capable of promoting, I think it is the science of science itself, the science of investigation—of method. I once heard Maurice say . . . that almost all differences of opinion when analysed, were differences of method. (Quoted by Robson in his textual introduction to the *Logic*, p. xlix)

And it is clear that all subsequent accounts of method and experimental design can be traced back to Mill.

THE CONCEPT OF STATISTICAL CONTROL

The standard design for agricultural experiments at Rothamsted in the days before Fisher was to divide a field into a number of *plots*. Each plot would receive a different treatment, say a different manure or fertilizer or manure/fertilizer mixture. The plot that produced the highest yield would be taken to be the best, and the corresponding treatment considered to be the most effective. Now Fisher, and others, realized that soil fertility is by no means uniform across a large field and that this as well as other factors, can affect the yields. In fact, the differences in the yields could be due to many factors other than the particular treatments and the highest yield might be due to some chance combination of these factors. The essential problem is to estimate the magnitude of these chance factors—the errors—to eliminate, for example, the differences in soil fertility.

Some of the first data that Fisher saw at Rothamsted were the records of daily rainfall and yearly yields from plots in the famous Broadbalk wheat field. Fertilizers had been applied to these plots, using the same pattern, since 1852. Fisher used the method of *orthogonal polynomials* to obtain fits of the yields over time. In his paper on these data, published in 1921(b), he describes *analysis of variance* (ANOVA) for the first time.

When the variation of any quantity (variate) is produced by the action of two or more independent causes, it is known that the variance produced by all the causes simultaneously in operation is the sum of the values of the variance produced by each cause separately . . . In Table II is shown the analysis of the total variance for each plot, divided according as it may be ascribed (i) to annual causes, (ii) to slow changes other than deterioration, (iii) to deterioration; the sixth column shows the probability of larger values for the variance due to slow changes occurring fortuitously. (Fisher, 1921b, pp. 110–111)

The method of data analysis that Fisher employed was ingenious and painstaking, but he realized quickly that the data that were available suffered from deficiencies in the design of their collection. Fisher set out on a new series of field trials.

He divided a field into *blocks* and sub-divided each block into plots. Each plot within the block was given a different treatment, and each treatment was assigned to each plot *randomly*. This, as Bartlett (1965) puts it, was Fisher's "vital principle."

When statistical data are collected as natural observations, the most sensible assumptions about the relevant statistical model have to be inserted. In controlled experimentation, however, randomness could be introduced deliberately into the design, so that any systematic variability other than [that] due to imposed treatments could be eliminated.

The second principle Fisher introduced naturally went with the first. With statistical analysis geared to the design, all variability not ascribed to the influence of treatments did not have to inflate the random error. With equal numbers of replications for the treatments each replication could be contained in a distinct block, and only variability among plots in the same block were a source of error—that between blocks could be removed. (Bartlett, 1965, p. 405)

The statistical analysis allowed for an even more radical break with traditional experimental methods.

No aphorism is more frequently repeated in connection with field trials, than that we must ask Nature few questions, or, ideally, one question, at a time. The writer is convinced that this view is wholly mistaken. Nature, he suggests, will best respond to a logical and carefully thought out questionnaire; indeed, if we ask her a single question, she will often refuse to answer until some other topic has been discussed. (Fisher, 1926b, p. 511)

Fisher's "carefully thought out questionnaire" was the *factorial* design. All possible combinations of treatments would be applied with *replications*. For example, in the application of nitrogen (N), phosphate (P), and potash (K) there would be eight possible treatment combinations, no fertilizer, N, P, K, N & P, N

& K, P & K, and N & P & K. Separate compact blocks would be laid out and these combinations would be randomly applied to plots within each block. This design allows for an estimation of the *main effects* of the basic fertilizers, the first order interactions (the effect of two fertilizers in combination), and the second order interaction (the effect of the three fertilizers in combination). The 1926(b) paper sets out Fisher's rationale for field experiments and was, as he noted, the precursor of his book, *The Design of Experiments* (1935a), published 9 years later. The paper is illustrated with a diagram (Figure 11.1) of a "complex experiment with winter oats" that had been carried out with a colleague at Rothamsted (Eden & Fisher, 1927).

Here 12 treatments, including absence of treatments—the "control" plots— were tested.

Any general difference between sulphate and chloride, between early and late application, or ascribable to quantity of nitrogenous manure, can be based on thirty-two comparisons, each of which is affected by such soil heterogeneity as exists between plots in the same block. To make these three sets of comparisons only, with the same accuracy, by single question methods, would require 224 plots, against our 96; but in addition many other comparisons can be made with equal accuracy, for all combinations of the factors concerned have been explored. Most

＼／	2 M EARLY	2 S LATE	＼／	2 S LATE	＼／	＼／	1 S EARLY
1 S EARLY	1M EARLY	1 M LATE	1 S LATE	2M EARLY	2M LATE	1M EARLY	1 M LATE
＼／	2M LATE	＼／	2 S EARLY	＼／	1 S LATE	＼／	2 S EARLY
2 S EARLY	2 M EARLY	＼／	1M LATE	＼／	2 S EARLY	2 S LATE	2 M LATE
＼／	1 S LATE	1 S EARLY	1 M EARLY	1M LATE	＼／	＼／	1 S LATE
2 M LATE	＼／	2 S LATE	＼／	2M EARLY	＼／	1 M EARLY	1 S EARLY
2 S EARLY	2M LATE	1 S EARLY	2M EARLY	2 S LATE	2 S EARLY	2 M EARLY	＼／
＼／	＼／	1 M LATE	＼／	1 M EARLY	2M LATE	＼／	1M LATE
2 S LATE	1M EARLY	＼／	1 S LATE	＼／	＼／	1 S EARLY	1 S LATE
2M EARLY	1M EARLY	2M LATE	2 S LATE	1 S EARLY	＼／	＼／	1 S LATE
1 S LATE	＼／	＼／	1M LATE	1M EARLY	2 S EARLY	2M LATE	＼／
1 S EARLY	＼／	2 S EARLY	＼／	＼／	2M EARLY	2 S LATE	1M LATE

FIG. 1.—A COMPLEX EXPERIMENT WITH WINTER OATS.

FIG. 11.1.   Fisher's Design 1926. Journal of the Ministry of Agriculture.

important of all, the conclusions drawn from the single-factor comparisons will be given, by the variation of non-essential conditions, a very much wider inductive basis than could be obtained, by single question methods, without extensive repetitions of the experiment. (Fisher, 1926b, p. 512)

The algebra and the arithmetic of the analysis will be dealt with in the following chapter. The crucial point of this work is the combination of statistical analysis with experimental design. Part of the stimulus for this paper was Russell's (1926) article on field experiments which had appeared in the same journal just months earlier. Russell's review presents the orthodox approach to field trials and advocated carefully planned, systematic layouts of the experimental plots. Sir John Russell was the Director of the Rothamsted Experimental Station, he had hired Fisher, he was Fisher's boss, but Fisher dismissed his methodology. In a footnote in the 1926(b) paper he says,

This principle was employed in an experiment on the influence of weather on the effectiveness of phosphates and nitrogen alluded to by Sir John Russell. The author must disclaim all responsibility for the design of this experiment, which is, however, a good example of its class. (Fisher, 1926b, p. 506)

And as Fisher Box (1978) remarks:

It is a measure of the climate of the times that Russell, an experienced research scientist who . . . had had the wisdom to appoint Fisher statistician for the better analysis of the Rothamsted experiments, did not defer to the views of his statistician when he wrote on how experiments were made. Design was, in effect, regarded as an empirical exercise attempted by the experimenter; it was not yet the domain of statisticians. (p. 153)

In fact the statistical analysis, in a sense, arises from the design. Nowadays, when ANOVA is regarded as efficient and routine, the various designs that are available and widely used are dictated to us by the knowledge that the reporting of statistical outcomes and their related levels of *significance* is the *sine qua non* of scientific respectability and acceptability by the psychological establishment. Historically, the new methods of analysis came first. The confounds, defects, and confusions of traditional designs became apparent when ANOVA was used to examine the data and so new designs were undertaken.

Randomization was demanded by the logic of statistical inference. Estimates of error and valid tests of statistical significance can only be made when the assumptions that underlie the theory of sampling distributions are upheld. Put crudely, this means that "blind chance" should not be restricted in the assignment of treatments to plots, or experimental groups. It is, however, important to note that randomization does not imply that *no* restrictions or structuring of the arrangements within a design are possible.

Figure 11.2 shows two systematic designs: (*a*) a block design and (*b*) a latin square design, and two randomized designs of the same type (*c*) and (*d*). The essential difference is that chance determines the application of the various treatments applied to the plots in the latter arrangements but the restrictions are apparent. In the randomized block and in the randomized latin square each block contains one replication of all the treatments.

The estimate of error is valid, because, if we imagine a large number of different results obtained by different random arrangements, the ratio of the real to the estimated error, calculated afresh for each of these arrangements, will be actually distributed in the theoretical distribution by which the significance of the result is tested. Whereas if a group of arrangements is chosen such that the real errors in this group are on the whole less than those appropriate to random arrangements, it has now been demonstrated that the errors, as estimated, will, in such a group, be higher than is usual in random arrangements, and that, in consequence, within such a group, the test of significance is vitiated. (Fisher, 1926b, p. 507)

Fisher later examines the utility of the Latin Square design, pointing out that it is by far the most efficient and economical for "those simple types of manurial trial in which every possible comparison is of equal importance" (p. 510). In 1925 and early 1926, Fisher had enumerated the 5X5 and 6X6 squares and in the 1926 paper made an offer that undoubtedly helped to spread the name, and the fame, of the Rothamsted Station to many parts of the world.

The Statistical Laboratory at Rothamsted is prepared to supply these, or other types of randomized arrangements, to intending experimenters; this procedure is con-

	Treatments					**A Standard Latin Square**			
	1	2	3	4	5				
Block 1	A	B	C	D	E	A	B	C	D
Block 2	A	B	C	D	E	B	A	D	C
Block 3	A	B	C	D	E	C	D	B	A
Block 4	A	B	C	D	E	D	C	A	B
Block 5	A	B	C	D	E				
			(a)				(b)		

	Treatments					**A Random Latin Square**			
	1	2	3	4	5				
Block 1	D	C	E	A	B	D	A	C	B
Block 2	A	D	B	C	E	C	B	D	A
Block 3	B	A	E	C	D	B	D	A	C
Block 4	E	D	C	A	B	A	C	B	D
Block 5	B	A	D	E	C				
			(c)				(d)		

FIG. 11.2.   Experimental Designs.

sidered the more desirable since it is only too probable that new principles will, at their inception, be, in some detail or other, misunderstood and misapplied; a consequence for which their originator, who has made himself responsible for explaining them, cannot be held entirely free from blame. (Fisher, 1926b, pp. 510–511)

THE LINEAR MODEL

Fisher described ANOVA as a way of "arranging the arithmetic" (Fisher Box, 1978, p. 109), an interpretation with which not a few students would quarrel. However, the description does point to the fact that the components of variance are *additive* and that this property is an arithmetical one and not part of the calculus of probability and statistical inference as such.

The basic construct that marks the culmination of Fisher's work is that of specifying values of an unknown dependent variable, y, in terms of a linear set of parameters, each one of which weights the several independent variables x_1, x_2, x_3, . . . x_n, that are used for prediction, together with an error component ϵ that accounts for the random fluctuations in y for particular fixed values of x_1, x_2, x_3, . . . x_n. In algebraic terms,

$$y = \beta_0 + \beta_1 x_1 + \beta_2 x_2 + \beta_3 x_3 + . . . + \beta_n x_n + \epsilon$$

The random component in the model makes it a *probabilistic* model and the properties of the distribution of this component, real or assumed, govern the inferences that may be made about the unknown dependent variable. Fisher's work is the crucial link between classical least squares analysis and regression analysis.

As Seal (1967) notes, "The linear regression model owes so much to Gauss that we believe it should bear his name" (p. 1).

However, there is little reason to suppose that this will happen. Twenty years ago Seal found that very few of the standard texts on regression, or the linear model, or ANOVA made more than a passing reference to Gauss and the situation is little changed today. Some of the reasons for this have already been mentioned in this book. The European statisticians of the 18th and 19th centuries were concerned with vital statistics and political arithmetic, and inference and prediction in the modern sense was, generally speaking, a long way off in these fields. The mathematics of Legendre and Gauss and others on the Theory of Errors did not impinge on the work of the statisticians. Perhaps more strikingly, the early links between social and vital data and error theory that were made by Laplace and Quetelet were largely ignored by Karl Pearson and Ronald Fisher.

Why, then, could not the Theory of Errors be absorbed into the broader concept of statistical theory . . . ? . . . the original reason was Pearson's preoccupation with the multivariate normal distribution and its parameters. The predictive regression equation of his pathbreaking 'regression' paper (1896) was not seen to be identical in form and solution to Gauss's *Theoria Motus* (1809) model. . . . R.A. Fisher and his associates . . . were rediscovering many of the mathematical results of least squares (or error) theory, apparently agreeing with Pearson that this theory held little interest to the statistician. (Seal, 1967, p. 2)

There might be other more mundane, nonmathematical reasons. Galton and others were strongly opposed to the use of the word *error* in describing the variability in human characteristics and the many treatises on the theory might thus have been avoided by the new social scientists who were, in the main, not mathematicians.

In his 1920 paper on the history of correlation Pearson is clearly most anxious to downplay any suggestion that Gaussian theory contributed to its development. He writes of the "innumerable treatises" (p. 27) on least squares, of the lengthy analysis, of his opinion that Gauss and Bravais "contributed nothing of real importance to the problem of correlation" (p. 82), and of his view that it is not clear that a least squares generalization "indicates the real line of future advance" (p. 45). The generalization had been introduced by Yule who Pearson and his Gower Street colleagues clearly saw as the enemy. Pearson regarded himself as the father of correlation and regression insofar as the mathematics were concerned. Galton and Weldon were, of course, recognized as important figures but they were not mathematicians and posed no threat to Pearson's authority. In other respects, Pearson was driven to try to show that his contributions were supreme and independent.

The historical record has been traced by Seal (1967), from the fundamental work of Legendre and Gauss at the beginning of the 19th century to Fisher over 100 years later.

THE DESIGN OF EXPERIMENTS

A lady declares that by tasting a cup of tea made with milk she can discriminate whether the milk or the tea infusion was first added to the cup. We will consider the problem of designing an experiment by means of which this assertion can be tested. (Fisher, 1966, 8th Ed., p. 11)

With these words Fisher introduces the example that illustrated his view of the principles of experimentation. Holschuh (1980) describes it as, "the somewhat artificial 'lady tasting tea' experiment" (p. 35), and indeed it is, but perhaps an American writer does not appreciate the fervor of the discussion on the best method of preparing cups of tea that still occupies the British! Fisher Box (1978) reports that an informal experiment was carried out at Rothamsted. A coworker, Dr B. Muriel Bristol, declined a cup of tea from Fisher on the grounds that she preferred one to which milk had first been added. Her insistence that the order in which milk and tea were poured into the cup made a difference led to a light-hearted test actually being carried out.

Fisher examines the design of such an experiment. Eight cups of tea are prepared. Four of them have tea added first and four milk. The subject is told that this has been done and the cups of tea are presented in a random order. The task is, of course, to divide the set of eight into two sets of four according to the method of preparation. Because there are 70 ways of choosing a set of four objects from eight,

> A subject without any faculty of discrimination would in fact divide the 8 cups correctly into two sets of 4 in one trial out of 70, or, more properly, with a frequency which would approach 1 in 70 more and more nearly the more often the test were repeated. . . . The odds could be made much higher by enlarging the experiment, while if the experiment were much smaller even the greatest possible success would give odds so low that the result, might with considerable probability, be ascribed to chance. (Fisher, 1966, 8th Ed., pp. 12–13)

Fisher goes on to say that it is "usual and convenient to take 5 per cent. as a standard level of significance, . . ." (p. 13) and so an event that would occur by chance once in 70 trials is decidedly significant. The crucial point for Fisher is the act of randomization.

> Apart, therefore, from the avoidable error of the experimenter himself introducing with his test treatments, or subsequently, other differences in treatment, the effects of which the experiment is not intended to study, it may be said that the simple precaution of randomisation will suffice to guarantee the validity of the test of significance, by which the result of the experiment is to be judged. (Fisher, 1966, 8th Ed., p. 21)

This is indeed *the* crucial requirement. Experimental *design* when variable measurements are being made and statistical methods are to be used to tease out the information from the error demands randomization. But there are ironies here in this, Fisher's elegant account of the lady tasting tea. It has been hailed as *the* model for the statistical inferential approach.

> It demands of the reader the ability to follow a closely reasoned argument, but it will repay the effort by giving a vivid understanding of the richness, complexity and subtlety of modern experimental method. (Newman, 1956, Vol. 3., p. 1458)

In fact it uses a situation and a method that Fisher repudiated elsewhere. More discussion of Fisher's objections to the *Neyman-Pearson* approach will be given later. For the moment it might be noted that Fisher's misgivings center on the equation of hypothesis testing with industrial quality control acceptance procedures where the population being sampled has an objective reality, and that population is repeatedly sampled. However, the tea-tasting example appears to follow this model! Kempthorne (1983) highlighted problems and indicated the difficulties that so many have had in understanding Fisher's pronouncements. In his book, *Statistical Methods and Scientific Inference*, first published in 1956, Fisher devotes a whole chapter to "Some Misapprehensions about Tests of Significance." Here he castigates the notion that "the level of significance should be determined by 'repeated sampling from the same population', evidently with no clear realization that the population in question is hypothetical" (Fisher, 1973, 3rd Ed., pp. 81–82).

He determines to illustrate "the more general effects of the confusion between the level of significance appropriately assigned to a specific test, with the frequency of occurrence of a specified type of decision" (Fisher, 1973, 3rd Ed., p. 82).

He states, "In fact, as a matter of principle, the infrequency with which, in particular circumstances, decisive evidence is obtained, should not be confused with the force, or cogency of such evidence" (Fisher, 1973, 3rd Ed., p. 96).

Kempthorne (1983), whose perceptions of both Fisher's genius and inconsistencies are as cogent and illuminating as one would find anywhere, wonders if this book's lack of recognition of randomization arose because of Fisher's belated, but of course, not admitted, recognition that it did not mesh with "fiduciating." He quotes a "curious" statement of Fisher's and comments, "Well, well!." A slightly expanded version is given here.

Whereas in the "Theory of Games" a deliberately randomized decision (1934) may often be useful to give an unpredictable element to the strategy of play; and whereas planned randomization (1935–1966) is widely recognized as essential in the selection and allocation of experimental material, it has no useful part to play in the formation of opinion, and consequently in tests of significance designed to aid the formation of opinion in the Natural Sciences. (Fisher, 1973, 3rd Ed., p. 102)

Kendall (1963) wishes that Fisher had never written the book, saying, "If we had to sacrifice any of his writings, [this book] would have a strong claim to priority" (Kendall, 1963, p. 6).

But he did write the book, and he used it to attack his opponents. In marshalling his arguments, he introduced inconsistencies of both logic and method that have led to confusion in lesser mortals. Karl Pearson and the biometricians used exactly the same tactics. In chapter 13 the view will be presented that it is this rather sorry state of affairs that has led to the historical development of statistical procedures, as they are used in psychology and the behavioral sciences, being ignored by the texts that made them available to a wider, and undoubtedly eager, audience.

12

Assessing Differences

and Having Confidence

FISHERIAN STATISTICS

Any assessment of the impact of Fisher's arrival on the statistical battlefield has to recognize that his forces did not really seek to destroy totally Pearson's work or its *raison d'etre*. The controversy between Yule and Pearson, discussed earlier, had a philosophical, not to say ideological, basis. If, at the height of the conflict, one or other side had "won," then it is likely that the techniques advocated by the vanquished would have been discarded and forgotten. Fisher's war was more territorial. The empire of observation and correlation had to be taken over by the manipulations of experimenters. Although he would never have openly admitted it, indeed he continued to attack Pearson and his works to the very end of his life (which came 26 years after the end of Pearson's), the paradigms and procedures he developed did indeed incorporate and improve on the techniques developed at Gower Street. The chi-square controversy was not a dispute about the utility of the test or its essential rationale, but a bitter disagreement over the efficiency and method of its application. For a number of reasons, which have been discussed, Fisher's views prevailed. He *was* right.

In the late 1920s and 1930s Fisher was at the height of his powers and vigorously forging ahead. Pearson, though still a man to be reckoned with, was nearly 30 years away from his best work, an old man facing retirement, rather isolated as he attacked all those who were not unquestioningly "for" him. Last, but by no means least, Fisher was the better mathematician. He had an intuitive flair that brought him to solutions of ingenuity and strength. At the same time he was able to demonstrate to the community of biological and behavioral scientists, a community that so desperately needed a coherent system of data management and assessment, that his approach had enormous practical utility.

Pearson's work may be characterized as *large sample* and correlational, Fisher's as *small sample* and experimental. Fisher's contribution easily absorbs the best of Pearson and expands on the seminal work of "Student." Assessing the import and significance of the variation in observations across groups subject to different experimental treatments is the essence of *analysis of variance*, and a haphazard glance at any research journal in the field of experimental psychology attests to its impact.

THE ANALYSIS OF VARIANCE

The fundamental ideas of analysis of variance appeared in the paper which examined correlation among Medelian factors (Fisher, 1918). At this time, eugenic research was occupying Fisher's attention. Between 1915 and 1920, he published half a dozen papers that dealt with matters relevant to this interest, an interest that continued throughout his life. The 1918 paper uses the term *variance* for $(\sigma_1^2 + \sigma_2^2)$, σ_1 and σ_2 representing two independent causes of variability, and referred to the normally distributed population.

> We may now ascribe to the constituent causes fractions or percentages of the total variance which they together produce. It is desirable on the one hand that the elementary ideas at the basis of the calculus of correlations should be clearly understood, and easily expressed in ordinary language, and on the other that loose phrases about the "percentage of causation," which obscure the essential distinction between the individual and the population, should be carefully avoided. (Fisher, 1918, pp. 399–400)

Here we see Fisher already moving away from Pearsonian correlational methods as such and appealing to the Gaussian additive model. Unlike Pearson's work, it cannot be said that the particular philosophy of eugenics directly governed Fisher's approach to new statistical techniques, but it is clear that Fisher always promoted the value of the methods in genetics research (see, e.g., Fisher, 1952). What the new techniques were to achieve was a recognition of the utility of statistics in agriculture, in industry, in the biological and behavioral sciences, to an extent that could not possibly have been foreseen before Fisher came on the scene.

The first published account of an experiment that used analysis of variance to assess the data was that of Fisher and MacKenzie (1923) on *The Manurial Response of Different Potato Varieties.*

> Two aspects of this paper are of historical interest. At that time Fisher did not fully understand the rules of the analysis of variance—his analysis is wrong—nor the role of randomization. Secondly, although the analysis of variance is closely tied to additive models, Fisher rejects the additive model in his first analysis of variance, proceeding to a multiplicative model as more reasonable. (Cochrane, 1980, p. 17)

Cochrane points out that randomization was not used in the layout and that an attempt to minimize error used an arrangement that placed different treatments near one another. The conditions could not provide an unbiased estimate of error. Fisher then proceeds to an analysis based on a multiplicative model.

> Rather surprisingly, practically all of Fisher's later work on the analysis of variance uses the additive model. Later papers give no indication as to why the product model was dropped. Perhaps Fisher found, as I did, that the additive model is a good approximation unless main effects are large, as well as being simpler to handle than the product model. (Cochrane, 1980, p. 21)

Fisher's derivation of the procedure of *analysis of variance* and his understanding of the importance of randomization in the planning of experiments is fully discussed in *Statistical Methods for Research Workers*, first published in 1925(a). This work will be examined in more detail.

Over 45 years and 14 editions, the general character of the book did not change. The 14th edition was published in 1970, using notes left by Fisher at the time of his death. Expansions, deletions, and elaborations are evident over the years. Notable are Fisher's increasing recognition of the work of others and greater attention to the historical account. Fisher's concentration on his row with the biometricians as time went by is also evident. The preface to the last edition follows earlier ones in stating that the book was a product of the research needs of Rothamsted. Further:

> It was clear that the traditional machinery inculcated by the biometrical school was wholly unsuited to the needs of practical research. The futile elaboration of innumerable measures of correlation, and the evasion of the real difficulties of sampling problems under cover of a contempt for small samples, were obviously beginning to make its pretensions ridiculous. (Fisher, 1970, 14th Ed., p. v)

The opening sentence of the chapter on correlation in the first edition reads:

> No quantity is more characteristic of modern statistical work than the correlation coefficient, and no method has been applied successfully to such various data as the method of correlation.

and in the 14th edition:

> No quantity has been more characteristic of biometrical work than the correlation coefficient, and no method has been applied to such various data as the method of correlation. (Fisher, 1970, 14th Ed., p. 177)

This not-so-subtle change is reflected in the divisions in psychology that are still evident. The two disciplines discussed by Cronbach in 1957 (see chap. 2) are those of the correlational and experimental psychologists.

In his opening chapter, Fisher sets out the scope and definition of statistics. He notes that they are essential to social studies and that it is because the methods are used there that "these studies may be raised to the rank of sciences" (p. 2). The concepts of populations and parameters, of variation and frequency distributions, of probability and likelihood, of the characteristics of efficient statistics are outlined very clearly. A short chapter on diagrams ought to be required reading, for it points up how useful diagrams can be in the appraisal of data.[1] The chapter on distributions deals with the normal, Poisson, and binomial distributions. Of interest is the introduction of the formula,

$$s^2 = \frac{1}{n - 1} \, S(x - x)^2$$

(Fisher uses S for summation) for variance, noting that s is the best estimate of σ.

Chapter 4 deals with tests of goodness-of-fit, independence, and homogeneity, giving a complete description of the application of the χ^2 tests, including Yates' correction for discontinuity and the procedure for what is now known as the *Fisher Exact Test*. Chapter 5 is on tests of significance, about which more will be said later. Chapter 6 manages to discuss, quite thoroughly, the techniques of interclass correlation without mentioning Pearson by name except to acknowledge that the data of Table 31 are Pearson and Lee's. Failure to acknowledge the work of others, which was a characteristic of both Pearson and Fisher, and which, to some extent, arose out of both spite and arrogance, at least partly explains the anonymous presentation of statistical techniques that is to be found in the modern textbooks and commentaries.

And then, Chapter 7, two-thirds of the way through the book, introduces that most important and influential of methods—*analysis of variance*. Fisher describes analysis of variance as "the separation of the variance ascribable to one group of causes from the variance ascribable to other groups" (Fisher, 1970, 14th Ed., p. 213), but he examines the development of the technique from a consideration of the *intraclass correlation*. His example is clear and worth describing. Measurements from n' pairs of brothers may be treated in two ways in a correlational analysis. The brothers may be divided into two classes, say the elder brother and the younger, and the usual *interclass* correlation on some measured variable may be calculated. When, on the other hand, the separation of the brothers into two classes is either irrelevant or impossible, then a common mean and standard deviation and an *intraclass* correlation may be computed. Given pairs of measurements, x_1, x_1'; x_2, x_2'; x_3, x_3'; . . . ; $x_{n'}$, $x'_{n'}$, the following statistics may be computed.

---

[1] Scatterplots, that so quickly identify the presence of "outliers," are critical in correlational analyses. The geometrical exploration of the fundamentals of variance analysis provides insights that cannot be matched (see, e.g., Kempthorne, 1976).

$$x = \frac{1}{2n'} \Sigma(x + x'),$$

$$s^2 = \frac{1}{2n'} \{\Sigma(x - x)^2 + \Sigma(x' - x)^2\},$$

$$r_I = \frac{1}{2n's^2} \Sigma\{(x - x)(x' - x)\}.$$

In the preceding equations Fisher's S has been replaced with Σ and r_I used to designate the intraclass correlation coefficient. The computation of r_I is very tedious as the number of classes k, and the number of observations in each class increases. Each pair of observations has to be considered twice, (x_1, x_1') and (x_1', x_1) for example. A set of k values gives $k(k - 1)$ entries in a symmetrical table. "To obviate this difficulty Harris introduced an abbreviated method of calculation by which the value of the correlation given by the symmetrical table may be obtained directly from two distributions" (Fisher, 1970, 14th Ed., p. 216). In fact,

$$k\Sigma(x_p - x)^2 = n's^2\{1 + (k - 1)r_I\}$$

Fisher goes on to discuss the sampling errors of the intraclass correlation and refers them to his z distribution. Figure 12.1 shows the effect of the transformation of r to z.

Curves of very unequal variance are replaced by curves of equal variance, skew curves by approximately normal curves, curves of dissimilar form by curves of similar form. (Fisher, 1970, 14th Ed., p. 218)

The transformation is given by,

$$z = \frac{1}{2} \log_e \frac{1 + (k - 1)r}{1 - r}$$

Fisher provides tables of the r to z transformation. After giving an example of the use of the table and finding the significance of the intraclass correlation, conclusions may be drawn. Because the symmetrical table does not give the best estimate of the correlation, a negative bias is introduced into the value for z and Fisher shows how this may be corrected. Fisher then shows that intraclass correlation is an example of the analysis of variance: "A very great simplification is introduced into questions involving intraclass correlation when we recognise that in such cases the correlation merely measures the relative importance of two groups of variation" (Fisher, 1970, 14th Ed., p. 223).

Figure 12.2 is Fisher's general summary table, showing, "in the last column, the interpretation put upon each expression in the calculation of an intraclass correlation from a symmetrical table" (p. 225).

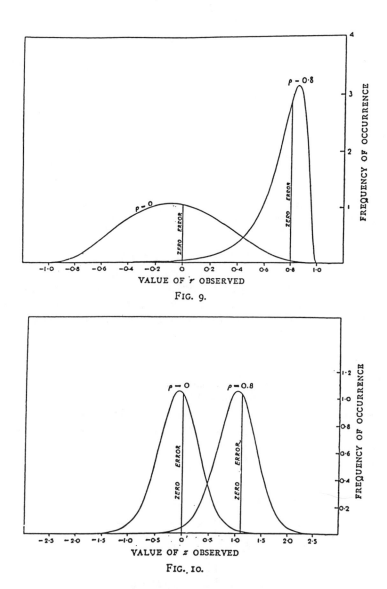

VALUE OF r OBSERVED

FIG. 9.

VALUE OF z OBSERVED

FIG. 10.

FIG. 12.1.   r to z transformation (from Fisher, Statistical Methods for Research Workers).

167

	Degrees of Freedom.	Sum of Squares.	
Within families . .	$n'(k-1)$	$\overset{kn'}{\underset{1}{S}}(x-\bar{x}_p)^2$	$ns^2(k-1)(1-r)$
Between families .	$n'-1$	$\overset{n'}{\underset{1}{kS}}(\bar{x}_p-\bar{x})^2$	$ns^2\{1+(k-1)r\}$
Total . .	$n'k-1$	$\overset{kn'}{\underset{1}{S}}(x-\bar{x})^2$	ns^2k

FIG. 12.2. ANOVA summary table 1 (from Fisher, Statistical Methods for Research Workers).

A quantity made up of two independently and normally distributed parts with variances A and B respectively, has a total variance of (A + B). A sample of n' values is taken from the first part and different samples of k values from the second part added to them. Fisher notes that in the population from which the values are drawn the correlation between pairs of members of the same family is,

$$\rho = \frac{A}{A + B}$$

and the values of A and B may be estimated from the set of kn' observations. The summary table is then presented again (Fig. 12.3) and Fisher points out that "the ratio between the sums of squares is altered in the ratio $n' : (n' - 1)$, which precisely eliminates the negative bias observed in z derived by the previous method" (Fisher, 1970, 14th Ed., p. 227).

	Degrees of Freedom.	Sum of Squares.	
Within families	$n'(k-1)$	$\overset{kn'}{\underset{1}{S}}(x-\bar{x}_p)^2$	$n'(k-1)B = n's^2(k-1)(1-r)$
Between families	$n'-1$	$\overset{n'}{\underset{1}{kS}}(\bar{x}_p-\bar{x})^2$	$(n'-1)(kA+B)=(n'-1)s^2\{1+(k-1)r\}$
Total	$n'k-1$	$\overset{kn'}{\underset{1}{S}}(x-\bar{x})^2$	$(n'-1)kA+(n'k-1)B=s^2\{n'k-1-(k-1)r\}$

FIG. 12.3. ANOVA summary table 2 (from Fisher, Statistical Methods for Research Workers).

The general class of significance tests applied here is that of testing whether an estimate of variance derived from n_1 degrees of freedom is significantly greater than a second estimate derived from n_2 degrees of freedom. The significance may be assessed without calculating r. z may be calculated as $\frac{1}{2} \log_e\{(n' - 1)(kA + B) - n'(k - 1)B\}$. Fisher provides tables of the z distribution for the 5% and 1% points. In the later editions of the book he notes that these values were calculated from the corresponding values of the variance ratio, e^{2z}, and refers to tables of these values prepared by Mahalonobis, using the symbol x in 1932, and Snedecor, using the symbol F in 1934. In fact,

$$z = \frac{1}{2} \log_e F.$$

"The wide use in the United States of Snedecor's symbol has led tothe distribution being often referred to as the distribution of F" (Fisher, 1970, 14th Ed., p. 229).

Fisher ends the chapter by giving a number of examples of the use of the method.

The final two chapters of the book discuss further applications of analysis of variance and statistical estimation. Of most interest here is Fisher's demonstration of the way in which the technique can be used to test the linear model and the "straightness" of the regression line. The method is *the* link between least squares and regression analysis. Also, of importance is Fisher's discussion of Latin Square designs and the analysis of covariance in improving the efficiency and precision of experiments.

Fisher Box notes that the book did not receive a single good review. An example, which reflected the opinions of many, was the reviewer for the *British Medical Journal.*

If he feared that he was likely to fall between two stools, to produce a book neither full enough to satisfy those interested in its statistical algebra nor sufficiently simple to please those who dislike algebra, we think Mr. Fisher's fears are justified by the result. (Anon., 1926, p. 815)

Yates (1951) comments on these early reviews, noting that many of them expressed dismay at the lack of formal mathematical proofs and interpreted the work as though it was only of interest to those who were involved in small sample work. Whatever its reception by the reviewers, by 1950, when the book was in its 11th edition, about 20,000 copies had been sold.

But it is fair to say that something like 10 years went by from the date of the original publication before Fisher's methods really started to have an effect on the behavioral sciences. Lovie (1979) traces its impact over the years 1934 to 1945. He mentions, as do others, that the early textbook writers contributed to its acceptance. Notable here are the works of Snedecor, published in 1934 and 1937. Lush (1972) quotes a European researcher who told him, "When you see

Snedecor again, tell him that over here we say, 'Thank God for Snedecor; *now* we can understand Fisher'" (Lush, 1972, p. 225).

Lindquist published his *Statistical Analysis in Educational Research* in 1940 and this book, too, was widely used. Even then, some authorities were sceptical, to say the least. Charles C. Peters in an editorial for the *Journal of Educational Research* rather condescendingly agrees that Fisher's statistics are "suitable enough" for agricultural research.

> And occasionally these techniques will be useful for rough preliminary exploratory research in other fields, including psychology and education. But if educationists and psychologists, out of some sort of inferiority complex, grab indiscriminately at them and employ them where they are unsuitable, education and psychology will suffer another slump in prestige such as they have often hitherto suffered in consequence of the pursuit of fads. (Peters, 1943, p. 549)

That Peters' conclusion partly reflects the situation at that time but somewhat misses the mark, is best evidenced by Lovie's (1979) survey. Lovie says that the incorporation of the technique of analysis of variance into psychology "was a long and painful process" and that this was due to the method's implications rather than to the arithmetic or the mathematics. Despite the best efforts of the early interpreters, the methods were not applied fully to many of the relatively large-scale, and sometimes quite complex, experiments that were being undertaken. It appears that workers in the 1930s and 1940s fell back upon traditional methods for handling data and interpreting outcomes, methods that sometimes did little more than to invite readers of the published accounts to share the insights of the researchers by merely looking at the data.

> One could perhaps even argue that many of the early workers were so unused to ANOVA that they gained more real insight into their results by the skilful use of the traditional means of analysis than they did by their relatively trivial use of ANOVA. (Lovie, 1979, p. 172)

Forty or fifty years on, sophisticated designs and complex analyses are common in the literature but misapprehensions and misgivings are still to be found there. The recipes are enthusiastically applied but their structure is not always appreciated.

If the early workers relied on writers like Snedecor to help them with Fisherian applications, later ones are indebted to workers like Eisenhart (1947) for assistance with the fundamentals of the method. Eisenhart sets out clearly the importance of the *assumptions* of analysis of variance, their critical function in inference, and the relative consequences of their not being fulfilled. Eisenhart's significant contribution has been picked up and elaborated on by subsequent writers but his account cannot be bettered.

He delineates the two fundamentally distinct classes of analysis of variance—

what are now known as the *fixed* and *random* effects models. The first of these is the most familiar to researchers in psychology. Here the task is to determine the significance of differences among treatment means: "Tests of significance of employed in connection with problems of this class are simply extensions to small samples of the theory of least squares developed by Gauss and others—the extension of the theory to small samples being due principally to R.A. Fisher" (Eisenhart, 1947, pp. 3–4).

The second class Eisenhart describes as *the true analysis of variance*. Here the problem is one of estimating, and inferring the existence of, the components of variance, "ascribable to random deviation of the characteristics of individuals of a particular generic type from the mean value of these characteristics in the 'population' of all individuals of that generic type" (Eisenhart, 1947, p. 4).

The failure of the then current literature to adequately distinguish between the two methods is because the emphasis had been on tests of significance rather than on problems of estimation. But it would seem that, despite the best efforts of the writers of the most insightful of the now current texts (e.g., Hays, 1963, 1973), the distinction is still not fully applied in contemporary research. In other words, the emphasis is clearly on the assessment of differences among pairs of treatment means rather than on the relative and absolute size of variances.

Eisenhart's discussion of the assumptions of the techniques is a model for later writers. Random variation, additivity, normality of distribution, homogeneity of variance, and zero covariance among the variables are discussed in detail and their relative importance examined. This work can be regarded as a classic of its kind.

MULTIPLE COMPARISON PROCEDURES

In 1972 Maurice Kendall commented on how regrettable it was that during the 1940s mathematics had begun to "spoil" statistics. Nowhere is the shift in emphasis from practice, with its room for intuition and pragmatism, to theory and abstraction, more evident than in the area of multiple comparison procedures. The rules for making such comparisons have been discussed ad nauseam and they continue to be discussed. Among the more complete and illuminating accounts are those of Ryan (1959) and Petrinovich and Hardyck (1969). Davis and Gaito (1984) provide a very useful discussion of some of the historical background. In commenting on Tukey's (1949) intention to replace the intuitive approach (championed by "Student") with some hard, cold facts, and to provide simple and definite procedures for researchers, they say:

> [this is] symptomatic of the transition in philosophy and orientation from the early use of statistics as a practical and rigorous aid for interpreting research results, to a highly theoretical subject predicated on the assumption that mathematical reasoning was paramount in statistical work. (Davis & Gaito, 1984, p. 5)

It is also the case that the automatic invoking, from the statistical packages, of any one of half a dozen procedures following an F test has helped to promote the emphasis on the comparison of treatment means in psychological research.

No one would argue with the underlying rationale of multiple comparison procedures. Given that the task is to compare treatment means, it is evident that to carry out multiple t tests from scratch is inappropriate. Over the long run it is apparent that the larger the number of comparisons involved, using a procedure that assumes that the comparisons are based on independent paired data sets will increase the Type I error rate considerably when all possible comparisons in a given set of means are made. Put simply, the number of false positives will increase. As Davis and Gaito (1984) point out, with α set at the 0.05 level and H_0 true, comparisons, using the t test, among 10 treatment means would, in the long run, lead to the difference between the largest and the smallest of them being reported as significant some 60% of the time. One of the problems here is that the range increases faster than the standard deviation as the size of the sample increases. The earliest attempts to devise methods to counteract this effect comes from Tippett (1925) and "Student" (1927) and later workers referred to the "studentizing" of the range, using tables of the sampling distribution of the range/standard deviation ratio, known as the q statistic. Newman (1939) published a procedure that uses this statistic to assess the significance of multiple comparisons among treatment means.

In general, the earlier writers followed Fisher who advocated performing t tests following an analysis that produced an overall z that rejected the null hypothesis, the variance estimate being provided by the error mean square and its associated degrees of freedom. Fisher's only cautionary note comes in a discussion of the procedure to be adopted when the z test fails to reject the null hypothesis.

> Much caution should be used before claiming significance for special comparisons. Comparisons, which the experiment was designed to make, may, of course, be made without hesitation. It is comparisons suggested subsequently, by a scrutiny of the results themselves, that are open to suspicion; for if the variants are numerous, a comparison of the highest with the lowest observed value, picked out from the results, will often appear to be significant, even from undifferentiated material. (Fisher, 1966, 8th Ed., p. 59)

Fisher is here giving his blessing to *planned* comparisons but does not mention that these comparisons should, strictly speaking, be *orthogonal* or independent. What he does say is that unforeseen effects may be taken as guides to future investigations. Davis and Gaito (1984) are at pains to point out that Fisher's approach was that of the practical researcher and to contrast it with the later emphasis on fundamental logic and mathematics.

Oddly enough, a number of procedures, springing from somewhat different rationales, all appeared on the scene at about the same time. Among the best known are those of Duncan (1951, 1955), Keuls (1952), Scheffé (1953), and Tukey (1949, 1953). Ryan (1959) examines the issues. After contending that, fundamentally, the same considerations apply to both a posteriori (sometimes called post hoc) and a priori (sometimes called planned) comparisons, and drawing an analogy with debates over *one-tail* and *two-tail* tests (to be discussed briefly later), Ryan defines the problem as the control of *error rate*. *Per comparison* error rates refer to the probability that a given comparison will be wrongly judged significant. *Per experiment* error rates refer not to probabilities as such, but to the frequency of incorrect rejections of the null hypothesis in an experiment, over the long run of such experiments. Finally, the so-called *experimentwise* error rate *is* a probability, the probability that any one particular experiment has at least one incorrect conclusion. The various techniques that were developed have all largely concentrated on reducing, or eliminating, the effect of the latter. The exception seems to be Duncan who attempted to introduce a test based on the error rate per *independent* comparison. Ryan suggests that this special procedure seems unnecessary and Scheffé (1959), a brilliant mathematical statistician, is unable to understand its justification. Debates will continue and, meanwhile, the packages provide us with all the methods for a keypress or two.

For the purposes of the present discussion, the examination of multiple comparison procedures provides a case history for the state of contemporary statistics. First it is an example, to match all examples, of the quest for *rules* for decision making and statistical inference that lie outside the structure and concept of the experiment itself. Ryan argues "that comparisons decided upon a priori from some psychological theory should not affect the nature of the significance tests employed for multiple comparisons" (Ryan, 1959, p. 33).

"Multiple comparison procedures" could easily replace, with only some slight modification, the subject of ANOVA in the following quote:

> The quick initial success of ANOVA in psychology can be attributed to the unattractiveness of the then available methods of analysing large experiments, combined with the appeal of Fisher's work which seemed to match, with a remarkable degree of exactness, the intellectual ethos of experimental psychology of the period, with its atheoretical and situationalist nature and its wish for more extensive experiments. (Lovie, 1979, p. 175)

Fisher would have deplored this, indeed he *did* deplore it. Secondly, it reflects the emphasis, in today's work, on the avoidance of the Type I error. Fisher would have had mixed feelings about this. On the one hand he rejected the notion of "errors of the second kind" (to be discussed in the next chapter), only rejection or acceptance of the null hypothesis enters into his scheme of things. On the other he would have been dismayed, indeed he *was* dismayed, by a concentration on automatic acceptance or rejection of the null hypothesis as the final arbiter in assessing the outcome of an experiment.

Criticizing the ideologies of both Russia and the United States, where he felt such technological approaches were evident he says:

> How far, within such a system [Russia], personal and individual inferences from observed facts are permissible we do not know, but it may be safer, . . . to conceal rather than to advertise the selfish and perhaps heretical aim of understanding for oneself the scientific situation. In the U.S. also the great importance of organized technology has I think made it easy to confuse the process appropriate for drawing correct conclusions with those aimed rather at, let us say, speeding production, or saving money. (Fisher, 1955, p. 70)

Thirdly, the multiple comparison procedure debate reflects, as has been noted, the increasingly mathematical approach to applied statistics. In the United States, a Statistical Computing Center at the State College of Agriculture at Ames, Iowa (now Iowa State University) became the first center of its kind. It was headed by George W. Snedecor, a mathematician, who suggested that Fisher be invited to lecture there during the summer session of 1931. Lush (1972) reports that academic policy at that institution was such that graduate courses in statistics were administered by the Department of Mathematics. At Berkeley, the mathematics department headed by Griffith C. Evans, who went there in 1934, was to be instrumental in making that institution a world center in statistics. Fisher visited there in the late summer of 1936 but made a very poor personal impression. Jerzy Neyman was to join the department in 1939. And, of course, *Annals of Mathematical Statistics* was founded at Michigan in 1930. On more than one occasion during those years at the end of the 1930s, Fisher contemplated moving to the United States and one may wonder on what his influence would have been on statistical developments had he become part of that milieu.

And, finally, the technique of multiple comparisons establishes without a backward glance, a system of statistics that is based unequivocally on a long-run relative frequency definition of probability where subjective, a priori notions, at best run in parallel with the *planning* of an experiment, for they certainly do not affect, in the statistical context, the real *decisions*.

CONFIDENCE INTERVALS AND SIGNIFICANCE TESTS

Inside the laboratory, at the researcher's terminal, as the outcome of the job reveals itself, and most certainly within the pages of the journals, success means *statistical significance*. A very great many reviews and commentaries, some of which have been brought together by Henkel and Morrison (1970), deplore the concentration on the Type I error rate, the α level, as it is known, that this implies. To a lesser extent, but gaining in strength, is the plea for an alternative approach to the reporting of statistical outcomes, namely, the examination of *confidence intervals*. And, to an even lesser extent, judging from the journals, is the challenge that the statistical outcomes made in the assessment of differences, should be translated into the reporting of *strengths of effects*. Here the wheel is turning full circle, back to the appreciation of experimental results in terms of a correlational analysis.[2]

Fisher himself seems to have believed that the notion of statistical significance was more or less self-evident. Even in the last edition of *Statistical Methods*, the words "null" and "hypothesis" do not appear in the index, and "significance" and "tests of significance, meaning of" have one entry which refers to the following:

> From a limited experience, for example, of individuals of a species, . . . we may obtain some idea of the infinite hypothetical population from which our sample has been drawn, and so of the probable nature of future samples . . . . If a second sample belies this expectation we infer that it is, in the language of statistics, drawn from a second population; that the treatment . . . did in fact make a material difference, . . . Critical tests of this kind may be called tests of significance, and when such tests are available we may discover whether a second sample is or is not significantly different from the first. (Fisher, 1970, 14th Ed., p. 41)

A few pages later, Fisher does explain the use of the *tail area* of the probability interval and notes that the $p = 0.05$ level is the "convenient" limit for judging significance. He does this in the context of examples of how often deviations of a particular size occur in a a given number of trials—that twice the standard deviation is exceeded about once in 22 trials, and so on. There is little wonder that researchers interpreted significance as an extension of the proportion of outcomes in a long-run repetitive process, an interpretation to which Fisher objected! In *The Design of Experiments*, he says:

> In order to assert that a natural phenomenon is experimentally demonstrable we need, not an isolated record, but a reliable method of procedure. In relation to the test of significance, we may say that a phenomenon is experimentally demonstrable when we know how to conduct an experiment which will rarely fail to give us a statistically significant result. (Fisher, 1966, 8th Ed., p. 14)

Here Fisher certainly seems to be advocating "rules of procedure," again a situation which elsewhere he condemns. Of more interest is the notion that experiments might be repeated to see if they fail to give significant results. This seems to be a very curious procedure for surely experiments, if they are to be repeated, are repeated to find *support* for an assertion. The problems that these statements cause are based on the fact that the *null* hypothesis is a statement that is the negation of the effect that the experiment is trying to demonstrate, and that

---

[2]Of interest here, however, is the increasing use, and the increasing power, of regression models in the analysis of data, see, for example, Fox (1984).

it is *this* hypothesis that is subjected to statistical test. The Neyman-Pearson approach (discussed in the next chapter) was an attempt to overcome these problems, but it was an approach that again Fisher condemned.

It appears that Fisher is responsible for the first formal statement of the 0.05 level as the criterion for judging significance but the convention predates his work (Cowles & Davis, 1982a). Earlier statements about the improbability of statistical outcomes were made by Pearson in his 1900(a) paper and "Student" (1908a) judged that three times the probable error in the normal curve would be considered significant. Wood and Stratton (1910) recommend "taking 30 to 1 as the lowest odds which can be accepted as giving practical certainty that a difference in a given direction is significant" (p. 433).

Fisher Box mentions that Fisher took a course at Cambridge on the theory of errors from Stratton during the academic year 1912–1913.

Odds of 30 to 1 represent a little more than three times the probable error referred to the normal probability curve. Because the probable error is equivalent to a little more than two thirds of a standard deviation, three P.E.'s is almost two standard deviations and, of course, reference to any table of the "areas under the normal curve" shows that a z score of 1.96 cuts off 5% in the two tails of the distribution. With some little allowance for rounding, the 0.05 probability level is seen to have enjoyed acceptance some time before Fisher's prescription.

A test of significance is a test of the probability of a statistical outcome under the hypothesis of chance. In post-Fisherian analyses the probability is that of making an error in rejecting the null hypothesis, the so-called Type I error. It is, however, not uncommon to read of the null hypothesis being rejected at the 5% level of *confidence*, an odd inversion that endows the act of rejection with a sort of statement of belief about the outcome. Interpretations of this kind reflect, unfortunately in the worst possible way, the notions of significance tests in the Fisherian sense, and *confidence intervals* introduced in the 1930s by Jerzy Neyman. Neyman (1941) states that the theory of confidence intervals was established to give frequency interpretations of problems of estimation. The classical frequency interpretation is best understood in the context of the long-run relative frequency of the outcomes in, say, the rolling of a die. Actual relative frequencies in a finite run are taken to be more or less equal to the probabilities, and in the "infinite" run *are* equal to the probabilities. In his 1937 paper Neyman considers a system of random variables, $x_1, x_2, x_3, \ldots x_n$, designated E and a probability law $p(E|\theta_1, \theta_2, \theta_3, \ldots \theta_l)$ where $\theta_1, \theta_2, \theta_3, \ldots \theta_l$ are unknown parameters. Then the problem is to establish:

> . . . single-valued functions of the x's $\underline{\theta}(E)$ and $\overline{\theta}(E)$ having the property that, whatever the values of the θ's, say $\theta'_1, \theta'_2, \ldots \theta'_l$, the probability of $\underline{\theta}(E)$ falling short of θ'_1 and at the same time of $\overline{\theta}(E)$ exceeding θ'_1 is equal to a number α fixed in advance so that $0 < \alpha < 1$,

$$P\{\underline{\theta}(E) \leq \theta'_1 \leq \overline{\theta}(E)|\theta'_1, \theta'_2, \ldots \theta'_l\} = \alpha$$

It is essential to notice that in this problem the probability refers to the values of $\theta(E)$ and $\bar{\theta}(E)$ which, being single-valued functions of the x's are random variables. θ'_1 being a constant, the left-hand side of [the above] *does not* represent the probability of θ'_1 falling within some fixed limits. (Neyman, 1937, p. 379)

The values $\theta(E)$ and $\bar{\theta}(E)$ represent the confidence limits for θ'_1 and span the confidence interval for the confidence coefficient α. Care must be taken here not to confuse this α with the symbol for the Type I error rate, in fact *this* α is one minus the Type I error rate. The last sentence in the quotation from Neyman, just given, is very important. First an example of a statement of the confidence interval in more familiar terms is, perhaps, in order. Suppose that measurements on particular fairly large random sample have produced a mean of 100 and that the standard error of this mean has been calculated to be 3. The routine method of establishing the upper and lower limits of the 90% confidence interval would be to compute $100 \pm 1.65(3)$. What has been established? The textbooks will commonly say that the probability that the population mean, μ, falls within this interval is 90%, which is of course *precisely* what Neyman says is not the case.

For Neyman the confidence limits represent the solution to the statistical problem of estimating θ_1 independent of a priori probabilities. What Neyman is saying is that, over the long run, confidence intervals, calculated in this way, will contain the parameter 90% of the time. It is not just being pedantic to insist that, in Neyman's terms, to say that the *one interval actually calculated* contains the parameter 90% of the time is mistaken. Nevertheless, that is the way in which confidence intervals have sometimes come to be interpreted and used.

A number of writers have vigorously propounded the benefits of confidence intervals as opposed to significance testing.

Whenever possible, the basic statistical report should be in the form of a *confidence interval*. Briefley, a confidence interval is a subset of the alternative hypotheses computed from the experimental data in such a way that for a selected confidence level α, the probability that the the true hypothesis is included in a set so obtained is α. Typically, an α-level confidence interval consists of those hypotheses under which the p value for the experimental outcome is larger than $1 - \alpha$ . . . Confidence intervals are the closest we can at present come to quantitative assessment of hypothesis- probabilities . . . and are currently our most effective way to eliminate hypotheses from practical consideration—if we choose to act as though none of the hypotheses not included in a 95% confidence interval are correct, we stand only a 5% chance of error. (Rozeboom, 1960, p. 426)

Both Ronald Fisher and Jerzy Neyman would have been very unhappy with this advice! It does, however, reflect once again, the way in which researchers in the psychological sciences prescribe and propound rules that, they believe, will lead to acceptance of the findings of research. Rozeboom's paper is a thoughtful attempt to provide alternatives to the routine *null hypothesis significance test* and deals with the important aspect of *degree of belief* in an outcome.

One final point on confidence interval theory. It is apparent that some early commentators (e.g., E.S. Pearson, 1939b; Welch, 1939) believed that Fisher's "fiducial theory" and Neyman's confidence interval theory were closely related. Neyman himself (1934) felt that his work was an extension of that of Fisher. Fisher objected strongly to the notion that there was anything at all confusing about fiducial distributions or probabilities and denied any relationship to the theory of confidence intervals which, he maintained was itself inconsistent. In 1941 Neyman attempted to show that there is no relationship between the two theories and here he did not pull his punches.

> The present author is inclined to think that the literature on the theory of fiducial argument was born out of ideas similar to those underlying the theory of confidence intervals. These ideas, however, seem to have been too vague to crystallize into a mathematical theory. Instead they resulted in misconceptions of "fiducial probability" and "fiducial distribution of a parameter" which seem to involve intrinsic inconsistencies . . . In this light, the theory of fiducial inference is simply non-existent in the same sense as, for example, a theory of numbers defined by mutually contradictory definitions. (Neyman, 1941, p. 149)

To the confused onlooker, Neyman does seem to have been clarifying one aspect of Fisher's approach, and perhaps for a brief moment of time there was a hint of a rapprochement. Had it happened there is reason to believe that unequivocal statements from these men would have been of overriding importance in subsequent applications of statistical techniques. In fact, their quarrels left the job to their interpreters. Debate and disagreement would, of course, have continued, but those who like to feel safe could have turned to the orthodoxy of the masters, a notion that is not without its attraction.

A NOTE ON "ONE-TAIL" AND "TWO-TAIL" TESTS

In the early 1950s, mainly in the pages of *Psychological Bulletin* and the *Psychological Review*, then, as now, immensely important and influential journals, a debate took place on the utility and desirability of one-tail versus two-tail tests (Burke, 1953; Hick, 1952; Jones, 1952, 1954; Marks, 1951, 1953;). It had been stated that when an experimental hypothesis had a *directional* component, that is not merely that a parameter μ_1 differed significantly from a second parameter μ_2, but that, for example, $\mu_1 > \mu_2$, then the researcher was permitted to use the area cut off in only one tail of the probability distribution when the test of significance was applied. Referred to the normal distribution, this means that the *critical value* becomes 1.65 rather than 1.96. It was argued that because most assertions that appealed to theory were *directional*, for example that spaced was *better* than massed practice in learning, or that extraverts conditioned *poorly* whereas introverts conditioned *well*, that the actual statistical test should take into account these one-sided alternatives. Arguments against the use of one-tailed tests primarily centered on what the researcher does when a very large difference is obtained, but in the unexpected direction. The temptation to "cheat" is overwhelming! It was also argued that such data ought not to be treated with the same reaction as a zero difference on scientific grounds: "It is to be doubted whether experimental psychology, in its present state, can afford such lofty indifference toward experimental surprises (Burke, 1953, p. 385).

Many workers were concerned that a move toward one-tail tests represented a loosening or a lowering of conventional standards, a sort of reprehensible breaking of the rules and pious pronouncements about scientific conservatism abound. Predictably, the debate led to attempts to establish the rules for the use of one-tail tests (Kimmel, 1957).

What is found in these discussions is the implicit assumption that formally-stated *alternative* hypotheses are an integral part of statistical analysis. What is not found in these discussions is any reference to the logic of using a probability distribution for the assessment of experimental data. Put baldly and simply, using a one-tail test means that the researcher is using only half the probability distribution and it is inconceivable that this procedure would have been acceptable to any of the founding fathers.[3] The debate is yet another example of the eagerness of practical researchers to codify the methods of data assessment so that statistical significance has the maximum opportunity to reveal itself, but in the presence of rules that discouraged, if not entirely eliminated, "fudging."

Significance levels, or *P* levels, are routinely accepted as part of the interpretation of statistical outcomes. The statistic that is obtained is examined with respect to a hypothesized distribution of the statistic, a distribution that can be completely specified. What is not so readily appreciated is the notion of an *alternative* model. This matter will be examined in the final chapter. For now, a summary of the process of significance testing given in one of the weightier and more thoughtful texts might be helpful.

1. Specification of a hypothesized class of models and an alternative class of models.
2. Choice of a function of the observations T.
3. Evaluation of the significance level, i.e., $SL = P(T \geq t)$, where t is the observed value of T and where the probability is calculated for the hypothesized class of models.

---

[3]Over the years the author has occasionally discussed this debate with a colleague, Caroline Davis, attempting to defend or excuse the "commonsense" view of the use of one-tail tests despite their illogicality. He is now convinced that there is neither defense nor excuse.

In most applied writings the significance level is designated by P, a custom which has engendered a vast amount of confusion.

It is quite common to refer to the hypothesized class of models as the *null hypothesis* and to the alternative class of models as the *alternative hypothesis*. We shall omit the adjective "null" because it may be misleading. (Kempthorne & Folks, 1971, pp. 314–315)

13

The Statistical

Hotpot

TIMES OF CHANGE

The latter years of the 1920s were watershed years for statistics. Karl Pearson was approaching the end of his career (he retired in 1933) and some of the older statisticians were not able to cope with the new order. The divisions had been, and were still being, drawn. Yule retired from full-time teaching at Cambridge in 1930, and, writing to Kendall after K.P.'s death in 1936 said "I feel as though the Karlovingian era has come to an end, and the Piscatorial era which succeeds it is one in which I can play no part" (quoted by Kendall, 1952, p. 157).

Yule's text had not by then tackled the problems of small samples. The *t* tests were not discussed until the 11th edition of 1937, a revision that was, in fact, undertaken by Maurice Kendall. The changes that were taking place in statistical methodology led to positions being adopted that were often based more on personality and style and loyalties than rational argument on the basic logic and utility of the approaches. Yates, who succeeded Fisher at Rothamsted in 1933, was to write, in 1951, in a commentary on *Statistical Methods for Research Workers*:

> Because of the importance that correlation analysis had assumed it was natural that the analysi̇ of variance should be approached via correlation, but to those not trained in ; school of correlational analysis (*of which I am fortunate to be able to count myself one*) this undoubtedly makes this part of the book more difficult to comprehend. (Yates, 1951, p. 24, emphasis added)

And Yates was a solid supporter of Fisher to the very end.

Fisher published his text in 1925 and in the same year his paper on the applications of "Student's" distribution appeared. Egon Pearson and Jerzy Neyman met that year. They were to introduce new features into statistics that Fisher would vehemently oppose to the end of his life.

NEYMAN AND PEARSON

It is a curious fact that what most social scientists now take to be *inferential statistics* is a mixture of procedures that, as presented in many of the current statistical cookbooks,[1] would be criticized by its innovators, Ronald A. Fisher, Jerzy Neyman, and Egon Pearson. Fisher established the present-day paramount importance of the rejection or acceptance of the *null hypothesis* in the determination of a decision on a statistical outcome—the hypothesis that the outcome is due to *chance*. The new participants—they could not be described as partners—in the union that became statistics argued for an appreciation of the probability of an *alternative hypothesis*.

In 1925 Jerzy Neyman, on a Polish Government fellowship and with a new PhD from Warsaw, arrived at University College, London, to study statistics with Karl Pearson. Neyman was born in Russia in 1894 and read mathematics at the University of Kharkov. In 1921 he moved to the new Republic of Poland where he became an assistant at the University of Warsaw and where he worked for the State Meteorological Institute. His initial months in London were difficult, partly because of his struggles with English and partly because of misunderstandings with "K.P.," but gradually he struck up a friendship that led to a research collaboration with Egon Pearson. Neyman's professional progress and his social and academic relationships have been recounted in a sympathetic and revealing account by Constance Reid (1982).

The younger Pearson has been described by many as a somewhat diffident and introverted man who was very much in the shadow of his father. Reid tells us of his feelings:

> Pearson had decided that if he was going to be a statistician he was going to have to break with his father's ideas and construct his own statistical philosophy. In retrospect, he describes what he wanted to do as "bridging the gap" between "Mark I" statistics—a shorthand expression he uses for the statistics of K.P., which was based on large samples obtained from natural populations—and the statistics of Student and Fisher, which had treated small samples obtained in controlled experiments—"Mark II statistics." (Reid, 1982, p. 60)

---

[1]The phrase "statistical cookbook" has a a a pejorative ring, which is not wholly justified. There are many excellent basic texts available and there are many excellent cookery books. Both are necessary to our well-being. The point is that conflicting recipes lead to statistical and gastronomic confusion and the fact that such conflicts exist has, by and large, been ignored by consumers in the social sciences.

Pearson (1966) himself describes "the first steps." In 1924 papers by E.C. Rhodes and by Karl Pearson (1924b) had explored the problem of choosing between alternative tests for the significance of differences, tests that had the same logical validity but that gave different levels of significance for the outcome.

> I set about exploring the multi-dimensional sample space and comparing what came to be termed the rejection regions associated with alternative tests. Could one find some general principle or principles appealing to intuition, which would guide one in choosing between tests? (E.S. Pearson, 1966, p. 6)

Pearson had pondered the question of, what, exactly, was the interpretation of "Student's" test?

> In large samples . . . the ratio $t = (\bar{x} - \mu)\sqrt{n}/s$ could be regarded as the best estimate available of the desired ratio $(\bar{x} - \mu)\sqrt{n}/\sigma$ and, as such, referred to the normal probability scale. If the sample was . . . small— . . . a sample with a less divergent mean x_1, might well provide a larger value of t than—a second sample with a more divergent mean, x_2, simply because s_1 in the first sample happened through sampling fluctuations to be smaller than s_2 in the second. To someone brought up with the older point of view this seemed at first sight paradoxical. . . . I realize that a reorientation of outlook must for me at any rate have been necessary. It was a shift which I think K.P. was not able or never saw the need to make. (Pearson, 1966, p. 6)

In 1926 Pearson put the problem to "Student" and the latter's reply shows, once more, the fertility of his ideas. Just as they had aided Fisher's inspirations, his comments now set the younger Pearson and later Neyman on the path that led to the *Neyman-Pearson Theory*. After noting what, of course, was widely accepted, that with large samples one is able to find the chance that a given value for the mean of the sample lies at any given distance from the mean of the population, and that, even if the chance is very small, there is no *proof* that the sample has not been randomly drawn, he says:

> What it does is to show that if there is any *alternative hypothesis* which will explain the occurrence of the sample with a more reasonable probability, say 0.05 (such as that it belongs to a different population or that the sample wasn't random or whatever will do the trick) you will be very much more inclined to consider that the original hypothesis is not true. (Quoted by Pearson, 1966, p. 7, emphasis added)

Pearson recalls that during the autumn of 1926, the problems of the specification of the class of *alternative hypotheses* and their definition, the *rejection region* in the sample space, and the *two sources of error* were discussed. At the end of the year, Pearson was examining the *likelihood ratio criterion* as a way of approaching the question as to whether the *alternative* or what Fisher later called the *null*, hypothesis was the more likely. Pearson always recognized that he was a weak mathematician and that he needed help with the mathematical formulation of the new ideas. He recalled to Reid (1982) that he approached Neyman, the new post-doctoral student at Gower Street, perhaps because he was "so 'fresh' to statistics" (p. 62) and because other possible collaborators would all have preferences for either Mark I or Mark II statistics. Neyman was not a member of either of the camps. He really knew very little of the statistical work of the elder Pearson, nor that of "Student" or Fisher. But an immediate and close collaboration was not possible. Although Egon Pearson and Neyman had a good deal of social contact over the summer of 1926 and Pearson remembered that they had touched on the new questions, Neyman was disenchanted with the Biometric Laboratory. It was not the frontier of mathematical statistics that he had expected and he determined to go to Paris (where his wife was an art student) and press on with his work in probability and mathematics.

At the end of 1926, correspondence began between Neyman and Pearson, and Pearson visited his coworker in Paris in the spring of 1927. Reid (1982) reports that she gave copies of Neyman's letters to Pearson to Erich Lehmann, an early student of Neyman's at Berkeley and an authority on the *Neyman-Pearson* theory (Lehmann, 1959), for his comment. Lehmann's conclusion was that, at any rate until early in 1927, Neyman "obviously didn't understand what Pearson was talking about" (p. 73).

The first joint paper, in two parts, was published in *Biometrika* in 1928. Neyman had returned to Poland for the academic year 1927–1928, teaching both at Warsaw and Krakow, and he clearly felt that he had not played as big a role in the first paper as had Pearson. The paper (Part I) ends with Neyman's disclaimer.

> N.B. I feel it necessary to make a brief comment on the authorship of this paper. Its origin was a matter of close co-operation, both personal and by letter, and the ground covered included the general ideas and the illustration of these by sampling from a normal population. A part of the results reached in common are included in Chapters I, II and IV. Later I was much occupied with other work, and therefore unable to co-operate. The experimental work, the calculation of tables and the development of the theory of Chapters III and IV are due entirely to Dr Egon S. Pearson. (p. 240)

It might be, too, that at this time Neyman wanted to distance himself just a little from the *maximum likelihood criterion*, which was the main theoretical underpinning of the ideas developed in the paper. In the early correspondence with Pearson, Neyman referred to it as, "your principle" and was not convinced that it was the only possible approach.

The 1928 (Part I) paper begins by stating the important problem of statistical inference, that of determining whether or not a particlar sample (Σ) has been randomly drawn from a population (π). Hypothesis A is that indeed it has. But Σ may have been drawn from some other population π', and thus, two sorts of error may arise. The first is when A is rejected but Σ was drawn from π, and the second is when A is accepted but Σ has been drawn from π'.

In the long run of statistical experience the frequency of the first source of error (or in a single instance its probability) can be controlled by choosing as a discriminating contour, one outside which the frequency of occurrence of samples from π is very small—say, 5 in 100 or 5 in 1000.

The second source of error is more difficult to control, . . . It is not of course possible to determine π', . . . but . . . we may determine a "probable" or "likely" form of it, and hence fix the contours so that in moving "inwards" across them the difference between π and the population from which it is "most likely" that Σ has been sampled should become less and less. This choice also implies that on moving "outwards" across the contours, other hypotheses as to the population sampled become more and more likely than Hypothesis A. (Neyman & Pearson, 1928, p. 177)

Hypothesis A corresponds to Σ having been drawn from π, and Hypothesis A' to Σ having been drawn from π'. A ratio of the probabilities of A and A' is a measure for their comparison. But,

Probability is a ratio of frequencies and this relative measure cannot be termed the ratio of the probabilities of the hypotheses, unless we speak of probability *à posteriori* and postulate some *à priori* frequency distribution of sampled populations. Fisher has therefore introduced the term *likelihood*, and calls this comparative measure the ratio of the likelihoods of the two hypotheses. (Neyman & Pearson, 1928, p. 186)

The *likelihood criterion* is given by,

$$\lambda = \frac{\text{Likelihood of } \pi}{\text{Likelihood of } \pi'(\text{max.})}$$

This ratio defines surfaces in a probability space such that it decreases from 1 to 0 as a specific point moves outwards and alternatives to the statistical hypothesis become more likely.

One had then to decide at which contour H_0 should be regarded as no longer tenable, that is where should one choose to bound the rejection region? To help in reaching this decision it appeared that the probability of falling into the region chosen, if H_0 were true, was one necessary piece of information. In taking this view it can of course be argued that our outlook was conditioned by current statistical practice, (E.S. Pearson, 1966, p. 10)

The paper does consider other approaches and notes that the authors do not claim that the principle advanced is necessarily the best to adopt, but it is clear that it is favored.

We have endeavoured to connect in a logical sequence several of the most simple tests, and in so doing have found it essential to make use of what R.A. Fisher has termed "the principle of likelihood." The process of reasoning, however, is necessarily an individual matter, and we do not claim that the method which has been most helpful to ourselves will be of greatest assistance to others. It would seem to be a case where each individual must reason out for himself his own philosophy. (Neyman & Pearson, 1928, p. 230)

There are faint echoes here of the subjective element in Neyman's initial reasoning, commented on by Lehmann and reported by Reid (1982)—the notion that belief in a prior hypothesis affects the consideration of the evidence.

There is a subjective element in the theory which expresses itself in the choice of significance level you are going to require; but it is qualitative rather than quantitative.[2] While it is not very satisfying and rather pragmatic, I think this reflects the way our minds work better than the more extreme positions of either denying any subjective element in statistics or insisting upon its complete quantification. (Lehmann, quoted by Reid, 1982, p. 73)

Neyman, in Poland in 1929, wanted to present a joint paper at the International Statistical Institute meeting, scheduled to be held there that year. The paper that Neyman was preparing dealt with the Bayesian approach to the problem that he and Pearson had considered and was to attempt to show that it led to essentially the same solution. Egon Pearson just could not agree to a collaboration that admitted, in the slightest, the notion of *inverse probability*.

Pearson . . . pointed out to Neyman that if they published the proposed paper, with its admission of inverse probability, they would find themselves in a disagreement with Fisher, . . . Many years later he explained, "The conflict between K.P. and R.A.F. left me with a curious emotional antagonism and also fear of the latter so that it upset me a bit to see him or to hear him talk." (Reid, 1982, p. 84)

He would not put his name to the paper. The curious fact is that neither Neyman nor Pearson ever wholeheartedly subscribed to the *inverse probability* approach, but Neyman felt that it should be addressed. Pearson's attempt to avoid a confrontation was doomed to failure, just as his father's earlier attempts to deflect Fisher's views had been.

The years that spanned the turn of the 1920s to the 1930s were not particularly happy ones for the collaborators. Pearson was enduring the agonies of an unhappy romance and finding his relationship with his father increasingly frustrating.

---

[2]Cowles and Davis (1982b) carried out a simple experiment that supports the suggestion that the 0.05 level of significance is subjectively reasonable. Sandy Lovie has pointed out to the author that the same experiment, in a slightly different context, was performed by Bilodeau (1952).

Neyman found his work greatly constrained by economic and political difficulties in Poland, and the elder Pearson rejected a paper he submitted to *Biometrika*. But, albeit in an intermittent fashion, the collaboration continued as they worked toward what they described as their "big paper."

This was communicated to the Royal Society by Karl Pearson in August of 1932, read in November of that year, and published in *Philosophical Transactions* in 1933. Neyman had written to Fisher, with whom he was then on reasonably amicable terms, about the paper, and the latter had indicated that were it to be sent to the Royal Society, he would likely be a referee.

> To Neyman it has always been a source of satisfaction and amusement that his and Egon's fundamental paper was presented to the Royal Society by Karl Pearson, who was hostile and skeptical of its contents, and favourably refereed by the formidable Fisher, who was later to be highly critical of much of the Neyman-Pearson theory. (Reid, 1982, p. 103)

Reid reports that when she wrote to the librarian of the Royal Society to discover the name of the second referee, she found that there had only been one referee, and that he was A.C. Aitken of Edinburgh (a leading innovator in the field of matrix algebra).

In fact, two papers were published in 1933. The Royal Society paper dealt with procedures for the determination of the most efficient tests of statistical hypotheses. There is no doubt that it is one of the most influential statistical papers ever written. It transformed the way in which both the reasoning behind, and the actual application of, statistical tests were perceived. Forty years later Le Cam and Lehmann enthusiastically assessed it:

> The impact of this work has been enormous. It is, for example, hard to imagine hypothesis testing without the concept of power . . . However, the influence of the work goes far beyond . . . By deriving tests as the solutions of clearly defined optimum problems, Neyman and Pearson established a pattern for Wald's general decision theory and for the whole field of mathematical statistics as it has developed since then. (Le Cam & Lehmann, 1974, p. viii)

The later paper (Neyman & Pearson, 1933b), presented to the Cambridge Philosophical Society, again sets out the Neyman-Pearson rationale and procedures for hypothesis testing. Their stated aim is to separate hypothesis testing from problems in estimation and to examine the employment of tests independently of a priori probability laws. They have rejected the Bayesian approach and they employ the frequentist's view of probability. A concept of central importance is that of the *power* of a statistical test, and the term is introduced here for the first time. A *Type I* error is that of rejecting a statistical hypothesis, H_0, when it is true. The *Type II* error occurs when H_0 is not rejected but some rival, alternative hypothesis is, in fact, true.

If now we have chosen a region w, in the sample space W, as critical region to test H_0, then the probability that the sample point Σ defined by the set of variates $[x_1, x_2, \ldots x_3]$ falls into w, if H_0 is true, may be written as

$$P(w|H_0) = \epsilon$$

The chance of rejecting H_0 if it is true is therefore equal to ϵ, and w may be termed of size ϵ for H_0. The second type of error will be made when some alternative H_i is true, and Σ falls in $\bar{w} = W - w$. If we denote by $P_I(w)$, $P_{II}(w)$ and $P(w)$ the chance of an error of the first kind, the chance of an error of the second kind and the total chance of error using w as critical region, then it follows that

$$P_I(w) = \phi_0 \, P(w|H),$$

$$P_{II}(w) = \sum_{i=1}^{m} \phi_1 \, P(w|H_i),$$

$$P(w) = P_I(w) + P_{II}(w).$$

(Neyman & Pearson, 1933b, p. 495)

The rule then is to set the chance of the first kind of error (the *size* or what we would now call the α level) at a small value and then choose a rejection class so that the chance of the second kind of error is minimized. In fact, the procedure attempts to maximize the *power* of the test for a given *size*. The probability of rejecting the statistical hypothesis, H_0, when in fact the true hypothesis is H_i, that is $P(w|H_i)$, is called the *power* of the critical region w with respect to H_i.

If we now consider the probability $P_{II}(w)$ of type II errors when using a test T based on the critical region w, we may describe

$$1 - \phi_0 - P_{II}(w) = \sum_{i=1}^{m} \{\phi_i P(w|H_i)\}$$

as the *resultant power* of the test T. . . . It is seen that while the power of a test with regard to a given alternative H_i is independent of the probabilities *a priori*, and is therefore known precisely as soon as H_i and w are specified, this is not the case with the resultant power, which is a function of the ϕ_i's. (Neyman & Pearson, 1933b, p. 499)

Note here that the ϕ_i's are the probabilities a priori of the admissible alternative hypotheses. Now Neyman and Pearson of course fully recognized that the ϕ_i's cannot often be expressed in numerical form and that the statistician has to consider the sense, from a practical point of view, in which tests are independent of probabilities a priori, noting:

This aspect of the error problem is very evident in a number of fields where tests must be used in a routine manner, and errors of judgment lead to waste of energy or financial loss. Such is the case in sampling inspection problems in mass-production industry. (Neyman & Pearson, 1933b, p. 493)

This apparently innocuous statement alludes to the features of the Neyman-Pearson theory of hypothesis testing that, over the course of the next few years, Fisher vigorously attacked, that is: (a) the notion that hypothesis testing can be regarded as a decision process akin to methods used in quality control, and reduced to a set of practical rules, and (b) the implication that "repeated sampling from the same population"—which occurs in industry when similar samples are drawn from the same production run—determines the level of significance. These suggestions were anathema to Fisher. They were, however, the very features which made statistics so welcome in psychology and the social sciences—that is, the promise of a set of rules with apparently respectable mathematical foundations that would allow decisions to be made on the *meaning* in noisy quantitative data. Few ventured into an examination of the logic of the methods; very few would wish to be trampled as the giants fought in the field. These matters will be examined later in this chapter.

Perhaps we should spare a thought for Sir Ronald Fisher, curmudgeon that he was. He must indeed be constantly tossing in his grave as lecturers and professors across the world, if they remember him at all, refer to the content of most current curricula as *Fisherian statistics.*

STATISTICS AND INVECTIVE

The full force of Fisher's opposition to the Neyman-Pearson theory was not immediately felt in 1933. The circumstances of his developing fury are, however, evident. In a decision that could hardly have been less conducive to harmony in the development of statistics, the University of London split Karl Pearson's department when he retired in 1933.

Statistics was taught at no other British university, nor was there another professor of eugenics, charged with the duty and the means of research into human heredity. If Fisher were to teach at a university, it would have to be as Pearson's successor. (Fisher Box, 1978, p. 257)

Fisher became Galton Professor in the Department of Eugenics, and Egon Pearson, promoted to Reader, headed the Department of Applied Statistics. There, in Gower Street, Fisher's department on the top floor and Egon Pearson's on the floor below, the rows began to simmer. Fisher Box (1978) reports that her father had ascertained, before accepting the appointment, that Egon Pearson was well disposed to it. Fisher corresponded with him, apparently in the hope that they might resolve conflicts in the teaching of statistics. Fisher Box (1978) learned from correspondence with Egon Pearson that Fisher had even suggested that, despite the decision to split the old department, he and Pearson should reunite it. Pearson's response was to the effect that no lectures in the theory of statistics should be given by Fisher, that the territories had been defined, and that each should stay within them.

Early in 1934 Pearson invited Jerzy Neyman to join his department, temporarily, as an assistant. Neyman accepted and, in the summer of 1934, received an appointment as lecturer.

The moods at Gower Street must have been impossible and the intensity of the strain is difficult to imagine and reconstruct.

[Karl] Pearson was made an honorary member of the Tea Club, and when he joined them in the Common Room, it was observed that Fisher did him the unique honour of breaking out of conversation to step forward and greet him cordially. (Fisher Box, 1978, p. 260)

or,

The Common Room was carefully shared. Pearson's group had tea at 4; and at 4:30, when they were safely out of the way, Fisher and his group trooped in. Karl Pearson had withdrawn across the college quadrangle with his young assistant Florence David. He continued to edit *Biometrika*; but, as far as Miss David remembers, he never again entered his old building. (Reid, 1982, p. 114)

It appears that, at first, Neyman and Fisher got on quite well and that Neyman tried to bring Fisher and Egon Pearson together. His work on estimation, rather than the joint work with Pearson on hypothesis testing, occupied his attention. His 1934 paper (discussed earlier) was, in the main, well-received by Fisher, and Fisher's December, 1934 paper, presented to the Royal Statistical Society (Fisher, 1935b), was commented on favorably by Neyman.

But any harmony disappeared at meetings of the Industrial and Agricultural Section of the Royal Statistical Society in 1935. Neyman presented his "Statistical Problems in Agricultural Experimentation" in which he questioned the efficiency of Fisher's handling of Randomized Block and Latin Square designs, illustrating his talk with wooden models that had been prepared for him at University College.[3] Fisher's response to the paper (for which he was supposed to give the vote of thanks) began by expressing the view, to put it bluntly (which

---

[3]Reid (1982) relates a story told by both Neyman and Pearson. One evening they returned to the department after dinner and found the models strewn about the floor. They suspected that the angry act was Fisher's.

he did), that he had hoped that Neyman would be speaking on something that he knew something about. His closing comments disparaged the Neyman-Pearson approach.

Frank Yates (1936) presented a paper on factorial designs to the Society later that year. Neyman expressed doubts about the interpretation of interactions and main effects when the number of replications was small. The problem has been examined more recently by Traxler (1976). The details of these criticisms, and they had validity, did not concern Fisher.

[Neyman had] asserted that Fisher was wrong. This was an unforgivable offense— Fisher was never wrong and indeed the suggestion that he might be was treated by him as a deadly assault. Anyone who did not accept Fisher's writing as the God-given truth was at best stupid and at worst evil. (Kempthorne, 1983, p. 483)

Oscar Kempthorne, quoted here, and undoubtedly an admirer of Fisher's work, had what he has described as a "partial relationship" with Fisher when he worked at Rothamsted from 1941 to 1946 and knew Fisher's fiery intransigence. It is understandable that Fisher Box (1978) presents a view of these troubled times that is more sympathetic to Fisher, couching her commentary in terms that do reflect an important aspect of the situation. Statistics was becoming more mathematical and the shift of its intellectual power base to the United States was to make it even more mathematical. Fisher Box (1978) comments, "Fisher was a research scientist using mathematical skills, Neyman a mathematician applying mathematical concepts to experimentation" (p. 265).

She quotes Neyman's reply to Fisher in which he explains his concerns about inconsistencies in the application of the z test. The test is deduced from the sums of two *independent* squares but the restricted sampling of Randomized Blocks and Latin Squares leads to the mutual dependence of results.

Mathematicians tended to formulate the argument in these terms, that is in terms of normal theory, ignoring randomization. Nevertheless, in doing so they exhibited a fundamental misunderstanding of Fisher's work, for it happens to be false that the derivation of the z distribution depends on the assumptions Neyman criticized. (Fisher Box, 1978, p. 266)

Fisher Box defends this view but it was not a view that convinced many mathematicians and statisticians outside the Fisherian camp.

In 1935 Egon Pearson was promoted to Professor and Neyman appointed Reader in statistics at University College. Fisher opposed Neyman's appointment. Neyman recalled to Reid (1982) that at about this time Fisher had demanded that Neyman should lecture using only *Statistical Methods for Research Workers* and that when Neyman refused said, "'Well, if so, then from now on I shall oppose you in all my capacities' And he enumerated—member of the Royal

Society and so forth. There were quite a few. Then he left. Banged the door" (Reid, 1982, p. 126).

Fisher withdrew his support for Neyman's election to the International Statistical Institute. It was this sort of intense personal animosity that led to confusion, indeed despair, as onlookers attempted to grasp the developments in statistics. The protagonists introduced ambivalence and contradiction as they defended their positions. Debate and discussion, in any rational sense, never took place. As if this was not enough, Neyman and Egon Pearson were beginning to draw apart. Neyman certainly did not feel committed to University College. Karl Pearson died in April 1936 and very shortly thereafter Egon Pearson began work on a survey of his father's contribution (E.S. Pearson, 1938a). Neyman was working on the development of a theory of estimation using *confidence intervals*. In a move that seems utterly astonishing, Pearson, who had inherited the editorship of *Biometrika*, after a certain amount of equivocation, rejected the resulting paper. Pearson thought that the paper was too long and too mathematical. It subsequently appeared in the *Philosophical Transactions of the Royal Society* (Neyman, 1937). Joint work between the two friends had almost ceased. Neyman visited the United States in 1937 and made a very good impression. His visit to Berkeley resulted in his being offered a post there in 1938, an offer which he accepted.

Neyman's move to the University of California, the growth in the development and applications of statistics at the State Agricultural College at Ames, Iowa, and the important influence of the University of Michigan, where *Annals of Mathematical Statistics,* edited by Harry C. Carver, had been founded in 1930, moved the vanguard of mathematical statistics to America, where it has remained. The tribulations of actual and devastating warfare were on Britain's horizon. There was no one left on the statistical battlefield who wanted to fight with Fisher. He was disliked by many but his close collaborators, he was often avoided, and he was misunderstood.

Fisher enjoyed a considerable reputation as a geneticist, carrying out experiments and publishing work that had considerable impact. His study of natural selection from a mathematical point of view led to a reconciliation of the Mendelian and the biometric approaches to evolution. In 1943 he accepted the post of Arthur Balfour Professor of Genetics at Cambridge University, an appointment for which Egon Pearson must have given thanks. Not that Pearson suffered too much from the lash of Fisher's tongue, for Fisher regarded him as a lightweight and, whenever he could, coldly ignored him.

Fisher was always willing to promote the application of his work to experimentation in a wide variety of fields. He was unable to accept any criticism of his view of its mathematical foundations. Perhaps the most unfortunate episode took place at the end of Karl Pearson's life. Taking as his reason an attack Pearson had made, in a work published very shortly after his death, on a paper written by an Indian statistician R.S. Koshal, Fisher undertook, "to examine frankly the status of the Pearsonian methods" (p. 303). Nearly 15 years later, in an author's note accompanying a republication of "Professor Karl Pearson and the Method of Moments," Fisher really exceeds the bounds of academic propriety:

> If peevish intolerance of free opinion in others is a sign of senility, it is one which he had developed at an early age. Unscrupulous manipulation of factual material is also a striking feature of the whole corpus of Pearsonian writings, and in this matter some blame does seem to attach to Pearson's contemporaries for not exposing his arrogant pretensions. (Fisher, 1950, p. 29.302a)

Of course Karl Pearson was guilty of the same sort of invective. Personal criticism in the defense of their mathematical and statistical stances are features of the style of both men. No academic writer expects to escape criticism, indeed lack of criticism generally indicates lack of interest, but these sort of polemics can only damage the discipline. Ordinary, and even some *extraordinary* men and women, run for cover. These conflicts may well be responsible for the rather uncritical acceptance of the statistical tools that we use today, a point that will be discussed further.

FISHER versus NEYMAN AND PEARSON

In an author's note preceding a republication of a 1939 paper, Fisher reiterates his opposition to the Neyman-Pearson approach, referring specifically to the Cambridge paper.

> The principles brought to light [in the following paper] seem to the author essential to the theory of tests of significance in general, and to have been most unwarrantably ignored in at least one pretentious work on "Testing statistical hypotheses." Practical experimenters have not been seriously influenced by this work, but in mathematical departments, at a time when these were beginning to appreciate the part they might play as guides in the theoretical aspects of experimentation, its influence has been somewhat retrograde. (Fisher, 1950, p. 35.173a)

Fisher set out his objections to Neyman and Pearson's views in 1955. *Statistical Methods and Scientific Induction* sets out to examine the differences in logic in the two approaches. He acknowledges that Barnard had observed that:

> Neyman, thinking that he was correcting and improving my own early work on tests of significance, as a means to the "improvement of natural knowledge", in fact reinterpreted them in terms of that technological and commercial apparatus which is known as an acceptance procedure. (Fisher, 1955, p. 69)

Now Fisher acknowledges the importance of acceptance procedures in industrial settings, noting that whenever he travels by air he gives thanks for their reliability. He objects, however, to the translation of this model to the physical and biological sciences. Whereas in a factory the population that is the product has an objective reality, such is not the case for the population from which the psychologist's or the biologist's sample has been drawn. In the latter case he argues there is,

. . . a multiplicity of populations to each of which we can legitimately regard our sample as belonging; so that the phrase "repeated sampling from the same population" does not enable us to determine which population is to be used to define the probability level, for no one of them has objective reality, all being products of the statistician's imagination. (Fisher, 1955, p. 71)

Fisher maintains that significance testing in experimental science depends only on the properties of the unique sample that has been observed and that this sample should be compared only with other possibilities, that is to say, "to a population of samples in all relevant respects like that observed, neither more precise nor less precise, and which therefore we think it appropriate to select in specifying the precision of the estimate" (Fisher, 1955, p. 72).

Fisher was never able to come to terms with the critical contribution of Neyman and Pearson, namely the notion of *alternative hypotheses* and *errors of the second kind*. Once again his objections are rooted in what he considers to be the adoption of the misleading quality control model. He says, "The phrase 'Errors of the second kind', although apparently only a harmless piece of technical jargon, is useful as indicating the type of mental confusion in which it was coined" (Fisher, 1955, p. 73).

Fisher agrees that the frequency of wrongly rejecting the null hypothesis can be controlled but disagrees that any specification of the rate of errors of the second kind is possible. Nor is such a specification necessary or helpful. The crux of his argument rests on his objection to using hypothesis testing as a decision process.

The fashion of speaking of a null hypothesis as "accepted when false", whenever a test of significance gives us no strong reason for rejecting it, and when in fact it *is* in some way imperfect, shows real ignorance of the research worker's attitude, by suggesting that in such a case he has come to an irreversible decision. (Fisher, 1955, p. 73)

What really should happen when the null hypothesis is accepted? The researcher concludes that the deviation from truth of the working hypothesis is not sufficient to warrant modification. Or, says Fisher, perhaps, that the deviation being in the expected direction, to an extent confirms the researcher's suspicion, but the data available are not sufficient to demonstrate its reality. The implication is clear. Experimental science is an ongoing process of evaluation and re-evaluation of evidence. Every conclusion is a provisional conclusion.

> Acceptance is irreversible, whether the evidence for it was strong or weak. It is the result of applying mechanically rules laid down in advance; no *thought* is given to the particular case, and the tester's state of mind, or his capacity for *learning*, is inoperative. (Fisher, 1955, pp. 73–74)

Finally, Fisher launches an attack, from the same basic position, on Neyman's use of the term *inductive behaviour* to replace the phrase *inductive reasoning*. It is clear that Neyman *was* looking for a statistical system that would provide rules. The 1933b paper shows that Neyman and Pearson believed that they were on the same track as Fisher:

> In dealing with the problem of statistical estimation, R.A. Fisher has shown how, under certain conditions, what may be described as *rules of behaviour* can be employed which will lead to results independent of those probabilities [here Neyman is referring to probabilities *a priori*]; in this connection he has discussed the important conception of what he terms fiducial limits. (Neyman & Pearson, 1933b, p. 492, emphasis added)

It appears that the users of statistical methods have implicitly accepted the notion that the Neyman-Pearson approach was a natural, almost an inevitable, progression from the work of Fisher. It is, however, little wonder that, even leaving the personalities and polemics aside, that Fisher objected to the mechanization of the scientific endeavor. It was just not the way he looked at science. The 1955 paper almost goes out of its way to attack Abraham Wald's (1950) book on *Statistical Decision Functions*, objecting specifically to its characterization as a book about experimental design. Neyman (1956) rebutted the criticisms of Fisher and effectively restates his position, but it is apparent that the two are really arguing at cross-purposes. Responding to Neyman's rebuttal, Fisher (1957) begins, "If Professor Neyman were in the habit of learning from others he might profit from the quotation he gives from Yates" (Fisher, 1957, p. 179).

Of interest here is Fisher's continuing determination to defend the concept of *fiducial* probability at all costs. He raises the concept again and again in his writings on inference and *never* admitted that it presented difficulties.

> The expressions "fiducial probability" and "fiducial argument" are Fisher's. Nobody knows just what they mean, because Fisher repudiated his most explicit, but definitely faulty, definition and ultimately replaced it with only a few examples. (Savage, 1976, p. 466)

The Bayesian argument lends itself to decision analysis. Fisher objected to both. The fiducial argument has been characterized as an elliptical attempt to arrive at Bayesian-type posterior probabilities without invoking the Bayesian-type priors. What muddies the water was Fisher's insistence that fiducial probabilities are verifiable in the same way, for example, as the probabilities in games of chance are verifiable. What makes the situation even more vexing is that the perceived relationship between Neyman's *confidence intervals* and Fisher's fiducial theory would make the latter easier to grasp. But Neyman's theory of estimation by confidence sets grows out of the same conceptual roots as Neyman-Pearson hypothesis testing. No rational compromise was possible.

The null hypothesis (it has been noted that the term is Fisher's and that it was not used by Neyman and Pearson) is, in Fisherian terms, the hypothesis that is tested and it implies a particular value (most often zero) for the population parameter. When a statistical analysis produces a *significant* outcome, this is taken to be evidence against the null hypothesis, evidence against the stated value for the parameter, evidence against the assertion that nothing has happened, evidence against a conclusion that the experimental manipulation has had no effect. The point is that a *significant* outcome does not appear to be evidence *for* anything. The Neyman-Pearson position is that hypothesis testing demands a research hypothesis for which we can find support. Suppose that the statistical hypothesis states that in the population the correlation is zero and indeed it *is*, then an obtained sample value of $+0.8$, given a reasonable n would lead to a Type I error. If, on the other hand, the statistical hypothesis states that the population value is $+0.8$, but again it is really zero, then an obtained value of 0.8 will lead to a Type II error. It will immediately be argued that no one would set the population parameter under the null hypothesis as $+0.8$ unless there were evidence that it was of this order. However, this implies that experimenters take into account other evidence than that immediately to hand. No matter how formal the rules, it is plain that in real life the rules do not *inevitably* guide behavior and decisions, or conclusions about outcomes. As was noted earlier, my holding a winning lottery ticket that was drawn from a million tickets—an extemely improbable event—does *not necessarily* lead to my rejecting the hypothesis of chance.

There are, then, difficult problems in the assessment of the rules of statistical procedures. It is small wonder that they are not widely appreciated because the founding fathers themselves were not clear on the issues, or at any rate in public, and in their writings, they were not *always* clear on the issues. Some few examples will suffice to illustrate the point.

In 1935 Karl Pearson asserted that "tests are used to ascertain whether a reasonable *graduation* curve has been achieved, not to assert whether one or another hypothesis is true or false" (K. Pearson, 1935, p. 296).

All he is doing here is arguing with Fisher. He himself used his own χ^2 test for hypothesis testing (e.g. K. Pearson, 1909).

In his famous discussion of the "tea-tasting" investigation Fisher discusses the "sensitiveness" of an experiment. He notes that by increasing the size of the experiment,

. . . we can render it more sensitive, meaning by this that it will allow of the detection of a lower degree of sensory discrimination, or, in other words, of a quantitatively smaller departure from the null hypothesis. Since in every case the experiment is capable of disproving, but never of proving this hypothesis, we may say that the value of the experiment is increased whenever it permits the null hypothesis to be more readily disproved.

The same result could be achieved by repeating the experiment, as originally designed, upon a number of different occasions. (Fisher, 1966. 8th Ed., p. 22)

Here Fisher appears to be alluding to what Neyman and Pearson formalized as the *power* of the test—a notion that he never would accept in their context. He is also using the words "proved" and "disproved" rather loosely, and, though he might be forgiven, the slip flies in the face of the routine statements about the essentially probabilistic nature of statistical outcomes. Elsewhere Fisher presents the view that each experiment is, as it were, self-contained in the context of significance testing.

On the whole the ideas (a) that a test of significance must be regarded as one of a series of similar tests applied to a succession of similar bodies of data, and (b) that the purpose of the test is to discriminate or "decide" between two or more hypotheses, have greatly obscured their understanding, when taken as contingent possibilities but as elements essential to their logic. (Fisher, 1973, 3rd Ed., pp. 45–46)

To practicing researchers the notion that tests are not used to "decide" is incomprehensible. What else are they for? Fisher's supporters would say that what he means is that they are not used to decide finally and irreversibly, and scientists would surely agree.

In his 1955 paper where he objects to the Neyman-Pearson specification of the two types of error and gives his views (mentioned earlier) of what the researcher will conclude when a result fails to reach statistical significance, Fisher says:

These examples show how badly the word "error" is used in describing such a situation. Moreover, it is a fallacy, so well known as to be a *standard* example, to conclude from a test of significance that the null hypothesis is thereby established; at most it may be said to be *confirmed* [emphasis added] or strengthened. (Fisher, 1955, p. 73)

Now it might be argued that a careful reading of Fisher's voluminous works would make his position clear, and that these quotations are selective. The point is taken, but the point may also be made that it is hardly surprising that the later interpretations of, and commentaries on, his influential contribution contain difficulties and contradictions. Had the protagonists been more concerned with rational debate rather than heated argument, statistics would have had a quite different history.

PRACTICAL STATISTICS

A striking feature of the general statistics texts produced for courses in the psychological sciences is the anonymity of the prescriptions that are described. A startlingly high number of incoming graduate students in the author's department were unaware that the F ratio was named for a man called Fisher, but a cursory glance through the indexes of introductory texts reveals why. Pearson's name is sometimes mentioned as a convenient label for a correlation coefficient, distinguishing it from the rank-order method of Spearman. Neyman and Pearson Jr. are hardly ever acknowledged. "Power" is treated with caution. Controversial issues are *never* discussed.

Gigerenzer (1987) presents an interesting discussion of the situation:

> The confusion in the statistical texts presented to the poor frustrated students were caused in part by the attempt to sell this hybrid as the sine qua non of scientific inference. (Gigerenzer, 1986, p. 20)

Gigerenzer's thesis addresses what he sees as experimental psychology's fight against *subjectivity*. Probabilistic models and statistical methods provided the discipline with a mechanical process that seemed to allow for *objective* assessment independent of the experimenter. Parallel constructs of individual differences as *error* and uncertainty as *ignorance* further promoted psychology's view of itself as an objective science.

It is Gigerenzer's view that the illusion was more or less deliberately created by the early textbooks and has been perpetuated. The general neglect of alternative theories and methods of inference, anonymous presentation, the silence on the controversies, and "institutionalization," all conspired to provide psychology with its need for objectivity. Gigerenzer makes telling and important points. But a more mundane explanation can be advanced.

Surely social scientists can be forgiven for not being mathematicians or logicians, and those who took a peek at the literature of the 1920s and 1930s must have been dismayed at the bitterness of the controversies. At the same time the methods were being popularized by such people as Snedecor—and they seemed to be methods that worked. It is absolutely clear that psychologists wanted to construct a research methodology that would be accepted by traditional science. The controversies were ignored because experimentalists in the social sciences believed that they were sifting the methodological wheat from the polemical chaff. The principals in the arguments were ignored because of an eagerness to get on with the practical job, and in this they were supported by the master, Fisher. Moreover, the textbook writers, interpreting Fisher, can be forgiven for their lack of acknowledgment of the founding fathers—they were, after all, following the master who rarely gave credit to anybody!

What is, perhaps, more contentious is the *effect* that all this has had on the discipline. If it is to be admitted that the logical foundations of psychology's most widespread method of data assessment are shaky, what are we to make of the "findings" of experimental psychology? Is the whole edifice of data and theory to be compared with the buildings in the towns of the "wild west"—a gaudy false front, and little of substance behind. This is an unreasonable conclusion and it is not a conclusion that is borne out by even a cursory examination of the successful predictions of behavior and the confident applications of psychology, in areas stretching from market research to clinical practice, that have a utility that is indisputable. The plain fact of the matter is that psychology is using a set of tools that leaves much to be desired. Some parts of the kit perhaps should be discarded, some of them, like blunt chisels, will let us down and we might be injured. But, they seem to have been doing a job. Psychology *is* a success.

References

Acree, M.C. (1978). *Theories of statistical inference in psychological research: A historico-critical study.* Unpublished PhD Dissertation, Clark University, Worcester, MA, USA.

Adams, W.J. (1974). *The life and times of the central limit theorem.* New York: Kaedmon.

Airy, G.B. (1875). *On the algebraical and numerical theory of errors of observations and the combination of observations* (2nd. ed.), London: Macmillan.

Anon. (1926). Review of Fisher's *Statistical methods for research workers. British Medical Journal, 1,* 578–579.

Arbuthnot, J. (1692). *Of the laws of chance: Or a method of calculation of the hazards of gaming.* London: Printed by B. Motte and sold by Randall Taylor.

Arbuthnot, J. (1710). An argument for divine providence, taken from the constant regularity observ'd in the births of both sexes. *Philosophical Transactions of the Royal Society, 27,* 186–190.

Barnard, G.A. (1958). Thomas Bayes—a biographical note. *Biometrika, 45,* 293–295.

Bartlett, M.S. (1965). R.A. Fisher and the last fifty years of statistical methodology. *Journal of the American Statistical Association, 60,* 395–409.

Bartlett, M.S. (1966). Review of *Logic of Statistical Inference,* by Ian Hacking. *Biometrika, 53,* 631–633.

Bayes, T. (1763). An essay towards solving a problem in the doctrine of chances. *Philosophical Transactions of the Royal Society, 53,* 370–418. [Reprinted with a biographical note by G.A. Barnard in *Biometrika,* 1958, *45,* 293–315.]

Bennett, J.H. (1971). *Collected papers of R.A. Fisher.* Adelaide: University of Adelaide.

Bernard, C. (1927). *An introduction to the study of experimental medicine.* (H.C. Greene, Trans.), New York: Macmillan. (Original work published in 1865)

Bernoulli, J. (1966). *Part four of the Art of Conjecturing showing the use and application of the preceding treatise in civil, moral and economic affairs.* (Bing Sung, trans.), Harvard University, Department of Statistics, Technical Report No. 2. (Original work published in 1713)

Bilodeau, E.A. (1952). Statistical versus intuitive confidence. *American Journal of Psychology, 65,* 271–277.

Boring, E. G. (1920). The logic of the normal law of error in mental measurement. *American Journal of Psychology, 31,* 1–33.

Boring, E.G. (1950). *A history of experimental psychology.* New York: Appleton-Century-Crofts.

Boring, E.G. (1957). When is human behavior predetermined? *The Scientific Monthly, 84,* 189–196.

Bowley, A.L. (1902). *Elements of statistics.* London: P.S. King. (6th ed., 1937).

Bowley, A.L. (1906). Presidential address to the economic science and statistics section of the British Association for the Advancement of Science, York. *Journal of the Royal Statistical Society, 69,* 540–558.

Bowley, A.L. (1926). Measurement of the precision obtained in sampling. *Bulletin of the International Statistical Institute, 22,* 1–62.

Bowley, A.L. (1936). The application of sampling to economic and social problems. *Journal of the American Statistical Association, 31,* 474–480.

Box, G.E.P (1984). The importance of practice in the development of statistics. *Technometrics, 26,* 1–8.

Bravais, A. (1846). Sur les probabilités des erreurs de situation d'un point [On the probability of errors in the position of a point]. *Memoires de l'Academie Royale des Sciences de l'Institut de France, 9,* 255–332.

Buck, P. (1977). Seventeenth-century political arithmetic: Civil strife and vital statistics. *Isis, 68*, 67–84.

Burke, C.J. (1953). A brief note on one-tailed tests. *Psychological Bulletin, 50*, 384–387.

Chang, W-C (1973). *A history of the chi-square goodness-of-fit test.* Unpublished PhD Dissertation, University of Toronto, Toronto, Ontario.

Chang, W-C. (1976). Sampling theories and sampling practice. In D.B. Owen (Ed.), *On the history of statistics and probability* (pp. 299–315). New York: Marcel Dekker.

Clark, R.W. (1971). *Einstein the life and times.* New York: World.

Cochrane, W.G. (1980). Fisher and the analysis of variance. In S.E. Fienberg, & D.V. Hinckley (Eds.)., *R.A. Fisher: An Appreciation* (pp. 17–34). New York: Springer-Verlag.

Cowan, R.S. (1972). Francis Galton's statistical ideas: The influence of eugenics. *Isis, 63*, 509–528.

Cowan, R.S. (1977). Nature and nurture: the interplay of biology and politics in the work of Francis Galton. In W. Coleman, & C. Limoges (Eds.). *Studies in the history of biology* (Vol. 1, pp. 138–208). Baltimore: The Johns Hopkins University Press.

Cowles, M., & Davis, C. (1982a). On the origins of the .05 level of statistical significance. *American Psychologist, 37*, 553–558.

Cowles, M., & Davis, C. (1982b). Is the 0.05 level subjectively reasonable? *Canadian Journal of Behavioural Science, 14*, 248–252.

Cowles, M., & Davis, C. (1987). The subject matter of psychology: volunteers. *British Journal of Social Psychology, 26*, 97–102.

Cronbach, L.J. (1957). The two disciplines of scientific psychology. *American Psychologist, 12*, 671–684.

Crum, L.S. (1931). On analytical interpretations of straw vote samples. *Journal of the American Statistical Association, 26*, 243–261.

Darwin, C. (1859). *The origin of species.* [Mentor Edition first published in 1958, New York: The New American Library].

David, F.N. (1949). *Probability theory for statistical methods.* Cambridge, England: Cambridge University Press.

David, F.N (1962). *Games, Gods and Gambling.* London: Charles Griffin.

Davis, C., & Gaito, J. (1984). Multiple comparison procedures within experimental research. *Canadian Psychology, 25*, 1–12.

Daw, R.H., & Pearson, E.S. (1972). Abraham De Moivre's 1733 derivation of the normal curve: A bibliographical note. *Biometrika, 59*, 677–680. [Reprinted in M. Kendall, & R.L. Plackett (Eds). (1979). *Studies in the history of statistics and probability*, Vol. II, New York: Macmillan].

Dawson, M.M. (1901). The development of insurance mathematics. In L.W. Zartman (Ed.), *Yale readings in insurance* (pp. 95–119). New Haven: Yale University Press. (Revision by W.H. Price published in 1914).

Dempster, A.P. (1964). On the difficulties inherent in Fisher's fiducial argument. *Journal of the American Statistical Association, 59*, 56–66.

De Moivre, A. (1756). *The doctrine of chances: or, A method of calculating the probabilities of events in play.* (3rd ed.), London: A. Millar. [Reprinted edition published by the Chelsea Publishing Co., New York, 1967 includes a biographical note on De Moivre by Helen M. Walker].

De Morgan, A. (1838). An essay on probabilities and on their application to life contingencies and insurance offices. D. Lardner (Ed.) *The Cabinet Cyclopaedia,* London: Longman, Orme, Brown, Green & Longmans and John Taylor.

Dodd, S.C. (1928). The theory of factors. *Psychological Review, 35*, I, 211–234; II, 261–279.

Duncan, D.B. (1951). A significance test for differences between ranked treatments in an analysis of variance. *Virginia Journal of Science, 2*, 171–189.

Duncan, D.B. (1955). Multiple range and multiple *F* tests. *Biometrics, 11*, 1–42.

Eden, T., & Fisher, R.A. (1927). Studies in crop variation. IV. The experimental determination of the value of top dressings with cereals. *Journal of Agricultural Science, 17*, 548–562.

Edgeworth, F.Y. (1887). Observations and statistics: An essay on the theory of errors of observation and the first principles of statistics. *Transactions of the Cambridge Philosophical Society, 14,* 138–169.

Edgeworth, F.Y. (1892). Correlated averages. *Philosophical Magazine, 34,* 190–204.

Eisenhart, C. (1947). The assumptions underlying the analysis of variance. *Biometrics, 3,* 1–21.

Eisenhart, C. (1970). On the transition from "Student's" z to "Student's" t. *The American Statistician, 33,* 6–10.

Ellis, B. (1968). *Basic concepts of measurement.* Cambridge, England: Cambridge University Press.

Fechner, G. (1966). *Elements of Psychophysics.* (H. Adler, Trans.). New York: Holt, Rinehart and Winston). (Original work published in 1860)

Feigl, H. (1959). Philosophical embarrassments of psychology. *American Psychologist, 14,* 115–128.

Finn, R.W. (1973). *Domesday book: A guide.* Chichester, England: Phillimore.

Fisher Box, J. (1978). *R.A. Fisher the life of a scientist.* New York: Wiley.

Fisher Box, J. (1981). Gosset, Fisher, and the t distribution. *The American Statistician, 35,* 61–66.

Fisher, R.A. (1915). Frequency distribution of values of the correlation coefficient in samples from an indefinitely large population. *Biometrika, 10,* 507–521.

Fisher, R.A. (1918). The correlation between relatives on the supposition of Mendelian inheritance. *Transactions of the Royal Society of Edinburgh, 52,* 399–433.

Fisher, R.A. (1919). The genesis of twins. *Genetics, 4,* 489–499.

Fisher, R.A. (1921a). On the "probable error" of a coefficient of correlation deduced from a small sample. *Metron, 1,* 3–32.

Fisher, R.A. (1921b). Studies in crop variation. I. An examination of the yield of dressed grain from Broadbalk. *Journal of Agricultural Science, 11,* 107–135.

Fisher, R.A. (1922a). On the interpretation of χ^2 from contingency tables and the calculation of P. *Journal of the Royal Statistical Society, 85,* 87–94.

Fisher, R.A. (1922b). The goodness of fit of regression formulae and the distribution of regression coefficients. *Journal of the Royal Statistical Society, 85,* 597–612.

Fisher, R.A. (1923). Statistical tests of agreement between observation and hypothesis. *Economica, 3,* 139–147.

Fisher, R.A. (1924a). The conditions under which χ^2 measures the discrepancy between observation and hypothesis. *Journal of the Royal Statistical Society. 87,* 442–450.

Fisher, R.A. (1924b). On a distribution yielding the error functions of several well known statistics. *Proceedings of the International Congress of Mathematics, Toronto, 2,* 805–813.

Fisher, R.A. (1925a, 1970, 14th ed.). *Statistical methods for research workers.* Edinburgh: Oliver and Boyd.

Fisher, R.A. (1925b). Applications of "Student's" distribution. *Metron, 5,* 90–104.

Fisher, R.A. (1925c). Theory of statistical estimation. *Proceedings of the Cambridge Philosophical Society, 22,* 700–725.

Fisher, R.A. (1926a). Bayes'theorem and the fourfold table. *Eugenics Review, 18,* 32–33.

Fisher, R.A. (1926b). The arrangement of field experiments. *Journal of the Ministry of Agriculture of Great Britain, 33,* 505–513.

Fisher, R.A. (1930). Inverse probability. *Proceedings of the Cambridge Philosophical Society, 26,* 528–535.

Fisher, R.A. (1935a, 1966, 8th ed.). *The design of experiments.* Edinburgh: Oliver and Boyd.

Fisher, R.A. (1935b). The logic of inductive inference. *Journal of the Royal Statistical Society, 98,* 39–54.

Fisher, R.A. (1950). Contributions to mathematical statistics. New York: Wiley.

Fisher, R.A. (1952). Statistical methods in genetics. *Heredity, 6,* 1–12.

Fisher, R.A. (1955). Statistical methods and scientific induction. *Journal of the Royal Statistical Society, B, 17,* 69–78.

Fisher, R.A. (1956). *Statistical methods and scientific inference*. New York: Hafner Press. (3rd ed., 1973).

Fisher, R.A. (1957). Comment on the notes by Neyman, Bartlett, and Welch in this Journal (Vol. 18, No. 2, 1956). *Journal of the Royal Statistical Society*, B, *19*, 179.

Fisher, R.A., & MacKenzie, W.A. (1923). Studies in crop variation. II. The manurial response of different potato varieties. *Journal of Agricultural Science*, *13*, 311–320.

Forrest, D.W. (1974). *Francis Galton: The life and work of a Victorian genius*. London: Elek.

Fox, J. (1984). *Linear statistical models and related methods*. New York: Wiley.

Funkhouser, H.G. (1936). A note on a 10th century graph. *Osiris*, *1*, 260–262.

Funkhouser, H.G. (1937). Historical development of the graphical representation of data. *Osiris*, *3*, 269–404.

Gaito, J. (1980). Measurement scales and statistics: Resurgence of an old misconception. *Psychological Bulletin*, *87*, 564–567.

Galbraith, V.H. (1961). *The making of Domesday book*. Oxford: Oxford University Press.

Galton, F. (1869). *Hereditary genius*. London: MacMillan. [Second ed., 1892, which was reprinted with an introduction by C.D. Darlington by Collins, London, 1962, and World Publishing Co. New York, 1962].

Galton, F. (1874). *English men of science*. London: MacMillan. [Edition with an introduction by Ruth Schwartz Cohen, Frank Cass, London, 1970].

Galton, F. (1877). Typical laws of heredity. *Proceedings of the Royal Institution of Great Britain*, *8*, 282–301. [Also in *Nature*, *15*, 492–495].

Galton, F. (1884). On the anthropometric laboratory at the late International Health Exhibition. *Journal of the Anthropological Institute of Great Britain and Ireland*, *14*, 205–221.

Galton, F. (1885a). Regression towards mediocrity in hereditary stature. *Journal of the Anthropological Institute of Great Britain and Ireland*, *15*, 246–263.

Galton, F. (1885b). Opening Address to the Anthropological Section of the British Association by the President of the Section. *Nature*, *32*, 507–510.

Galton, F. (1886). Family likeness in stature. *Proceedings of the Royal Society of London*, *40*, 42–73 (includes an appendix by J.D. Hamilton Dickson)..

Galton, F. (1888). Co-relations and their measurement, chiefly from anthropometric data. *Proceedings of the Royal Society of London*, *45*, 135–145.

Galton, F. (1889). *Natural inheritance*. London: Macmillan.

Galton, F. (1908). *Memories of my life*. London: Methuen.

Gauss, C.F. (1809). *Theoria motus corporum coelestium*. (*Theory of the Motion of Heavenly Bodies*, 1963, New York: Dover Reprint).

Gigerenzer, G. (1987). Probabilistic thinking and the fight against subjectivity. In L. Krüger, G. Gigerenzer,, & M. Morgan (Eds.). *The probabilistic revolution: Ideas in the sciences* (Vol 2, pp. 7–33). Cambridge, Mass.: MIT Press.

Gini, C. (1928). Une application de la méthode représentative aux matériaux du dernier recensement de la population italienne (1er décembre 1921) [An application of the representative method to material from the last census of the Italian population (1st December, 1921)]. *Bulletin of the International Statistical Institute*, *23*, 198–215.

Ginzburg, B. (1936). The scientific value of the Copernican induction. *Osiris*, *1*, 303–313.

Glaisher, J.W.L. (1872). On the law of facility of errors of observation and the method of least squares. *Royal Astronomical Society Memoirs*, *39*, 75–124.

Graunt, J. (1662). *Natural and political observations mentioned in a following index and made upon the bills of mortality*. London: Printed by Thomas Roycroft for John Martin, James Allestry, and Thomas Dicas. [Reprint Edition 1975 by Arno Press, New York].

Grünbaum, A. (1952). Causality and the science of human behavior. *The American Scientist*, *40*, 665–676.

Guthrie, S.C. (1946). *A history of medicine*. Philadelphia: J.B. Lipincott Co.

Hacking, I. (1965). *The logic of statistical inference*. Cambridge, England: Cambridge University Press.

Hacking, I. (1971). Jacques Bernoulli's *Art of Conjecturing*. *British Journal for the Philosophy of Science, 22*, 209–229.

Hacking, I. (1975). *The emergence of probability*. Cambridge, England: Cambridge University Press.

Halley, E. (1693). An estimate of the mortality of mankind, drawn from curious tables of the births and funerals at the city of Breslaw; with an attempt to ascertain the price of annuities on lives. *Philosophical Transactions of the Royal Society, 17*, 596–610.

Hartley, D. (1749). *Observations on man, his frame, his duty and his expectations*. 1966 Edition, Gainesville, FL: Scholars' Facsimiles and Reprints.

Hays, W.L. (1963). *Statistics*. New York: Holt, Rinehart and Winston.

Hays, W.L. (1973). *Statistics for the social sciences*. New York: Holt, Rinehart and Winston.

Hearnshaw, L.S. (1987). *The shaping of modern psychology*. London: Routledge and Kegan Paul.

Heisenberg, W. (1927). *The physical principles of the quantum theory*. Chicago: University of Chicago Press.

Henkel, R.E., & Morrison, D.E. (1970). *The significance test controversy*. London: Butterworths.

Heron, D. (1911). The danger of certain formulae suggested as substitutes for the correlation coefficient. *Biometrika, 8*, 109–122.

Hick, W.E. (1952). A note on one-tailed and two-tailed tests. *Psychological Review, 59*, 316–318.

Hilbert, D. (1902) Mathematical problems. *Bulletin of the American Mathematical Society, 8*, 437–445; 478–479.

Hogben, L. (1957). *Statistical theory*. London: Allen and Unwin.

Holschuh, N. (1980). Randomization and design: I. In S.E. Fienberg, & D.V. Hinkley (Eds.). *R.A. Fisher: An appreciation* (pp. 35–45). New York: Springer-Verlag.

Hume, D. (1748). *An enquiry concerning human understanding*. (In D.C. Yalden-Thomson (Ed.). (1951). *Hume, Theory of Knowledge*. Edinburgh: Thomas Nelson).

Huxley, J. (1947) Half a century of genetics. London: *Sunday Times*, July, 10th.

Huygens, C. (1657). *On reasoning in games of dice*. In J. Bernoulli (F. Maseres Ed. and Trans.). *The art of conjecture*. New York: Redex Microprint, 1970.

Jacobs, J. (1885). Review of Ebbinghaus's *Ueber das Gedächtnis*. *Mind, 10*, 454–459.

Jeffreys, H. (1939). Random and systematic arrangements. *Biometrika, 31*, 1–8.

Jevons, W. (1874). *The principles of science*. London: Macmillan.

Jones, L.V. (1952). Tests of hypotheses: One-sided vs. two-sided alternatives. *Psychological Bulletin, 49*, 43–46.

Jones, L.V. (1954). A rejoinder on one-tailed tests. *Psychological Bulletin, 51*, 585–586.

Kempthorne, O. (1976). The analysis of variance and factorial design. In D.B. Owen (Ed.), *On the history of statistics and probability*, pp. 29–54. New York: Marcel Dekker.

Kempthorne, O. (1983). A review of *R.A. Fisher: An Appreciation*. *Journal of the American Statistical Association, 78*, 482–490.

Kempthorne, O., & Folks, L. (1971). *Probability, statistics, and data analysis*. Ames, IA: Iowa State University Press.

Kendall, M.G. (1952). George Udny Yule, 1871–1951. *Journal of the Royal Statistical Society, 115A*, 156–161.

Kendall, M.G. (1959). Hiawatha designs an experiment. *American Statistician, 13*, 23–24.

Kendall, M.G. (1961). Daniel Bernoulli on maximum likelihood. *Biometrika, 48*, 1–18. [This paper is followed by a translation by C.G. Allen of Daniel Bernoulli's, *The most probable choice between several discrepant observations and the formation therefrom of the most likely induction*, 1777(?)., together with a commentary by Leonard Euler (1707–1783).]

Kendall, M.G. (1963). Ronald Aylmer Fisher, 1890–1962. *Biometrika, 50*, 1–15.

Kendall, M.G. (1968). Studies in the history of probability and statistics, XIX. Francis Ysidro Edgeworth (1845–1926). *Biometrika, 55*, 269–275.

Kendall, M.G., & Babington Smith, B. (1938). Randomness and random sampling numbers. *Journal of the Royal Statistical Society, 101*, 147–166.

Kenna, J.C. (1973). Galton's solution to the correlation problem: a false memory? *Bulletin of the British Psychological Society, 26*, 229–230.

Keuls, M. (1952). The use of studentized range in connection with an analysis of variance. *Euphytica, 1*, 112–122.

Kiaer, A.N. (1899). Sur les mèthodes représentatives ou typologies appliquées à la statistique (On representative methods or typologies applied to statistics). *Bulletin of the International Statistical Institute, 11*, 180–185.

Kiaer, A.N. (1903). Sur les mèthodes représentatives ou typologies (On representative methods or typologies). *Bulletin of the International Statistical Institute, 13*, 66–78.

Kimmel H.D. (1957). Three criteria for the use of one-tailed tests. *Psychological Bulletin, 54*, 351–353.

Kneale, W. (1949). *Probability and induction.* Oxford: Oxford University Press.

Kolmogorov, A.N. (1956). *Foundations of the theory of probability.* (N. Morrison, Trans.). New York: Chelsea Publishing Co. (Original work published in 1933)

Koren, J. (Ed.). (1918). *The history of statistics.* New York: Macmillan.

Kruskal, W., & Mosteller, F. (1979). Representative sampling, IV: The history of the concept in statistics, 1895–1939. *International Statistical Review, 47*, 169–195.

Lancaster, H.O. (1966). Forerunners of the Pearson χ^2. *Australian Journal of Statistics, 8*, 117–126.

Lancaster, H.O. (1969). *The chi-squared distribution.* New York: Wiley.

Laplace, P.S. de (1810) Mémoir sur les approximations des formules de très grandes nombres, et sur leur application aux probabilités (Memoir on approximations of formulae which are functions of very large numbers, and their application to probabilities). *Mémoirs de la classe des sciences mathématiques et physiques et de l'institut de France.* Année 1809, pp. 353–415; supplement pp.559–565.

Laplace P.S. de (1812). *Théorie analytique des probabilités.* Paris: Courcier.

Laplace P.S. de (1820). *A philosophical essay on probabilities.* (F.W. Truscott, & F.L. Emory, Trans.). New York: Dover Publications.

Le Cam, L., & Lehmann, E.L. (1974). J. Neyman On the occasion of his 80th birthday. *Annals of Statistics, 2*, vii-xi.

Legendre, A.M. (1805). *Nouvelles méthodes pour la détermination des orbites des comètes (New methods for determining the orbits of comets).* Paris: Courcier.

Lehmann, E.L. (1959). *Testing statistical hypotheses.* New York: Wiley.

Lindquist, E.F. (1940). *Statistical analysis in educational research.* Boston: Houghton Mifflin.

Lord, F.M. (1953). On the statistical treatment of football numbers. *American Psychologist, 8*, 750–751.

Lovie, A.D. (1979). The analysis of variance in experimental psychology: 1934–1945. *British Journal of Mathematical and Statistical Psychology, 32*, 151–178.

Lovie, A.D. (1984). Images of man in early factor analysis—psychological and philosophical aspects. Unpublished manuscript, University of Liverpool, England.

Lupton, S. (1898). *Notes on observations.* London: Macmillan.

Lush, J.L. (1972). Early statistics at Iowa State College. In T.A. Bancroft (Ed.)., *Statistical papers in honour of George W. Snedecor* (pp. 211–226). Ames, IA: Iowa State University Press.

Macdonell, W.R. (1901). On criminal anthropometry and the identification of criminals. *Biometrika, 1*, 177–227.

MacKenzie, D.A. (1981). *Statistics in Britain 1865–1930.* Edinburgh: Edinburgh University Press.

Marks, M.R. (1951). Two kinds of experiment distinguished in terms of statistical operations. *Psychological Review, 58*, 179–184.

Marks, M.R. (1953). One- and two-tailed tests. *Psychological Review, 60*, 207–208.

Maunder, W.F. (1972). Sir Arthur Lyon Bowley. An inaugural lecture delivered in the University of Exeter. (Reprinted in M.G. Kendall, & R.L. Plackett (Eds.), *Studies in the history of statistics and probability*, Volume II, (pp. 459–480). New York: Macmillan.

McMullen, L. [1], & Pearson, E.S. [2]. (1939). William Sealy Gosset, 1876–1937 (1). "Student" as a man; (2). "Student" as a statistician. *Biometrika, 30*, 205–250.

McNemar, Q. (1940). Sampling in psychological research. *Psychological Bulletin, 37*, 331–365.

Mercer, W.B. and Hall, A.D. (1911). The experimental error of field trials. *Journal of Agricultural Science, 4*, 107–132.

Merriman, M. (1877). A list of writings relating to the method of least squares, with historical and critical notes. *Transactions of the Connecticut Academy of Arts and Sciences, 4*, 151–232.

Merriman, M. (1884). *A textbook on the method of least squares* (8th ed.). New York: Wiley.

Michéa, R. (1938). Les variations de la raison au XVIIe siècle; essai sur la valeur du langage employé en histoire littéraire (Differences in meaning in the 17th century; essay on the value of language employed in literary history). *Revue Philosophique de la France et de l'Etranger, 126*, 183–201.

Mill, J.S. (1872). *A system of logic ratiocinative and inductive. Being a connected view of the principles of evidence and the methods of scientific investigation.* (8th ed.). (1973, Edited by J.M. Robson) Toronto: University of Toronto Press. (1st ed. 1843)

Miller, A.G. (Ed.). (1972). *The social psychology of the psychological experiment.* New York: Free Press.

Miller, G.A. (1963). Ronald A. Fisher: 1890–1962. *American Journal of Psychology, 76*, 157–158.

Nagel, E. (1936). The meaning of probability. *Journal of the American Statistical Association, 31*, 10–30. [Reprinted with a commentary in J.R. Newman (Ed.), *The World of Mathematics*, Vol.II, pp. 1398–1414. New York: Simon and Schuster].

Newman, D. (1939). The distribution of the range in samples from a normal population expressed in terms of an independent estimate of standard deviation. *Biometrika, 31*, 20–30.

Newman, J.R. (Ed.). (1956). *The world of mathematics.* (Vols. 1–4). New York: Simon and Schuster.

Neyman, J. (1934). On the two different aspects of the representative method: The method of stratified sampling and the method of purposive selection. *Journal of the Royal Statistical Society, 97*, 558–606.

Neyman, J. (1935). Statistical problems in agricultural experimentation. *Journal of the Royal Statistical Society*, Supplement, *2*, 107–154.

Neyman, J. (1937). x - Outline of a theory of estimation based on the classical theory of probability. *Philosophical Transactions of the Royal Society, A, 236*, 333–380.

Neyman, J. (1941). Fiducial argument and the theory of confidence intervals. *Biometrika, 32*, 128–150.

Neyman, J. (1956). Note on an article by Sir Ronald Fisher. *Journal of the Royal Statistical Society, B, 18*, 288–294.

Neyman, J., & Pearson, E.S. (1928). On the use and interpretation of certain test criteria for purposes of statistical inference. *Biometrika, 20a*, Part 1: 175–240, Part II: 263–294.

Neyman, J., & Pearson, E.S. (1933b). The testing of statistical hypotheses in relation to probabilities a priori. *Proceedings of the Cambridge Philosophical Society, 29*, 492–510.

Norton, B., & Pearson, E.S. (1976). A note on the background to, and refereeing of, R.A. Fisher's 1918 paper 'On the correlation between relatives on the supposition of Mendelian inheritance.' *Notes and Records of the Royal Society, 31*, 151–162.

Ore, O. (1953). *Cardano: The gambling scholar.* Princeton, NJ: Princeton University Press.

Parten, M. (1966). *Surveys, polls, and samples: Practical procedures.* New York: Cooper Square Publishers.

Pearl. R. (1917). The probable error of a Mendelian class frequency. *American Naturalist, 51*, 144–156.

Pearson, E.S. (1938a). *Karl Pearson: An appreciation of some aspects of his life and work.* Cambridge, England: Cambridge University Press.

Pearson, E.S. (1938b). Some aspects of the problem of randomization. II. An illustration of 'Student's' inquiry into the effect of balancing in agricultural experiments. *Biometrika, 30,* 159–171.

Pearson, E.S. (1939a). William Sealy Gosset, 1876–1937 (2). "Student" as a statistician. *Biometrika, 30,* 205–250.

Pearson, E.S. (1939b). Note on the inverse and direct methods of estimation in R.D. Gordon's problem. *Biometrika, 31,* 181–186.

Pearson, E.S. (1965). Some incidents in the early history of biometry and statistics, 1890–94. *Biometrika, 52,* 3–18.

Pearson, E.S. (1966). The Neyman-Pearson story: 1926–34. Historical sidelights on an episode in Anglo-Polish collaboration. In F.N. David (Ed.). *Festschrift for J. Neyman.* London: Wiley.

Pearson, E.S. (1968). Some early correspondence between W.S. Gosset, R.A. Fisher and Karl Pearson, with notes and comments. *Biometrika, 55,* 445–457.

Pearson, E.S., & Kendall, M.G. (1970). Karl Pearson's lectures on the history of statistics in the 17th and 18th centuries. Appendix to E.S. Pearson & M. G. Kendall (Eds.), *Studies in the history of statistics and probability.* London: Griffin.

Pearson, K. (1892). *The grammar of science.* London: Scott.

Pearson, K. (1894). Contributions to the mathematical theory of evolution. *Philosophical Transactions of the Royal Society, A, 185,* 71–110.

Pearson, K. (1895). Contributions to the mathematical theory of evolution. II. Skew variations in homogeneous material. *Philosophical Transactions of the Royal Society, A, 186,* 343–414.

Pearson, K. (1896). Mathematical contributions to the theory of evolution. III. Regression, heredity, and panmixia. *Philosophical Transactions of the Royal Society, A, 187,* 253–318.

Pearson, K. (1900a). On the criterion that a given system of deviations from the probable in the case of a correlated system of variables is such that it can be reasonably supposed to have arisen from random sampling. *Philosophical Magazine, 50,* 157–175.

Pearson, K. (1900b). Mathematical contributions to the theory of evolution. VII. On the correlation of characters not quantitatively measurable. *Philosophical Transactions of the Royal Society, A, 195,* 1–47.

Pearson, K. (1904). Mathematical contributions to the theory of evolution. XIII. On the theory of contingency and its relation to association and normal correlation. *Draper's Company Research Memoirs, Biometric Series I.* 35 pages.

Pearson, K. (1906). Walter Frank Raphael Weldon, 1860–1906. *Biometrika, 5,* 1–52.

Pearson, K. (1907). Reply to certain criticisms of Mr G.U. Yule. *Biometrika, 5,* 470–476.

Pearson, K. (1909). On the test of goodness of fit of observation to theory in Mendelian experiments. *Biometrika, 9,* 309–314.

Pearson, K. (1911). On the probability that two independent distributions of frequency are really samples from the same population. *Biometrika, 8,* 250–254.

Pearson, K. (1916a). On a brief proof of the fundamental formula for testing the goodness of fit of frequency distributions and of the probable error of "*P.*" *Philosophical Magazine, 31,* 369–378.

Pearson, K. (1916b). Mathematical contributions to the theory of evolution. XIX. Second supplement to a memoir on skew variation. *Philosophical Transactions of the Royal Society, A, 216,* 429–457.

Pearson, K. (1917). The probable error of a Mendelian class frequency. *Biometrika, 11,* 429–432.

Pearson, K. (1920). Notes on the history of correlation. *Biometrika, 13,* 25–45.

Pearson, K. (1922). On the χ^2 test of goodness of fit. *Biometrika, 14,* 186–191.

Pearson, K. (1924a). Historical note on the origin of the normal curve of errors. *Biometrika, 16,* 402–404.

Pearson, K. (1924b). On the difference and the doublet tests for ascertaining whether two samples have been drawn from the same population. *Biometrika, 16,* 249–252.

Pearson, K. (1926). Abraham de Moivre. Reply to Professor Archibald. *Nature, 117,* 551–552.

Pearson, K (1914–1930). *The life, letters and labours of Francis Galton.* Cambridge, England: Cambridge University Press. (Vol.1, 1914; Vol. 2, 1924; Vol. 3a, 3b, 1930).

Pearson, K. (1935). Statistical tests. *Nature, 136,* 296–297.

Pearson, K. (1978). *The history of statistics in the 17th and 18th centuries against the changing background of intellectual, scientific and religious thought.* (Edited by E.S. Pearson). London: Charles Griffin and Co.

Pearson, K., & Heron, D. (1913). On theories of association. *Biometrika, 9,* 159–315.

Peirce, B. (1852). Criterion for the rejection of doubtful observations. *The Astronomical Journal, 2,* 161–163.

Peters, C.C. (1943). Misuses of the Fisher statistics. *Journal of Educational Research, 36,* 546–549.

Petrinovich, L.F., & Hardyck, C.D. (1969). Error rates for multiple comparison methods: Some evidence concerning the frequency of erroneous conclusions. *Psychological Bulletin, 71,* 43–54.

Petty, W. (1690). *Political arithmetick.* London: Printed for Robert Clavel and Henry Mortlock.

Phillips, L.D. (1973). *Bayesian statistics for social scientists.* London: Nelson.

Picard, R. (1980). Randomization and design: II. In S.E. Fienberg & D.V. Hinkley (Eds.). *R.A. Fisher: An appreciation* (pp. 46–58). New York: Springer-Verlag.

Playfair, W. (1801a). *Commercial and political atlas.* (3rd ed.). London: Printed by T. Burton.

Playfair, W. (1801b). *Statistical breviary; shewing on a principle entirely new, the resources of every state and kingdom in Europe.* London: Printed by T. Bensley for J. Wallis, Egerton, Vernor and Hood, Black and Parry, and Tibbet and Didier.

Poisson, S.-D. (1837). *Recherches sur la probabilité des jugements en matière criminelle et en matière civile, précédées des règles génerales du calcul des probabilités* (Research on the probability of judgments in criminal and civil matters, preceded by general rules for the calculation of probabilities). Paris: Bachelier.

Popper, K.R. (1959). *The logic of scientific discovery.* London: Hutchinson.

Popper, K.R. (1962). *Conjectures and refutations: The growth of scientific knowledge.* New York: Basic Books.

Quetelet, L.A. (1849). *Letters addressed to H.R.H. the Grand Duke of Saxe Coburg and Gotha on the Theory of Probabilities as applied to the moral and political sciences.* (O.G. Downes, Trans.). London: Charles & Edwin Leyton. [Authorized facsimile of the original book produced in 1975 by Xerox University Microfilms, Ann Arbor, Michigan, U.S.A.]. (Original work published in 1835)

RAND Corporation (1965). *A million random digits with 100,000 normal deviates.* New York: Free Press.

Reichenbach, H. (1938). *Experience and prediction. An analysis of the foundations and structure of knowledge.* Chicago: University of Chicago Press.

Reid, C. (1982). *Neyman -from life.* New York: Springer-Verlag.

Rhodes, E.C. (1924). On the problem whether two given samples can be supposed to have been drawn from the same population. *Biometrika, 16,* 239–248.

Robinson, C. (1932). *Straw votes.* New York: Columbia University Press.

Robinson, C. (1937). Recent developments in the straw-poll field. *Public Opinion Quarterly, 1,* (3), 45–56, and *1,* (4), 42–52.

Rosenthal, R., & Rosnow, R.L. (Eds.). (1969). *Artifact in behavioral research.* New York: Academic Press.

Rowe, F.B. (1983). Whatever became of poor Kinnebrook? *American Psychologist, 38,* 851–852.

Rozeboom, W.W. (1960). The fallacy of the null hypothesis significance test. *Psychological Bulletin, 57,* 416–428.

Russell, B. (1931). *The scientific outlook.* London: Allen and Unwin.

Russell, B. (1946). *History of western philosophy and its connection with political and social circumstances from the earliest times to the present day.* London: Allen and Unwin.

Russell, Sir John, (1926). Field experiments: How they are made and what they are. *Journal of the Ministry of Agriculture of Great Britain, 32,* 989–1001.

Rutherford, E., & Geiger, H. (1910). The probability variations in the distribution of α particles. *Philosophical Magazine, 20,* 698–707.

Ryan, T.A. (1959). Multiple comparisons in psychological research. *Psychological Bulletin, 56,* 26–47.

Savage, L.J. (1962). *The foundations of statistical inference.* New York: Wiley.

Savage, L.J. (1976). On rereading R.A. Fisher. *Annals of Statistics, 4,* 441–500.

Scheffé, H. (1953). A method for judging all contrasts in the analysis of variance. *Biometrika, 40,* 87–104.

Scheffé, H. (1959). *The analysis of variance.* New York: Wiley.

Seal, H.L. (1967). The historical development of the Gauss linear model. *Biometrika, 54,* 1–24.

Seng, Y.P. (1951). Historical survey of the development of sampling theory and practice. *Journal of the Royal Statistical Society, 114,* 214–231.

Sheynin, O.B. (1966). Origin of the theory of error. *Nature, 211,* 1003–1004.

Sheynin, O.B. (1978). S.D. Poisson's work in probability. *Archives for History of Exact Sciences, 18,* 245–300.

Simpson, T. (1755). A letter to the Right Honourable George Earl of Macclesfield, President of the Royal Society, on the advantage arising in taking the mean of a number of observations, in practical astronomy. *Philosophical Transactions of the Royal Society, 49,* 82–93.

Simpson, T (1757). On the advantage arising from taking the mean of a number of observations, in practical astronomy, wherin the odds that the result in this way is more exact than from one single observation is evinced and the utility of the method in practise clearly made appear. In *Miscellaneous tracts on some curious and very interesting subjects in mechanics, physical astronomy and speculative mathematics* (pp. 64–75). London: Printed for J. Nourse.

Skinner, B.F. (1953). *Science and human behaviour.* New York: Macmillan.

Smith, D.E. (1929) *A source book in mathematics.* New York: McGraw Hill.

Smith, K. (1916). On the 'best' values of the constants in frequency distributions. *Biometrika, 11,* 262–276.

Snedecor, G.W. (1934). *Calculation and interpretation of analysis of variance and covariance.* Ames, IA: Collegiate Press.

Snedecor, G.W. (1937). *Statistical methods.* Ames, IA: Collegiate Press.

Soper, H.E. (1914). On the probable error of the correlation coefficient to a second approximation. *Biometrika, 9,* 91–115.

Soper, H.E., Young, A.W., Cave, B.M., Lee, A., & Pearson, K. (1917). On the distribution of the correlation coefficient in small samples. A co-operative study. *Biometrika, 11,* 328–413.

St. Cyres, Viscount (1909). *Pascal.* London: Smith, Elder and Co.

Stephan, F.F. (1948). History of the use of modern sampling procedures. *Journal of the American Statistical Association, 43,* 12–39.

Stephen, L. (1876). *History of English thought in the eighteenth century* (Vols. 1–2). London: Smith, Elder and Co.

Stevens, S.S. (1951). Mathematics, measurement and psychophysics. In S.S. Stevens (Ed.)., *Handbook of experimental psychology* (pp. 1–49). New York: Wiley.

Stigler, S.M. (1977). Eight centuries of sampling inspection: the trial of the Pyx. *Journal of the American Statistical Association, 72,* 493–500.

Struik, D.J. (1954). *A concise history of mathematics.* London: Bell.

"Student" (1907). On the error of counting with a haemacytometer. *Biometrika, 5,* 351–360.

"Student" (1908a). The probable error of a mean. *Biometrika, 6,* 1–25.

"Student" (1908b). Probable error of a correlation coefficient. *Biometrika, 6,* 302–310.

"Student" (1925). New tables for testing the significance of observations. *Metron*, *5*, 25–32.

"Student" (1927). Errors of routine analysis. *Biometrika*, *19*, 151–164.

Tedin, O. (1931). The influence of systematic plot arrangements upon the estimate of error in field experiments. *Journal of Agricultural Science*, *21*, 191–208.

Thomson, W. (Lord Kelvin). (1891). *Popular lectures and addresses*. London: Macmillan.

Thorndike, E.L. (1905). Measurements of twins. *Archives of Philosophy, Psychology, and Scientific Methods, No. 1*. New York: The Science Press.

Thorndike, E.L.,& Woodworth, R.S. (1901). The influence of improvement in one mental function upon the efficiency of other functions. *Psychological Review*, *8*, 247–261.

Thurstone, L.L. (1940). Current issues in factor analysis. *Psychological Bulletin*, *37*, 189–236.

Tippett, L.H.C. (1925). On the extreme individuals and the range of samples taken from a normal population. *Biometrika*, *17*, 364–387.

Todhunter, I. (1865). *A history of the mathematical theory of probability from the time of Pascal to that of Laplace*. Cambridge and London: Macmillan. [Reprinted in 1965 by the Chelsea Publishing Co., New York].

Traxler, R.H. (1976). A snag in the history of factorial experiments. In D.B. Owen (Ed.). *On the history of probability and statistics* (pp. 283–295. New York: Marcel Dekker.

Tukey, J.W. (1949). Comparing individual means in the analysis of variance. *Biometrics*, *5*, 99–114.

Tukey, J.W. (1953). *The problem of multiple comparisons*. Unpublished manuscript, Princeton University, Princeton, NJ.

Turner, F.M. (1978). The Victorian conflict between science and religion: A professional dimension. *Isis*, *69*, 356–376.

Venn, J. (1866). *The logic of chance*. London: Macmillan. (3rd ed. 1888).

Venn, J. (1891). On the nature and uses of averages. *Journal of the Royal Statistical Society*, *54*, 429–448.

von Mises, R. (1919) Grundlagen der wahrscheinlichkeitsrechnung (Principles of probability theory). *Mathematische Zeitschrift*, *5*, 52–99.

von Mises, R. (1957). *Probability, statistics and truth*. (Second revised English Edition prepared by Hilda Geiringer) London: Allen and Unwin.

Wald, A. (1950). *Statistical decision functions*. New York: Wiley.

Walker, E.L. (1970). *Psychology as a natural and social science*. Belmont, CA: Brooks/Cole.

Walker, H.M. (1929). *Studies in the history of statistical method*. Baltimore: Williams and Wilkins.

Wallis, W.A., & Roberts, H.V. (1956). *Statistics: A new approach*. New York: Free Press.

Watson. J.B. (1913). Psychology as the behaviorist views it. *Psychological Review*, *20*, 158–177.

Weaver, W. (1963). *Lady Luck: The theory of probability*. Harmondsworth: Penguin Books (1977). (First published by Educational Testing Services, 1963).

Welch, B.L. (1939). On confidence limits and sufficiency with particular reference to parameters of location. *Annals of Mathematical Statistics*, *10*, 58–69.

Welch, B.L. (1958). "Student" and small sample theory. *Journal of the American Statistical Association*, *53*, 777–788.

Weldon, W.F.R. (1890). The variations occurring in certain Decapod Crustacea.—I. *Crangon vulgaris*. *Proceedings of the Royal Society of London*, *47*, 445–453.

Weldon, W.F.R. (1892). Certain correlated variations in *Crangon vulgaris*. *Proceedings of the Royal Society of London*, *51*, 2–21.

Weldon, W.F.R. (1893). On certain correlated variations in *Carcinus moenas*. *Proceedings of the Royal Society of London*, *54*, 318–329.

Westergaard, H. (1932). *Contributions to the history of statistics*. London: P.S. King.

Whitney, C.A. (1984, October). Generating and testing pseudorandom numbers. *Byte*, p. 128.

Wolfle, D. (1940). *Factor analysis to 1940*. Chicago: University of Chicago Press.

Wood, T.B., & Stratton, F.J.M. (1910). The interpretation of experimental results. *Journal of Agricultural Science*, *3*, 417–440.

Yates, F. (1935). Complex experimentation. *Journal of the Royal Statistical Society Supplement*, *2*, 181–247.

Yates, F. (1939). The comparative advantages of systematic and randomized arrangements in the design of agricultural and biological experiments. *Biometrika*, *30*, 440–466.

Yates, F. (1951). The influence of *Statistical Methods for Research Workers* on the development of the science of statistics. *Journal of the American Statistical Association*, *46*, 19–34.

Yule, G.U. (1897a). Notes on the teaching of the theory of statistics at University College. *Journal of the Royal Statistical Society*, *60*, 456–458.

Yule, G.U. (1897b). On the theory of correlation. *Journal of the Royal Statistical Society*, *60*, 812–854.

Yule, G.U. (1900). On the association of attributes in statistics. *Philosophical Transactions of the Royal Society*, *A*, *194*, 257–319.

Yule, G.U. (1906). On a property which holds good for all groupings of a normal distribution of frequency for two variables. *Proceedings of the Royal Society*, *A*, *77*, 324–336.

Yule, G.U. (1912). On the methods of measuring association between two attributes. *Journal of the Royal Statistical Society*, *75*, 579–642.

Yule, G.U. (1921). Review of W. Brown and G.H. Thomson, *The essentials of mental measurement*. *British Journal of Psychology*, *2*, 100–107.

Yule, G.U. (1936). Karl Pearson, 1857–1936. *Obituary Notices of Fellows of the Royal Society of London*, *2*, 73–104.

Yule, G.U. (1938a). Notes of Karl Pearson's lectures on Theory of Statistics. *Biometrika*, *30*, 198–203.

Yule, G.U. (1938b). A test of Tippett's random sampling numbers. *Journal of the Royal Statistical Society*, *101*, 167–172.

Yule, G.U. (1939). [Review of] *Karl Pearson: An appreciation of some aspects of his life and work*. By E.S. Pearson. Cambridge: University Press, 1938. *Nature*, *143*, 220–222.

Yule, G.U., & Kendall, M.G. (1950). *An introduction to the theory of statistics* (14th ed.). London: Charles Griffin. (1st ed., Yule, 1911)

Author Index

Subject Index